THE FUTURE OF EDUCATION WITH AI

THE FUTURE OF EDUCATION WITH AI

Neeru Kapoor

HOW
ACADEMICS
an imprint of Highlyy Publishing LLP

ISBN: 978-93-6009-653-3
First Published : 2025

HOW ACADEMICS

Published by : an imprint of Highlyy Publishing LLP

Correspondence Address : 4/30 A II Floor, Double Storey Buildings
Vijay Nagar, Delhi-110009
Editorial: +91 9811026449
Sales : +91 9999953412
Email: info@howacademics.com
Website: www.howacademics.com

Printed in India

Contents

List of Figures

Preface

The world of education is on the cusp of a transformation unlike any it has seen before. The advent of artificial intelligence (AI) presents us with both profound opportunities and significant challenges, poised to reshape the fabric of how we teach, learn, and interact with knowledge. This book, "The Future of Education with AI," is born out of the recognition that we are standing at a critical juncture in educational history, where technology and pedagogy are intersecting in unprecedented ways.

The journey to this book began with a simple observation: despite the rapid advancement of AI in various sectors, education has been slow to fully embrace its potential. In my work with educators, students, technologists, and policymakers, I have seen both the excitement and the trepidation that AI brings to the educational sphere. It is clear that while AI has the capacity to revolutionize education, there are also fears about its implications—ranging from concerns over the loss of human touch in teaching to the potential for deepening inequalities. We will explore the multifaceted role AI can play in education. The narrative is divided into several parts, each addressing a different aspect of this transformation. We begin with a historical overview of technology in education, tracing the evolution of tools and methods that have led us to this point. This provides the necessary context to understand AI's potential impact.

The book also addresses the ethical and social implications of AI in education. As we adopt these powerful tools, we must remain vigilant about issues such as data privacy, algorithmic bias, and the potential for AI to reinforce existing educational inequalities. It is my firm belief that while AI offers incredible opportunities, it must be implemented thoughtfully and inclusively, ensuring that it benefits all students, regardless of their background.

Moreover, we will look into the role of educators in an AI-enhanced future. Far from replacing teachers, AI has the potential to empower them, offering new tools to enhance their teaching and free them from administrative burdens, allowing them to focus more on their core mission: educating and inspiring students.

Finally, the book provides a roadmap for the future, offering practical insights for educators, administrators, and policymakers on how to integrate AI into educational systems responsibly. It also invites readers to imagine new possibilities for education in the next decade and beyond.

"The Future of Education with AI" is not just a book about technology; it is a book about the future of humanity. The way we educate the next generation will shape the world they inherit, and AI is poised to play a crucial role in this process. My hope is that this book will serve as both a guide and a call to action, encouraging us to harness the power of AI to create a more equitable, effective, and inspiring educational landscape.

Chapter 1
Teaching Reimagined: Embracing AI in Education

OpenAI released Version 3 of ChatGPT in November 2022. It got over 100 million users in just a few weeks, making it one of the most popular software programs in the world in the fastest amount of time. Some people were shocked by what this technology could do (they came up with "AI-anxiety"), but others saw it as the start of a new era in which "human-like" tools would be used to help lawyers, teachers, health care workers, video makers, and others do their jobs.

This was not a new thing. The first version came out in 2018, and every year after that, a new one comes out. What makes v3.5 different from v1 is the knowledge base that it uses to answer users' questions. It was "trained" on 117 million factors. ChatGPT 4, which came out in 2023, is the most recent version. It was "trained" with over a trillion factors and live internet access. ChatGPT has become more accurate over time, giving fewer "nonsense" answers. It has also become less biased and can access more information in more languages from more places around the world.

OpenAI gave Microsoft $10 billion so that it could use ChatGPT and other AI products made by OpenAI. With "co-pilot," Microsoft will now use these large language learning (LLL) model-based AI systems in all of its Office products. This gives people who write documents in Word, make slide shows in PowerPoint, or look at data in Excel access to a digital assistant 24 hours a day, seven days a week. This speeds up work and makes these chores easier. Some people are very worried about the rise of AI systems like ChatGPT and have said that AI development should be "paused" until more is known about the legal, moral, hacking, and bias issues. Many school districts and colleges "banned" ChatGPT because they thought it was a way for people to "cheat" and copy other people's work. Concerned about privacy and security problems as well as following the rules for these kinds of products, governments in Europe and Asia blocked access to ChatGPT until they could prove they were following the rules. All in all, AI has caused a lot of trouble, especially in the classroom.

This chapter talks about the problems that come up when you use advanced AI in schooling and what might happen in the future. It talks about specific ways AI can be used to change the way we teach, learn, and grade, and it also offers a way forward. While ChatGPT is a useful tool that students should use, there are many other AI sites that are also very helpful for teachers and students. At the end of this chapter, a list of these will be given. This aims to question the basic ideas about how to teach, learn, and grade that have caused some teachers to have such bad reactions to the use of AI.

Implicit Models of Teaching, Learning and Assessment

The Banking Model

AI software for educational use is often designed and developed by those who do not understand the interpersonal, compassionate and contextual nature of teaching and learning. For them, learning is like "banking":

- Teachers make a knowledge deposit to a class of students.
- The student organize the deposited knowledge into appropriate "accounts" (chemistry, language arts, history, etc.).
- Students are encouraged to revise and check their mastery of the knowledge as deposited, using past test and assessment items to help them understand what matters most and what they need to know.
- Teachers test the student as to their ability to both recall the knowledge as deposited and to assess their capabilities in using this knowledge in appropriate ways.
- Students who can demonstrate mastery of knowledge and show that they can apply that knowledge then secure recognition of this mastery through credit, badges, or credentials - a kind of "interest payment."

In the early days, many teaching machines let kids learn without a teacher being there. They also gave simple multiple-choice tests as a way to check how well they understood the material. Behaviorism was at the heart of these gadgets' psychology.

It's not new to focus on technology to help people learn. Watters (2021) talks about the long history of teaching machines, which begins in the mid-1920s. Weller (2021) focuses on the idea that many people in the "EdTech" sector support: that teaching machines and learning systems will personalize instruction, letting students go at their own pace through their lessons and giving teachers more time to mentor, coach, and guide them. "Custom co-designed curriculum" is not the same thing as "individualized." It means using adaptable tests and other methods to let the student find their own way to mastering the material at their own pace.

Engaged, Authentic Learning — Student Agency for Co-Creation

In the 1960s, different ideas about how to teach and learn came up because of problems with the way things were done at the time. Ivan Illich (1971), Freire (1970, 1973, 1998), and Postman and Weingartner (1971), as well as Young (2014), were among the thinkers who made these points. These writers and others came up with an implicit model of teaching and learning that was based on guided inquiry and study, which was connected to a big picture of what the curriculum was supposed to teach. This kind of work came out of it:

- Teachers present students with challenges and tasks. Sometimes the teacher knows what it is the students are expected to "discover" (e.g., how to solve a quadratic equation), but sometimes they set a design challenge where the teacher learns alongside the student.
- Students develop their routes to learning, mentored, and coached by their teacher and other supports.
- Students self-assess their learning periodically. Sometimes peer assessment is also used.
- Teachers assess students against a competency framework - some assessments focus on specific skills, some of the students ability to use and integrate knowledge and some are focused on process (e.g., critical analysis, writing, research).

This chapter is based on a psychological method that sees the student as the one who is responsible for their own learning. It emphasizes learning by discovery and adaptation. Bandura's idea of social learning and humanistic psychology put together.

Constructions of Teaching

Both of these structures are extremes meant to show how completely different ways of thinking about the art and risk of teaching are. In banking, the focus is on results and how the teacher "produces" these results. In discovery, on the other hand, the focus is on both the social purpose of education and its role in helping each student find their own interests, worries, and personal and social commitments. Teachers need to check for learning in both models, but their role in making learning possible is different in each. In one (banking), it's all about teaching and testing. In the other (discovery), it's to push, teach, guide, inspire, share, mentor, and help, while also taking a moment to evaluate. When students learn banking, they are given information and skills; when they learn discovery, they are involved in making their own learning journey and decide what they want to learn.

To sum up, Biesta (2023) says that teaching is more than just guiding students through tough tests. Teachers teach kids to be more thoughtful, loving, compassionate, knowledgeable, creative, and thoughtful. They help kids figure out where they are going and what they want to do. The social purpose is to help people find their place in the world by getting them involved, creative, and critical.

AI and Technification

Artificial Intelligence (AI) enables learning, assessment, research, creativity, and collaboration. Its emerging presence is focused on:

- **Learning Analytics** - using algorithms and datasets to predict student behaviour and engage in early intervention to support retention and completion.
- **Automated Assessment** - using AI to generate assessments, administer assessments and automate marking and grading.
- **Supporting Learning Variety** - automated creation of multimedia materials (video, audio, infographics, slide decks, text-to-speech, speech-to-text) - especially important for ensuring access to learning and resources for students with disabilities and exceptionalities.
- **Assessing Soft Skills** - video interview assessment systems are capable of assessing a student's knowledge and emotional disposition and can provide feedback related to emotional intelligence.
- **Research** - automated finding of appropriate research materials and resources, showing inter-relationships between these resources and suggesting linkages.
- **Smarter data analysis** of data collected by researchers, students and others for projects, degrees, and diplomas.
- **Reducing Information Overload** - automated summarizing of complex documents, video and audio recordings and other materials.
- **Facilitating Creative Collaboration** - through intelligent meeting software, ideation sharing, co-curation of resources and other technologies.

- **Automated Course Creation** - automatic creation of course content, assessments, flash cards and other resources based on a limited amount of materials submitted to "kick-start" course creation.
- **Instant Language Translation** - ChatGPT can translate between thirty-three different languages. Google Translate between over 130 languages. Both have varying degrees of accuracy.

Large amounts of data are needed for all of these systems to start up and keep working. Some AI systems learn from interacting with people and can "appropriate" data and information to make them more reliable and accurate. All of them use certain types of algorithms to do their jobs, and they don't work well if the evidence they use is narrow and small, like in a very specialized knowledge area with fewer than 10,000 reference points. There is bias in some programs, which means they favor some points of view over others and some cultural groups over others.

Not all of the data that AI systems give us is correct. There are a lot of mistakes and hallucinations in early versions of ChatGPT (versions 1-3.5), where information that seems to make sense turns out to be nonsense. Developers are working methodically to cut down on mistakes, stop hallucinations, and make the system more reliable. ChatGPT 4 is trained on more than a trillion factors, while ChatGPT 3 was trained on only 300 billion. Because of this, ChatGPT 4 is 40% more likely than its predecessor to give correct true answers. A lot of information will have to be shared between schools, their staff, and students in order for these systems to work well. This is why EU countries and Japan are worried about privacy and security.

The other area of worry is "technification," which means seeing the art of teaching and the risk of learning as technical problems that can be solved by using technology more and more. Biesta (2023) talks about the technification mindset:

> "...researchers who promise that with more research, more of the "right" research, and also with more money for (their) research, they will eventually be able to deliver the so-called evidence base that will put education on a secure path of progress (albeit it is never entirely sure what this path will look like, where it will lead to, what the financial and human costs of getting there are and when this promised land will actually arrive."

The author William Rankin (2020) puts the issue of fads, trends, and technology more succinctly:

> "Each new craze proclaims that the house is falling down, even as it does nothing to repair the real, foundational problems. Digital white boards

> that promised to usher in Twenty-First-Century Learning™ now bear ghost-town witness in ten thousand classrooms to the foibles of wasting budgets on flashy, non-transformative technology rather than investing in people and training. MOOCs have proven so hollow that even Udacity has sworn off. Like the flat-earth myth of 'learning styles,' Dr John Hattie's "visible learning" is as academically rigorous as Dr. Pepper and as credible as Dr. Oz. Even most STEM programs — promising to give learners The Modern Skills They Need® — are as intellectually nutritious as styrofoam, more focused on improving a school's testing rank ("Our students have got to start scoring better against [insert group name] if they're going to be competitive in the Twenty-First Century!") than giving learners meaningful experiences and skills..
>
> The common feature all these failed educational panaceas share is a focus on facilitating and verifying the transfer of information. In other words, they're all built on the same lie."

Biesta (2019) says that the idea that high-stakes tests are the best way to measure the quality of education is linked to the idea of technological progress. After that, rankings can be made of the people, schools, regions, and countries. It is both reductionist and technified to boil down a rich and complex learning experience to a few easy indicators that can be measured in one day. These days, we measure what's handy instead of what really counts. Thinking of AI as a tool for this kind of technology will support a plan for education as banking and make it harder for students and communities to deal with the tough problems we face.

Instead of making education more technical, AI systems and apps could be used to shift the focus to a more humanistic, artistic, and caring way of teaching that gives students the power and motivation to take charge of their own learning. This idea says that now is not the time to follow the ideas of the global education reform movement (GERM). GERN bases its policies on test-based policies, a limited curriculum, seeing students as human resources ready to be hired, and teachers losing their professional status. Instead, we need to think about the future of teaching and learning in a very different way. That way of thinking is all about helping kids figure out what their purpose is, developing compassion, teamwork, critical reflection, analytical skills, the ability to be creative and imaginative, and the ability to learn new things throughout their lives. This method doesn't focus on test results; instead, it helps the student become an involved, knowledgeable, and active citizen, which is the kind of learning that John Dewey pushed for.

AI can help people change their minds in this way. One of the few times when teachers, students, and school administrators can all accept new ways of teaching, learning, and assessing is now, thanks to the tools and new ways of working that they make possible.

References

Bandura, A. (1951). Childhood and Adolescence: A Psychology of the Growing Person.

Biesta, G. (2019). Reclaiming Teaching for Teacher Education: Towards a Spiral Curriculum. Beijing International Review of Education, 1(2-3), 259-272.

Biesta, G. (2020). Risking Ourselves in Education: Qualification, Socialization and Subjectification Revisited. Educational Theory, 70(1), 89-104.

Biesta, G. (2023) "On Being a Teacher: How to Respond to the Global Construction of Teachers and Their Teaching? In Krause, S., Proyer, M. and Kremsner, G. (editors) The Making of Teachers in the Age of Migration: Critical Perspectives on the Politics of Education for Refugees, Immigrants and Minorities. London: Bloomsbury Academic,

Dewey, J. (1916). Democracy and Education. New York: MacMillan.

Frankl, V. (1988). Man's Search for Meaning. Washington, DC: Washington Square Press.

Freire, P. (1970). Pedagogy of the Oppressed. London: Penguin

Freire, P. (1973). Education for Critical Consciousness. London: Continuum.

Freire, P. (1978). Teachers as Cultural Workers - Letters to Those Who Aspire to Teach. Boulder, Co: Westview Press.

Gulson, K.N., Sellar, S., &Taylor-Webb, P. (2022). Algorithms of Education: How Datafication and Artificial Intelligence Shape Policy. Minneapolis: University of Minnesota Press.

Illich, I. (1971). Deschooling Society. New York: Harper & Row.

Jansen, J.D. (1988). Curriculum Reform in South Africa: A Critical Analysis of Outcomes Based Education. Cambridge Journal of Education, 28(3), 321-331.

Murgatroyd, S. (2010). Wicked Problems and the Work of the School. European Journal of Education, 45(2), 259-279.

Murgatroyd, S., & Sahlberg, P. (2016). Two Solitudes of Educational Policy and the Challenge of Development. Journal for Learning and Development, 3(3). Available at Volume 94(3), 29-36.

Murgatroyd, S. (2023). Futures possibilities for education in the face of global challenges: regenerative design as a driver for change. Revista Paraguaya de Education a Distancia, 4(1), 23-30.

Postman, N., & Weingartner, C. (1971). Teaching as a Subversive Activity. New York: Delta (Dell Publishing).

Rankin, W. (2020). Education is Over. Blog Posted at Regenerative.global, April 4th. Available at https://medium.com/regenerative-global/education-is-over-8b9d57502b2c

Ravitch, D. (2011). The Death and Life of the Great American School System: How Testing and Choice are Undermining Education. New York: Basic Books.

Rogers, C. (2004). On Becoming a Person. London: Constable and Robinson.

Sellar, S., Thompson, G., Rutowski, D., Berliner, D., & Sahlberg, P. (2017). The Global Education Race: Taking the Measure of PISA and International Testing. Edmonton: Brush Education.

Watters, A. (2021). Teaching Machines: The History of Personalized Learning. Boston: MIT Press.

Weller, M. (2020). 25 Years of EdTech. Athabasca, Canada: Athabasca University Press.

Young, M. (2014). Knowledge, Curriculum and the Future School. In Young, M. & Lambert, D with Roberts, C. & Roberts, M. (Editors) Knowledge and the Future School: Curriculum and Social Justice. London: Bloomsbury, pp. 9-40.

Chapter 2
Teaching and Learning in the Age of AI: What Lies Ahead

Introduction

Artificial intelligence is being used in schools, and the most direct product is the creation of an intelligent teaching system. Using computers to help teach led to the creation of the intelligent education system. It is an open method for interacting between people and computers that is made up of computer-based, student-centered, and computer-simulated ways of thinking that were created by teaching professionals. At this point, the clever teaching system is the main way that AI is used in education. Artificial intelligence is mostly used in intelligent teaching systems to represent information, figure out how to reason, and understand natural language. The intelligent teaching system is usually split into three main parts: the knowledge base, the teaching strategy, and the student model. It also has a natural language intelligent interface. This is because it combines the work of knowledge experts, teachers, and students. In particular, the intelligent teaching system's jobs are to figure out each student's learning style, cognitive traits, and current level of knowledge; to choose the best lessons and teaching methods based on those traits; and to give students individual help that is tailored to each student and lets them use normal language to talk to the "computer tutor." Computer science skills are needed to create an intelligent teaching system, but educational science theories are also needed.

Application of artificial intelligence in the field of education

Different ways of learning are one of the hardest things about school. It is hard for teachers to get a good sense of how each student really learns, which makes it hard to focus on each student's real needs during the planning and execution of lessons. This wastes teachers' energy, time, and teaching materials. But the AI system can give each student a personalized learning style so that they can learn in the best way for them. It can also keep accurate records of each student's learning progress, help teachers use hierarchical and precise teaching, and solve the main problems of teaching and learning. At the moment, image recognition, speech recognition, human-computer interaction, and other things are the major ways that artificial intelligence is used in education. Most of the applications are for training, online learning, teaching in the classroom, and other things. In the area of education, artificial intelligence is mostly used in the form of the Intelligent Tutoring System. There is an intelligent classroom, intelligent marking, intelligent diagnosis and intelligent treatment, intelligent preview, and intelligent operation in an intelligent teaching system. Intelligent sentiment analysis for the integration of intelligent teaching system is meant to make a good learning environment for students so that they can easily access all kinds of materials and learn from a wide range of services. This will help them learn well. Setting up the subject of teachers, students, and teaching management makes it possible to come up with and use teaching methods that are tailored to each student's needs. This way, each student can get individualized instruction. Smart teaching systems are now moving toward a new type of development called distributed intelligent teaching systems built on networks. It can bring students from different places together to learn in a virtual setting, make the most of network tools, encourage students to take the lead, and improve the effectiveness of teaching.

The use of artificial intelligence in education is still very new, and people are finding clever ways to combine the power of robots with human intelligence to change the way society grows. In recent years, artificial intelligence technology has always been growing quickly. Its use in education is very important for improving humanized and individualized teaching and combining teaching tasks. This is a big area of innovation in the field of education that is closely linked to the progress of science and technology.

Exploring Four Key Forms

Smart Assessment

In the usual way of teaching, teachers' jobs are mostly divided into two parts: teaching in the classroom and checking students' homework. They need to give teachers more time and effort to check their students' work. With the help of big data technology, text recognition technology, and semantic analysis technology, however, schoolwork can now be corrected automatically. Intelligent evaluation can make the process of improvement a lot easier. This is also a big change from the way evaluations have always been done. It works better, faster, and more accurately. It frees teachers from having to fix a lot of homework. Put more energy into teaching in the classroom, and you'll effectively help teachers become more efficient.

Smart Tutor System

One type of adaptive learning system is the intelligent teacher system. The one-way way that teachers impart knowledge to students in the traditional teaching mode has changed a lot because of this method. This means that teachers can now get better results when they teach. The system can make personalized learning plans for each student based on how well they understand the material being taught. It can also show which students are doing well with their own unique ways of learning and help them learn faster by giving them more resources to help them reach their learning goals.

With the clever tutor system, you can even look at the students' faces and figure out how well they are learning from that. With feedback, the teacher can get a better idea of how well the students understand what they are learning in class and use that information to plan and change what they are teaching. As it stands, the clever tutor system is still in its early stages of development. It's mostly useful for self-study and Q&A, but not so much for teaching in a classroom. Even if you want to use it better, you still need to work on making it better and more efficient on a technical level.

Educational Simulation Game

Quality education is a big part of current ideas about education. Because of this, the school shouldn't be dull; instead, it should be set up in a more fun way. Because AI is improving so quickly, teaching simulation games are not really fun in the usual sense of the word. They are aimed better. They support making education and teaching through games more open, and they make some digital games built on simulation environments. Students may be more excited about learning. Students can get a new perspective on things by playing smart computer games. These games also help them improve their observation and thinking skills, which encourages them to actively find answers and solve problems. Students can be more involved in learning by taking on different roles in a video game setting. They can also take part in learning activities with a strong desire to learn new things. There is evidence that using simulation games in the classroom can help students understand and relate to abstract ideas better by turning them into real examples. This can also help them pay more attention and gain deeper professional knowledge.

Educational Robot

Educational robots use a lot of different skills. The use of technology and information from different fields, the role that educational robots play in helping teachers is clear. Information technology can be used to improve students' understanding and ability to get information, keep the classroom interesting, and encourage students to think of new ideas. Educational robots are smart teaching tools that can be a useful addition to the work that teachers do in certain teaching situations. Through this human-computer contact, students can also actively look for answers to questions and improve their ability to learn on their own. Educational robots can tell when students' feelings change. Educational robots can tell when students' feelings change. As more interactions happen with students, teachers will have a better idea of how each student learns best. This will allow teachers to tailor their lessons to each student's needs, and students will enjoy learning through conversation with smart robots.

Obstacles in Teaching Artificial Intelligence

It's true that AI education isn't perfect, but it has had a big effect on every part of education. In the real world, people are trying to make education fit the needs of the age of AI. Our way of thinking has changed, the mode has been updated, our behavior has changed, and we've made progress in resource development and other areas that have led to positive thinking and exploration. But because education today is still very new, the role of artificial intelligence and the growth of artificial intelligence education are mostly shown by "technology," a lack of education, and some issues that exist in the field and in the practice of artificial intelligence education.

Artificial Intelligence Education Technology Upgrade

There is a difference between artificial intelligence and artificial intelligence schooling. Artificial intelligence is based on simulating how humans think and act in some ways, depending on the amount of data received, the way algorithms work, and how fast computers can process information. But artificial intelligence in education isn't an easy way to gather and analyze large amounts of data. It also requires a subjective analysis of each student's learning ability, type, style, specialty, and a number of other factors that are related. Based on this, teachers can make suggestions or take action. People and machines are not the same in important ways. Human intelligence is different from the intelligence that robots pretend to have. The computer is smart because a person can write down the problem and then the computer can do the math.

Then, human intelligence is something that can be learned and practiced, and it comes from taking the initiative. But the machine's brain is not as smart as the way humans think.

AI is automating administrative jobs, which means that schools can cut down on the time it takes to do hard work so that teachers have more time to spend with their students. With better ways to grade normal essays and written answers, AI can be used to automate the jobs that need to be done when there are multiple tests to grade. Also, Artificial Intelligence is making it possible to automate the sorting and filing of paperwork.

These days, smart information is a big deal. Robots can make digital content that is just as good as what some AU essay writing services can make. Virtual content, such as online conferences and lectures, is also smart content. Traditional course plans are being used by AI systems to make personalized textbooks for certain topics. Because of this, textbooks are being turned into digital files, and new learning tools are being made to assist students of all ages and academic levels. One of these systems uses AI to make textbook material easier to understand and has chapter summaries, flashcards, and practice tests that are easy to find your way around. The AI interface, on the other hand, lets teachers make electronic lesson plans and educational content that can be used on many devices. This includes online help programs, audios, and videos that show how things work.

Figure 1. Education Transformation workflow (Microsoft)

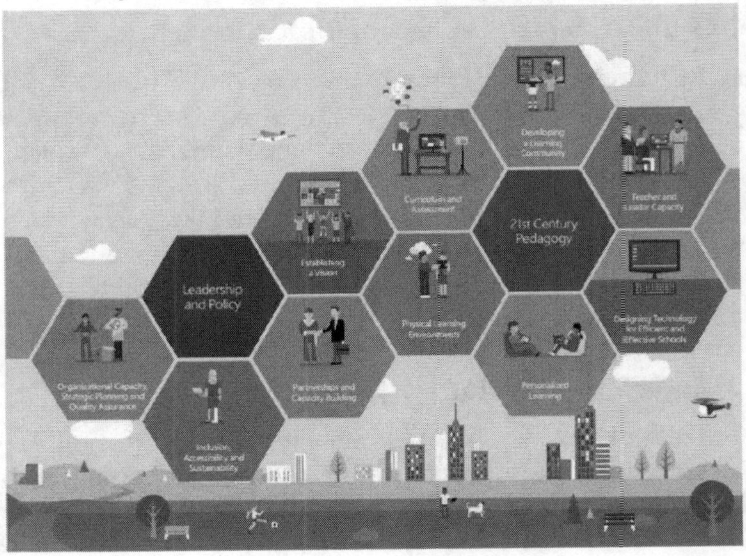

If AI is used in schools, teachers might not be removed, but they could do a much better job by giving each student personalized suggestions. AI tailors both in-class tasks and final exams to each student, making sure they get the best help possible. Also, getting comments right away is an important part of being a good tutor. Through AI-based apps, teachers can respond to each student in a way that is relevant to them. Lessons can be sped up with smart study tools and flashcards. They can also teach students if they are having trouble understanding what they are learning. College students can now talk to their teachers during a wider range of times. Smart tutoring tools can give students feedback right away and work with them one-on-one.

Any lesson can be learned with the help of AI from anywhere in the world at any time. AI teaches kids the basics of IT. With more inventions, there will be more online courses to choose from, and AI will make it possible for students to learn from anywhere.

AI helps schools figure out the best ways to make sure that kids don't get lost when they run through the hallways. AI can also be used to model complicated data so that the operations department can make predictions based on that data. Assigning seats at school events or getting food from nearby cafeterias are also examples. AI will come up with adaptable learning methods and personalized tools that will make learning better. AI could show students how their job paths might look based on their goals, which would help them in areas other than school. Time will tell what AI's long-term effects will be on the schooling field.

Limitations of Artificial Intelligence Education

Getting along It's been around for more than 60 years, but artificial intelligence is still not very useful in schooling right now. According to what each person knows, education is a way for people to learn and connect with and inspire each other. However, our intelligent teaching system is still a long way from reaching this level. Second, computers can't talk to kids like people can. Machines only look at the information that students put in and understand how they are learning. This means that people get wrong information because of "machine intelligence" data that doesn't take into account the real situation.

Learning Mode Solidification

An AI-based education system is turned into a training module by using information about each student's level of knowledge, cognitive ability, and preferred way of learning. The test scores for this module are used to grade students and see how well they are learning. The level of each student is different, and if they are taught based on a structured lesson plan instead of their own unique situation, then flexible teaching will not help them grow in a personalized way over time.

The Scope of Artificial Intelligence is Limited

Adding AI to education is in line with the times, but that doesn't mean that all subjects can be taught with AI or that the current AI education can't teach all subjects. Disciplines are clearly different from each other, and these differences can be seen in the study questions they ask, their theoretical frameworks, their ways of thinking, their research and writing methods, and so on. The way different subjects are taught and learned naturally differs because of these differences.

Analysis of the Limitations of Artificial Intelligence in Education

Because of how far along artificial intelligence is and what it is made of, it can't be used in every classroom.

References

Artificial Intelligence and the Future of Teaching and Learning Insights and Recommendations, May 2023

Artificial Intelligence in Education and Schools, Ahmet Gogen Harran University

AI Applications in Education, Zhengyu Xu(&), Yingjia Wei, and Jinming Zhang Hui Zhou Engineering Vocational College, Guangdong, China

Artificial Intelligence and the Future of Teaching and Learning Insights and Recommendations, May 2023

Artificial Intelligence in Education and Schools, Ahmet Gogen Harran University

AI Applications in Education, Zhengyu Xu(&), Yingjia Wei, and Jinming Zhang Hui Zhou Engineering Vocational College, Guan.

Leadership and Policy. Inclusion and Accessibility. What does success look like and how do you get there? Microsoft.

Chapter 3
Artificial Intelligence: Revolutionizing Schools-An Analysis

Introduction

People usually talk about artificial intelligence (AI) as the ability of machines or computers to think and act like humans. AI refers to the work that is being done to make computer systems that can think and act like humans. In this way, the most basic meaning of artificial intelligence is tools or programs that are very good at copying human behavior or thought. Timms (2016) says that thinking that artificial intelligence will be built into computers that people use at home may be an illusion of the way things work now. It could come into our lives in a number of different ways.

The year 2017 by Ng says that AI is the new energy of our time. It's possible that artificial intelligence will be the main building block of the Fifth Industrial Revolution because it has the ability to be a strong force for economic growth. That could be why China put $40 billion into AI in 2017, which was the high point of funding. China is projected to raise its gross domestic product (GDP) by 26% ($7 trillion) by 2030, which is in line with the money it makes from AI. In the same time frame, North America is projected to grow by 14.5%, or $3.7 trillion. These numbers help us understand the added value and global effects of AI on the next economy and, in our case, on the future of education. This, in turn, shapes the economy and workforce, paving the way for the next Industrial Revolution.

The further growth of artificial intelligence will have a wide range of effects, from changing the way society works in general to how classes and schools are run and how students are taught. One of the main places that could be most affected by the progress of AI is schools, which need to change with the times and make learning 21st century skills a major focus. Karsenti (2019) says that new kinds of technology will fill our lives and keep young people interested. Because of this, schools may have to make room for them. The main point of this study is to find out how people involved in law, business, education, and engineering feel about this change and what they think about how AI will affect education. In other words, the point of this study is to find out what using AI in education means and what effects it might have on the future of education based on the views of people from various fields who took part.

Artificial Intelligence in Education

Henry Ford once said, "If I had asked people what they wanted, they would have said faster horses." Roll and Wylie (2016) bring this quote to light. At first glance, it might seem like schools have turned into "faster classes" that get things done faster. But will these "fast classes" keep doing that, or do we need to think about them differently in the 21st century? As we move into the 22nd century, is it enough to teach skills, critical thought, and how to think about how you think? Or should we set up brand-new methods for the new era that have never been thought of before? What can artificial intelligence do for schooling that will set people apart from robots or smart cars and help people keep their social and emotional lives? Soon, these issues will likely be the major concerns of policymakers and implementors in the field. In fact, people are already talking about whether AI can really replace teachers or not.

Manyika et al. (2017) say that there will still be good teachers in the future who teach lessons that are meant to improve students' communication, creativity, and affective intelligence. These writers say that advances in automation and artificial intelligence will actually make "people more human." In a short summary of the research that has been done on artificial intelligence in education, Haseski (2019) says that using AI in education will make learning more personalized, provide effective learning experiences, help students find their talents, boost their creativity, and make teachers' jobs easier. However, there are also ideas that are the opposite of what you say. One risk that is being looked at in studies of artificial intelligence is giving computers the job of teachers. States and countries need to make a teacher profile that will work with these support systems in order to get ready for this future.

A lot of attention has been paid to artificial intelligence studies in education lately. However, theories of general artificial intelligence have been studied since at least the 14th century, and Alan Turing's work in 1937 brought these studies back to life. They are now being talked about a lot in scientific and academic journals. The field of AI is growing in group management, and the idea of "artificial intelligence leadership" is now being talked about in the literature.

With more use of AI in education, big changes are likely to happen in the way education works and the systems that run them. Sekeroglu, Dimililer, and Tuncal (2019), citing the study results, said that AI could help teachers give each student a more personalized education. People who aren't able to go to school, have disabilities, are refugees, or live in isolated communities can all get access to better and more appropriate learning chances with the help of artificial intelligence. Research has shown that using artificial intelligence and smart learning environments can help present successful approaches that are tailored to each person. It looks like human teachers are needed for quality education, but artificial intelligence (AI) could improve education and quality at all levels, especially by making it more personalized. Pedro et al. (2019) talk about a dual-teacher model with artificial intelligence in terms of individualized education: teachers spend a lot of time on routine and other administrative tasks, like repeating themselves and answering questions about a lot of different topics. But with in-class assistants supported by AI (secondary teachers), teachers will spend less time on routine tasks and more time on guiding students and talking to them one-on-one.

Research Method

Phenomenological study, a type of qualitative research, was used to plan the study. When you want to look into a problem or subject in more depth, qualitative study is the way to go. A type of study that tries to figure out what people think and feel is called phenomenological research. So, we tried to find out what the people thought about using AI in schools. A triangulated data collection method was used in this study to look at how people from four different professions felt about using artificial intelligence in schooling.

Participants

If possible, purposeful sampling was used to choose the individuals. Purposeful sampling is choosing a sample that has a lot of data based on the study question. Researchers looking into artificial intelligence in education have found four groups, with a total of 19 people in them:

- Academicians; academics working in the field of educational sciences (5 people)
- Legal Experts; lawyers and judges currently working in courts (5 people)
- Experts; technical experts on artificial intelligence (4 people), in private or public organizations
- Teachers; teachers currently working (5 people) in public schools

Tag names were used to report the results so that the subjects' real names would not be revealed. The names that were chosen were Ahmet and Ayse. Ali,

Huseyin, Ismail, Suleyman, Tahsin, Kemal, Elif, Kubra, Mahmut, Burak, Mehmet, Ziya, Recep, and Esref are some of the names of the people there.

Collection of Data and Analysis

For the study, semi-structured conversations were used. The people who took part were asked online what they thought about AI, how they thought it would be used in education, what they thought about the future, and what they thought were the good and bad effects of AI in education. Using the answers to the above questions, researchers looked at how the subjects felt about using AI in schools.

Three experts in the field of educational sciences helped come up with questions that would be used to find out what the subjects in the study thought. First, the questions were sent to the people who were taking part in an online form, which they filled out. Later, the people who filled out the form were interviewed in person about what they wrote on the form to get more information on the subject. In the first round of data collection, the participants were thought to be able to explain themselves better when writing alone. In the second, voluntary face-to-face meeting, the points that the researchers thought needed more clarification were brought up by the participants.

The content analysis method was used to look at all the data, from codes to bigger themes. The goal is to look at the information gathered from each individual one line at a time. To begin, codes were created, which led to themes that can be compared to writing. All of the lines were thought about at every stage of writing and when choosing the themes. As it got to the "findings" part, the codes that stood out in the analysis (like "individualization of instruction") were given more information. The subjects' thoughts on AI are looked into based on what they already know and think about AI, with possible outcomes in mind. As you can see in Table 1, only the last question (question 10) was coded with a set of numbers.

Trustworthiness

When doing qualitative study, trustworthiness is very important. An expert in the field helps with the data gathering, coding, tabulation, and reporting stages of qualitative research so that the study can be more reliable. In addition, the experts talked about their first thoughts about the subject. People who took part were asked to make preliminary opinions. An analyst triangle was used to do a full analysis that was not based on the work of three academics. It was done with the segmentation method of data sources.

To allow for viewpoint triangulation, we also looked at a lot of different studies on AI in fields ranging from health to business. In qualitative research, triangulation means using more than one method or source of data to get a full picture of a case or phenomenon. The study on artificial intelligence in education used a lot of different kinds of data because experts from many different fields took part. It was carefully checked to see if the data were compatible with other studies that looked at related topics. Data and results from several different data sources were used to compare the material. The researchers' biases were played down a lot. In case of future controls, both the raw data and the forms that have been analyzed are kept. The participants were given a clear explanation of the working process, goal, and methods. Transferability was explained in detail in terms of the people who took part and the process. They were told about rules for ethics and that they could quit the study whenever they wanted.

Findings

The main themes in this area are based on the codes that the participants stressed the most. The codes listed within the themes are not arranged by frequency, but the ones that stand out the most are shown below, along with a description of what they mean. The codes and expressions in the end results are seen to be confirmed by participants with different specialties after they give their permission. When the data was analyzed, it was clear that the participants were most interested in the goods, uses, and outputs that will come into our lives when AI comes to life. All of the other themes are explained below. We tried to give a few general quotes under each dimension that cover the theme because people talked about a lot of different things when they talked about products, problems, benefits, and ideas.

Products (Outcomes)

It was clear from this theme what the participants wanted to see happen in the education field in terms of products and solid outcomes. We wrote down the possible outcomes and products they expect from schooling under the "products" dimension. Not only physical tools were on the list of goods, but also software, systems, methods, and models. In terms of artificial intelligence in education, the following items would stand out or might have a big role:

- Advanced technology software
- Robot assistants and robot teachers
- Smart classes in schools
- Individualized education (pertains to individualization of instruction)

- Simulations for education and lessons
- Scenario and case study-producing systems
- Interest, ability, and needs analysis systems
- Vocational guidance system (for career choice)
- Programs or tools for taking attendance
- Unmanned systems of all sorts
- Learning outcome detection system (for levels of students)
- Personal teaching tools
- Attention and distraction analysis system
- Academic success detection and suggestion system for improvement
- Learning systems in cloud environments and virtual learning environments
- Curriculum editing system
- Systems that perceive and report students' learning patterns

As an example of the products/outcomes theme, Tahsin, an expert, told us, "Artificial intelligence in education can be used in many areas, from individual learning to taking attendance at the door of class to giving exams and using face recognition systems." and pointed out tools that can be used to make learning more custom. A lawyer named Ziya also said, "Providing individualized education by virtualizing teaching through artificial intelligence." Mahmut, a professional engineer, also said, "... course planning can be left to AI mechanisms [tools] by developing machine learning algorithms related to the educational system."

Drawbacks

Things that could go wrong and be dangerous with using AI in schools were talked about in this theme. Based on what the individuals said, these problems can be listed below:

- Mechanical thinking of individuals, suppressing intuitive knowledge
- The humanistic values could be replaced by a utilitarian or pragmatic perspective,
- The possible bad scenarios with the full evaluation of students, categorization of humans based on their IQ, etc.
- The information-oriented human type,
- No need for human intervention in education,

- The possibility of uncontrolled intelligence technologies in education (e.g., data security),
- Negative effects on social relationships.

In the talks, each participant talked about possible risks and downsides on their own. There are likely to be risks, especially for teachers who take part. A teacher named Ayse thinks that "artificial intelligence will increase its dominance over the world [Not much need for human intervention]." A knowledgeable person named Ali said, "some kind of machine-human style, mechanicalthinking people are waiting for us." "I think that we will not need teachers in the far future," says Emine, who is a teacher. A judge named Burak has similar views to teachers. He says, "Artificial intelligence will take over all educational tasks; even a teacher may not be needed." People may be worried about these things because of dystopian robot movies and other popular media, which some people thought could come true.

Benefits

In this theme, the results obtained from the opinions of the participants about the benefits of using artificial intelligence in education are presented. Accordingly, these benefits are:

- People measurement or measuring people
- Helping individual at learning at their own speed
- Correct determination of the individual's need
- Practical solutions to chronic problems
- No more paperwork in schools
- Prevention of waste of time
- Increase in education quality
- Providing ease of work
- Helping the right decisions with fast data analysis
- Planning teaching according to student capacity and speed
- Using or choosing effective learning methods using a learning analysis
- Ability to train in smaller groups with effective planning
- More effective individual learning process
- Helping policymakers, for example, population prediction simulations for making the right education investments in the right places

An academician named Ismail said, "...as a benefit of artificial intelligence, the student's information can be tracked, evaluated, and plans can be made for which career this student should focus on in the future." Elif, a participant who is an expert engineer, told the researchers, "...regular reporting of students' situations at school, making suggestions based on these reports, and sharing with the right people..." "Artificial intelligence tools can help in evaluating the results of exams, student movements, and communication between students," said Esref, a lawyer. Ahmet, a teacher, said, "An AI tool can listen to students' voices, figure out how much they've learned, and give them helpful or strict instructions based on that." These participants' thoughts are similar to the benefits that have been written about for "learning analytics."

Suggestions

This theme included the participants' suggestions regarding the use of artificial intelligence in education. These recommendations are as follows:

- There should be a certain measurement system when using artificial intelligence in education.
- Applications or systems developed regarding artificial intelligence in education should be tested with pilot applications and integrated into the system according to their results.
- Academic studies should be done on the developed systems and analysed.
- Necessary infrastructure works should be created.
- An audit mechanism should be established.
- Human psychology should not be ignored.
- Preventive and supportive software should be developed.
- The effects of artificial intelligence-related systems on the decision-making power of people in their lives should be measured.
- The AI integration process should proceed in a way that does not affect social relations negatively.
- Artificial intelligence in education is not a comprehensive solution; it should be used only in the areas of need.
- The process should be carried out in an interdisciplinary fashion with all stakeholders, not just educators and engineers.

"A conscious use of artificial intelligence must be present; AI should be preferred only for the areas that need it," Hatice, a teacher, said at this point. Ali, a professor, said, "We need to be careful about what we do." It is possible to do academic work. It is important to test software in pilot sites. Kubra, a very skilled engineer, gave a general explanation: "Artificial intelligence should not be at the center [sic] of educational activities; it should act as a helping element, for teachers and the human factor." To get rid of risks, AI systems should be fully controlled by people.

Since people are the ones most affected by technology, it is important that this whole process follows the law so that no one gets hurt. Recep, a lawyer, said, "If it can be based on a legal statute, the problems can be kept to a minimum." Mehmet, a lawyer, talked about his thoughts on data privacy in the context of legal cases: "The storage, protection, and confidentiality of personal data in coming AI systems must be essential; people are particularly concerned with mental analysis, and a measurement of people will lead to a whole life being exposed." Two steps should be taken to deal with this problem: 1-To set up the infrastructure the state needs to meet this duty and to make sure that the related body can only access it through strict protocols. 2-States should use deterrent fines to stop people from breaking privacy laws and to get rid of these laws as quickly and with as little damage as possible.

The last questions the volunteers were asked had a descriptive part to them: What do you mean when you talk about AI tools in education when you talk about educational settings that use AI?"Please give us a clear majority on whether AI is helpful or harmful." People were asked to rate, with a percentage, how much harm and good they thought the use of AI in society and education would cause. The comments were both focused on the pros and cons. Table 1 shows how the answers that the groups gave to this question were spread out.

Table 1. Distribution of benefit - drawback percentages by groups

Groups	**Benefit Average**	**Drawback Average**
Academicians	% 56.00	% 44.00
Law Personnel	% 72.20	% 27.80
Expert Engineers	% 95.00	% 5.00
Teachers	% 62.00	% 38.00
General	% 68.67	% 31.33

In this way, we can say that the participants had a generally good view of AI developments. Academicians may have only thought about the pros and cons of teaching in terms of teaching jobs and may have seen problems in teachers' futures, even though they seem to agree that teaching has benefits. On the other hand, professional engineers said that AI would improve processes and help everyone in the education field.

Conclusions

Four main themes and one descriptive theme about AI in education came out of the talks with the participants. The first theme was about the goods, which included powerful AI media, apps, or results that will happen soon. Some of these were simulation programs, systems that help with testing and review, VR classes, robots that help with homework, and personalized learning systems. One of the most talked-about effects of AI as a near future is how it will change individual learning with the tools it offers. When used in education, artificial intelligence can help make personalized learning possible. When Goksel and Bozkurt (2019) looked at papers on education and AI studies, they found that the most important ideas and concepts were personalized learning, adaptable learning, and learning styles. This means that instead of using a one-size-fits-all method, AI can be used in schools to make sure that each student gets the help they need. So, we can conclude that growth in education can meet the needs of optimal learning with AI and its supporting tools, which will be very helpful for both teachers and students. In this case, Abdelsalam (2014) suggested an intelligent tutoring system (ITS) that is built on the mastery learning strategy.

The second idea was about the bad things and danger. People who took part in the study thought that widespread use of AI would result in an overly mechanical way of processing information, a pragmatic approach, a greater focus on knowledge over aesthetic feelings, less room for teachers, problems with ethics and security, and bad effects on relationships between people. People who use their cell phones too much, inappropriately, or without control are already showing signs of behavioral, social, and emotional problems (Choliz, 2010). This may be made stronger by the fact that AI is already deeply ingrained in human life and phones. Participants said that phones already take away people's social interactions, and they are really curious about the next step for AI growth in the mobile world.

They think that there will be fewer jobs for teachers and more jobs for robot helpers in schools. Along these lines, Picciano (2019) says that most of the people who lose their jobs will be in professional and white-collar fields, like teaching, law, medicine, and the business world. A big worry in the community about AI is that it will take away jobs. Also, Picciano (2019) suggests that AI or machines won't be the ones doing the work of humans. Instead, it will be people who know how to use smart tools or intelligent systems that will be more powerful than those who don't. In their 2016 article about teachers' roles, Roll and Wylie say that teaching as it is now will not work in the future. Instead, they say that teachers should become mentors and teach their students lifelong skills like how to connect with others, break out of their comfort zone, and think about problems that come up in real life.

However, we have not yet hit the level of artificial intelligence that is shown on TV, but the field is quickly progressing. People who commented on the post all talked about Isaac Asimov's book I, Robot and the movie based on it. This could be because of movies or a fear of smart tools in the community. Some people brought up Isaac Asimov's "Robot Laws," which can be summed up as follows:

1. A robot may not injure a human being or, through inaction, allow a human being to come to harm, except when required to do so in order to prevent greater harm to humanity itself.
2. A robot must obey any orders given to it by human beings, except where such orders would conflict with the First Law or cause greater harm to humanity itself.
3. A robot must protect its own existence as long as such protection does not conflict with the First or Second Law or cause greater harm to humanity itself.

Later, a zeroth law was introduced:

0. A robot may not harm humanity, or by inaction, allow humanity to come to harm.

"Proportionality" is one of the most important ideas in avoiding risk from artificial intelligence technologies. Up to this point, participants said that academics, engineers, and other pros should use AI and related tools in a smart way.

The third theme was about how AI has helped people. This theme is like the first theme under "solid outcomes," but it's about functions and uses instead of outcomes. The people who took part in the study think that AI-powered systems will help content keep up with the learner's speed, help systems better figure out what learners need, stop time and resource waste, allow fast data analysis, and give people the power to make the right choices. One of the participants said that AI was very helpful because it can help states spend in related areas by predicting how people will move. According to Subrahmanyam and Swathi (2018), AI-powered prediction computing could learn about students' study habits and suggest the best time for them to study. Roll and Wylie (2016) say that both students and teachers need better, more personalized help. AI will better meet the needs of learners and let students learn at their own pace. Subrahmanyam and Swathi (2018) say that AI can help students master material by repeating lessons as needed and making a personalized learning plan for each student fast.

Some participants' thoughts are very similar to the idea of "learning analytics" that has been written about. Learning analytics is the process of gathering, measuring, analyzing, and sharing data about students and their surroundings in order to better understand and improve the places where they learn. As AI technologies become more common in schools, learning analytics can also help make sure that each student gets the right material to help them learn. To put it another way, the use of artificial intelligence (AI) in schools is important for creating a flexible and editable program. One very important thing that AI apps do is something called "learning analytics." One individual said that one result of the AI would be "measurable persons." This meant that the AI would look at people and make predictions about how they would do in order to help students and teachers learn better, which is similar to learning analytics. In this way, Karsenti (2019) says that using studies based on AI tools will help lower even the number of students who don't show up to school, which is great for schools.

The fourth theme is made up of ideas from people who wanted to use AI in education. These ideas include safety models, supervised systems, and steps that have already been thought out. At both the expert and judicial levels, there should be more than one kind of oversight. People who took part said that AI shouldn't be used in too many personal situations. In education, AI shouldn't be seen as a one-size-fits-all solution. Instead, it should be seen as a way to make things easier and more efficient in certain areas. If not, technologies that use artificial intelligence to make computers smarter might cause legal issues. Many issues need to be thought about, such as who AI will report to, what responsibility these tools will have, who owns the goods made by AI, and privacy and security concerns. At this point, the law should catch up with changes in technology, and rules about AI tools should be made based on robots or teacher assistants that we think will be around in the future.

The use of AI in education is exciting and could lead to positive changes for schools. It's important to deal with the new events by carefully talking about their causes and affects. People are interested in artificial intelligence technologies, but as the people who took part in this study have said, they are not a cure-all or a change that will make everything better. So, the good and bad effects on law, ethics, education, psychology, and society must be thought about. Since people are the ones most affected by technology, it is important that this whole process follows the law so that no one gets hurt.

The fifth result of this study is that people have a generally good view of AI. The people who took part seem to mostly have good feelings about AI. The teachers in the study think AI is good for education, but the academics don't seem to agree as much and are more focused on the bad things. Experts in the field think that AI systems are helpful because they will probably lead to full performance and get rid of problems in the systems, which will make work easier for people. The general good and bad mood seems to come from movies, TV shows, expert opinions, worries about the future of teaching, and real-life experience with online systems that are already in place.

Last but not least, different professionals took part in this study, which gave a full picture of how different educational stakeholders feel about AI in schools and education. There are four main themes that can be seen in the study's data: "Products" refers to the possible outcomes or products that could come from using AI in education. "Drawbacks" refers to the possible problems that could come from using AI in education. "Benefits" refers to the expected benefits of using AI in education. "Suggestions" refers to ideas on how to use AI in education. When AI comes to schools, there will definitely be pros, cons, and risks that go along with it. Most of the people who took part think that AI will give students and learners new chances that regular classroom or learning tools might not be able to provide. But things could go wrong too. Before the next industrial revolution, schools need to take a more proactive part. Policymakers should follow the advice in the research to get the most out of AI in the education area.

References

Abdelsalam, U. M. (2014, March). A proposal model of developing intelligent tutoring systems based on mastery learning. Paper presented the Third International Conference on E-Learning in Education (pp. 106-118). Retrieved from http://paper. researchbib.com/view/paper/14102

Asimov, I. (2004). I, Robot. New York: Bantam Books.

Buyukozturk, S., Cakmak, E. K., Akgun, O. E., Karadeniz, S., & Demirel, F. (2018). Bilimsel arafiirma yontemleri [Scientific research methods], Ankara: Pegem A Yayincilik.

Canbek, M. (2020). Artificial Intelligence Leadership: Imitating Mintzberg's Managerial Roles. In Business Management and Communication Perspectives in Industry 4.0 (pp. 173-187). IGI Global.

Chang, J., & Lu, X. (2019, August). The study on students' participation in personalized learning under the background of artificial intelligence. In 10th International Conference on Information Technology in Medicine and Education (ITME) (pp. 555-558). IEEE.

Choliz, M. (2010). Mobile phone addiction: a point of issue. Addiction, 105(2), pp. 373-374.

Creswell, J. W. (2013). Qualitative inquiry and research design: Choosing among five approaches, SAGE publications Felix, C.V. (2020). The Role of the Teacher and AI in Education. Sengupta, E., Blessinger, P. and Makhanya, M.S. (Ed.) International Perspectives on the Role of Technology in Humanizing Higher Education (Innovations in Higher Education Teaching and Learning, Vol. 33), Emerald Publishing Limited, pp. 33-48. https://doi.org/10.1108/S2055-364120200000033003

Goksel, N., & Bozkurt, A. (2019). Artificial intelligence in education: current insights and future perspectives. In S. Sisman-Ugur & G. Kurubacak (Eds.), Handbook of Research on Learning in the Age of Transhumanism (pp. 224236). Hershey, PA: IGI Global.

Grosz, B. J., & Stone, P. (2018). A century-long commitment to assessing artificial intelligence and its impact on society. Communications of the ACM, 61(12), pp. 68-73.

Golic, Z. (2019). Finance and artificial intelligence: The fifth industrial revolution and its impact on the financial sector. Zbornik radova Ekonomskog fakulteta u Istocnom Sarajevu, (19), pp. 67-81.

Haseski. H.I. (2019). What do Turkish pre-service teachers think about artificial intelligence? International Journal of Computer Science Education in Schools, 3(2), Doi: 10.21585/ijcses. v3i2.55

Humble, N., & Mozelius, P. (2019, October). Artificial Intelligence in Education-a Promise, a Threat or a Hype?. In European Conference on the Impact of Artificial Intelligence and Robotics 2019 (ECIAIR 2019), Oxford, UK (pp. 149-156). Academic Conferences and Publishing International Limited.

Karsenti, T. (2019). Artificial intelligence in education: the urgent need to prepare teachers for tomorrow's schools. Formation etprofession, 27(1), pp. 112-116. Doi:10.18162/fp.2019.a166.

Long, P., & Siemens, G. (2011). Penetrating the fog: Analytics in learning and education. EDUCAUSEReview, 46(5), pp. 31-40.

Manyika, J., Chui, M., Miremadi, M., Bughin, J., George, K., Willmott, P., & Dewhurst, M. (2017). A future that works: Automation, employment, and productivity. Chicago: McKinsey Global Institute.

Mohammed P.S., & Watson E. N. (2019). Towards inclusive education in the age of artificial intelligence: perspectives, challenges, and opportunities. In: Knox J., Wang Y., Gallagher M. (eds) Artificial Intelligence and Inclusive Education. Perspectives on Rethinking and Reforming Education. Singapore: Springer. https://doi.org/10.1007/978- 981-13-8161-4 2

Mou, X. (2019). Artificial intelligence: investment trends and selected industry uses. EMCompass; No. 71. Washington, D.C.: World Bank Group.

Ng, A. (2017, January 25). Artificial intelligence is the new electricity. Speech presented at Stanford MSx Future Forum in California, Stanford. https ://www.youtube.com/watch?v=21EiKfQYZXc.

Patton, M. Q. (1999). Enhancing the quality and credibility of qualitative analysis. Health services research, 34(5/2\ pp. 1189-1208.

Pedro, F., Subosa, M., Rivas, A., & Valverde, P. (2019). Artificial intelligence in education: Challenges and opportunities for sustainable development. Paris: UNESCO.

Picciano, A. (2019). Artificial intelligence and the academy's loss of purpose. Online Learning, 23(3), Doi:10.24059/olj.v23i3.2023

PwC. (2017). Sizing the prize What's the real value of AI for your business and how can you capitalise? Retrieved from https://www.pwc.com/gx/en/issues/analytics/assets/pwc-ai-analysis-sizing-the-prize-report.pdf.

Research on Education and Media. Vol. 12, N. 1, Year 2020 - ISSN: 2037-0830

Roll, I., & Wylie, R. (2016). Evolution and revolution in artificial intelligence in education. International Journal of Artificial Intelligence in Education, 26(2), pp. 582-599.

Sekeroglu, B., Dimililer, K., & Tuncal, K. (2019). Artificial intelligence in education: application in student performance evaluation. Dilemas Contemporaneos: Education, Politica y Valores, 7(1), pp. 1-21.

Streubert, H. J., & Carpenter, D. R. (2011). Qualitative research in nursing. (5th ed.). Philadelphia: Lippincott Williams and Wilkins.

Subrahmanyam, V. V., & Swathi, K. (2018). Artificial intelligence and its implications in education. In Int. Conf. Improv. Access to Distance High. Educ. Focus Underserved Communities Uncovered Reg. Kakatiya University (pp. 1-11). Timms, M. J. (2016). Letting artificial intelligence in education out of the box: educational cobots and smart classrooms. International Journal of Artificial Intelligence in Education, 26(2), pp. 701-712, Doi: 10.1007/s40593- 016-0095-y

Wartman, S. A., & Combs, C. D. (2018). Medical education must move from the information age to the age of artificial intelligence. Academic Medicine, 95(8), pp. 1107-1109.

Wogu, I. A. P., Misra, S., Olu-Owolabi, E. F., Assibong, P. A.. & Udoh, O. D. (2018). Artificial intelligence, artificial teachers and the fate of learners in the 21st century education sector: Implications for theory and practice. International Journal of Pure and Applied Mathematics, 119(16), pp. 2245-2259.

Yildirim, A., & Simsek, H. (2008). Sosyal bilimlerde nitel arafimna yontemleri [Qualitative research methods in the social sciences]. Ankara: Seckin Publication.

Chapter 4
AI: Catalyzing Change in School Education

These years, AI is becoming more and more a part of our daily lives. Because of this, the government and schools are paying more attention to build AI in education. Technology based on artificial intelligence (AI) is changing not only how schools teach and learn, but also the campus environment, the curriculum, and everything else in the education business. Schools are changing more and more with AI technology, from elementary school to college to adult education. People can learn better and reach their learning goals with these tools. It is thought that artificial intelligence technology will play a big part in changing the way schools teach and learn. New intelligent teaching tools will be brought to schools, along with new ways to teach and learn. It will also encourage new ways to evaluate teachers and run schools. Teachers need to change the way they think and look for new ways to use artificial intelligence and teaching together. They should also push for the deeper merging of technology and teaching and the creative growth of both education and teaching. If schools change the way they teach and learn, they will no longer be limited by time and space. This will create an information freeway, support fair practices in schools, and make learning and teaching more interesting and logical. In this system, students can grow based on their own abilities, while teachers' boring tasks will be taken over by AI systems, and the school will become smarter overall.

AI Education Technology Development and Application

As AI technology improves, more technologies will be used in modern education. These include smart robots, speech and picture recognition, augmented and virtual reality (AR/VR), machine learning, adaptive learning algorithms, quantum computing, block chain, and more. All of these technologies are called "intelligent technologies" as a group. Along with the education business, these technologies have started to speed up and are still doing so. Wu Yonghe et al. (2017) said that machine learning, deep learning, natural language processing, neural networks, learning computing, and image recognition are all technologies that are linked to "artificial intelligence and education." Mou Zhijia

(2017) says that to support personalized learning, AI has "two bottom layers": machine learning and deep learning; "three layer services": physical service-oriented voice recognition and emotional computing technologies; content-oriented natural language processing technologies; and behavioral service-oriented adaptive learning technologies. In 2018, Chen Kaiquan et al. said that adding five types of AI technologies—including intelligent recognition, natural language understanding, learning analysis, virtual reality, and education robots—can help the current digital intelligent teaching system get better at what it does. The education business will change as more and more products that use artificial intelligence to teach are released. Artificial intelligence (AI) is used in education and teaching goods. Schools and teachers can get AI-based education technology, tools, and services. By collecting user data from students and analyzing and giving feedback on it, it can then be used in the five stages of the learning process (teach, learn, test, train, and assess) to give students personalized answers and useful feedback.

As artificial intelligence has grown and spread, more and more software and tools that use AI have been introduced to the field of education. Jill Watson, a virtual assistant, helps the teaching assistant answer questions from the more than 300 children in a classroom. Knewton is an adaptive teaching platform that can collect data on how students behave while they are learning. This data can then be used to analyze and predict students' learning styles, hobbies, and progress so that they can provide personalized learning services. When it comes to educational robots, LEGO's newest line of programmable intelligent robots, MindstormsEV3, has improved interaction with smart devices by adding WiFi modules that let it connect to iOS and Android devices and be managed through an app. Human-computer contact can be made possible by getting better microphones and speakers. In China, many campus entrances, classroom entrances, and dorm entrances now have a variety of face entry control and attendance systems and other campus applications. The face recognition attendance system is clearly better than traditional card swipe, fingerprint recognition, and other methods because it lets parents and teachers see at all times if a student is at school. This effectively stops students from skipping classes, not coming home, and other issues. A lot of artificial intelligence technology has also been used in educational settings, like grading and diagnosing tests, managing campuses and classrooms, making decisions about education, and running schools.

The Aspects of Artificial Intelligence in Promoting Teaching and Learning Transformation

According to the research that has already been done, artificial intelligence is used to change many aspects of teaching and learning in schools. These include teaching and learning resources and environments, teaching and learning methods, managing and evaluating teachers, changing the structure and system of subjects, and changing the content of lessons, as shown in Figure 1.

Figure 1. Direction of Education and Teaching Transformation

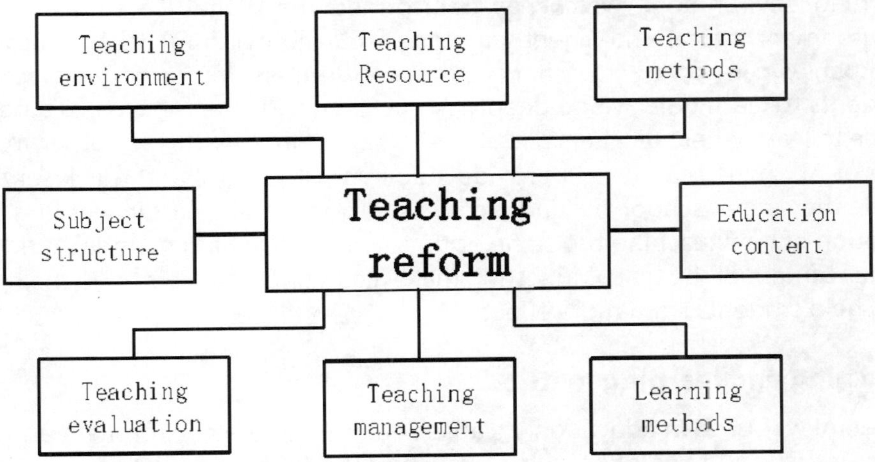

Teaching resources and teaching environment

Reforming the way we teach starts with making changes to the resources we use. The changes in tools and environment will lead to new ways of teaching, which will make the classroom a better place for students to learn, creating a circle. In a broader sense, modern science and technology have changed the way we teach and learn by changing things like school materials, media, and the environment. First, as artificial intelligence (AI) technology has grown, many companies have made a wide range of intelligent teaching and learning tools, as well as intelligent learning aids like intelligent teaching platforms, teaching robots, intelligent learning software, and more. These high-tech tools for teaching and learning have made things a lot easier for both teachers and students, giving teaching and learning a new lease on life. There are a lot of smart gadgets in the classroom these days thanks to artificial intelligence. In the classroom, teachers and smart helpers will work together. Both students and teachers will wear different smart tools with sensors. The whole process of learning and teaching is smart. Second, the progress made in artificial intelligence has made it much easier for students and teachers to find materials for learning. As part of intelligent development of learning resources, the machine has checked the resources for quality and added semantic information to them. The resources are now split into text, video, and other formats. So, when the intelligent learning environment figures out what the students need, it can push learning materials that are right for them. Thanks to the growth of search engines, students can quickly find the materials they need without having to spend a lot of time looking for them (Zhu and Wang 2019). Finally, the growth of artificial intelligence has made it easier to create an intelligent learning environment, which has transformed the digital learning resource environment into an intelligent learning resource environment. AI education companies can work with schools to make the classroom a better place for students to learn quickly and deeply. Artificial intelligence (AI) creates a better place to learn where teachers and students can connect with each other. In this age of AI, smart schools will provide students with useful and quick services while they are at school, making it easier for them to take part in learning. The creation of new teaching tools, the optimization of teaching materials, and the enhancement of the teaching setting make it easier for teachers to do their jobs and help students learn more effectively.

Teaching and learning methods

When AI was used in education, it caused changes in the environment and the technical support tools that were available. These changes led to a series of changes in how teachers taught. When it comes to teachers, AI can help them plan lessons. Teachers can use AI, big data, and other technological benefits to help students customize their learning and create scientifically sound learning programs. Smart computers and a lot of info can also be very helpful for teachers. With artificial intelligence (AI), teachers can watch how their students are learning in real time and give correct instructions so that students learn in an intelligent and exact way. Big data can help teachers understand their students' learning situations at any time, help them solve problems, help them grade homework, do teachers' boring routine tasks, free teachers from simple and dull teaching tasks, give teachers more time to talk to their students, get back to the work of "people," come up with new ways to teach, change the way they teach, and do more creative work. Machine learning can assist teachers, it will modify their duties, and it will encourage the switch from imparting information to building knowledge. In this age of AI, education needs to focus on teaching kids basic reading and writing skills. Teachers' job isn't to teach, but to help students grow. They should act as life coaches or psychologists for their students and help them see the good things in life and understand how valuable it is. Soon, teachers will have other things to do besides teaching. In this age of AI, the most important thing for teachers is not to learn more about their subjects and improve their professional skills and knowledge. Instead, they should focus on teaching students about ethics, duty, national identity, cross-cultural communication, and the arts.

When we build an intelligent setting for students to learn in, we need to think about how to guide them. By making different kinds of learning tasks, we create a helpful learning environment that lets students adaptively preview new information, use intelligent interaction to learn new information, do intelligent companionship exercises, and get intelligent advice on deep learning. This helps students understand, discover, and improve themselves all the time. Some ways of learning that were based on knowledge don't work anymore because of how things are changing. Things that you can learn by heart and then forgetting slowly lose their value over time. These things are things that AI can do better than people. Because of this, we need to change the way we think about education and speed up the shift from "learning to apply" to "use to learn." We also need to pay more attention to how each student learns best and encourage them to become talented individuals who can handle difficult situations in the future. If students don't have a connection between school and their social lives and if they don't learn from their own experiences, then school is dull and not very useful. As an open organization system, schools should connect with the real world and use all available social tools from outside the school to help teach. One university with "no campus" is the University of Minerva in the United States. Undergraduate programs that last four years are spread out in seven big cities around the world, such as San Francisco, Hong Kong, London, and others. Students can use first-class classrooms, labs, and other learning spaces thanks to partnerships with the local high school, labs, and high-tech companies. This is an example of how higher education can be changed from the ground up. In order for education to be smart, it needs to connect what students learn to real life. People can learn outside of school too, in places like businesses, communities, and science and technology sites. It's possible for education to go to different areas; any place where people can learn well is a school. By combining virtual scenes with the real world using mixed reality technology, students can see the small world and understand abstract ideas. This makes learning a real-life experience in a rich setting.

Teaching Management and Teaching Evaluation.

There is more and more info about how people teach and learn because technology is getting better and the learning environment is getting better. It is necessary for teachers to change the way they handle and evaluate their classes in order to make full and effective use of these data in order to improve teaching and learning.

As AI technology improves, it will be possible for many routine jobs in regular schools to be managed intelligently. This will have an impact on how teachers are managed. There is academic management, student status management, course management for students, teacher teaching management, study management, financial management, energy management, human resource management, and more. The smart tools will cut down on time-consuming tasks that need to be done by hand and make schools more efficient. At the same time, the smart platform can collect data and keep an eye on things in real time. It can also do statistics and analysis of information, make smart choices about management methods, make smart decisions about how to best use information, improve resource utilization, improve education management, and make sure that schoolwork develops in a way that is harmonious and long-lasting. In this age of AI, teacher control of students needs to be more adaptable, and changes should be made based on what each student needs to learn and how well they understand it. At the moment, more and more virtual schools in the US are trying to do this, which means they are trying to make the cycle of teaching management units longer. School grades are based on how many hours they put in, how well they understand, and how well they did on tests. It's up to each student to choose when and how long to study each time.

Evaluation in the classroom is a key way to check for understanding and help students grow. It has been found that diagnostic teaching evaluation is one of the places where artificial intelligence has the most potential. These days, artificial intelligence has also led to the growth of many intelligent diagnostic businesses. When it comes to evaluating teachers, we can now use AI to do automatic data collection, feature analysis, deep learning, and modeling simulations of teaching behavior traits to get a full and accurate picture of how well teachers teach in the classroom. There will no longer be a single evaluation between students and teachers. Instead, artificial intelligence technology will give a full evaluation of teachers. And this is how diversity in review will help teachers get more fair and objective evaluations, as well as more room to improve. This will help teachers grow in the right direction.

As a way to evaluate students, the platform uses artificial intelligence to gather and record different types of information about their learning at all times, creating a set of information about all the students together and about each individual student. Based on a specific analysis model, the platform quickly and accurately creates a diagnostic evaluation report for each student's learning. It then provides personalized learning resources and development suggestions to help each student become their best self by switching between a ruler to assess each student's current situation. In this way, the review is more scientific, fair, and up-to-date.

Reformation of the Subject System

More than anything else, AI will have an effect on how talented students are taught in schools. The most obvious example is how it will change the way subjects are organized in higher education. Artificial intelligence will have a big effect on the people who are studying it's work lives and future growth. The door to academia and the business world needs to be opened for scientific and engineering progress. AI has the potential to lead the economic revolution and social change. AI will change how universities set up their courses and the subjects they teach. In the past few years, many colleges have changed the way they structure their subjects to make them smarter.

Artificial intelligence is a new field of science and technology that is being studied and developed in the United States. Its goal is to extend and improve human intelligence's theory, method, technology, and application systems. In the United States' top 300 colleges, 27 graduate programs in computer science and AI are offered by 26 schools. Their work in computer theory, computer hardware, computer software, computer databases, and artificial intelligence is the best in the US and even the world. The university's bachelor's degree program in artificial intelligence includes a wide range of cutting-edge classes, such as computational biology, speech recognition, cognition, machine learning, and more. On June 28, 2018, Tsinghua University in China opened a place to study artificial intelligence. This is a big step forward for Tsinghua University's plan to become a world-class university. It's also a big step toward changing the way scientific study is done. A lot of colleges have added "Artificial Intelligence and Robot Engineering Majors." In 2019, Beijing University began teaching robotics engineering to first-year students. The professional courses teach students how to develop and use basic robot dynamics and control, bionic structural design, intelligent perception, human-computer interaction, and micro-nano operations. They also train people to become future leaders in robotics, intelligent manufacturing, and artificial intelligence. Over time, majors in artificial intelligence have started to show up on lists of regular college fields. Artificial intelligence not only helps new subjects and jobs come about, but it also changes the way old subjects and jobs are laid out and done. With the arrival of artificial intelligence, some standard subjects and jobs may become less strong in order to adapt to the changes that AI technology brings about.

In addition, as artificial intelligence (AI) gets better, there will be more cross-contact between subjects in higher education. The lines between subjects will become less clear, and the lines between jobs will be looked at again.

Reformation of Educational Content

The lessons taught in school are based on educational goals. Since AI has an effect on these goals, it will also have an effect on the lessons taught in schools. First, because AI will be a part of our everyday lives, it must be taught in schools. Students must learn the basics of AI and how it can be used in professional settings. This is a great way for students to learn about all parts of artificial intelligence. Second, the use of artificial intelligence across borders has blurred the lines between different topics. This needs a wide range of skills, since subjects that are taught separately and have nothing to do with each other don't help students build their wide range of skills. To make this possible, barriers must be taken down between courses and content must be integrated so that students can learn from each other. Again, education in the intelligent age is meant to improve it rather than add to it, with a focus on the growth of each student. So, in the future, the standard way of teaching in classes will not work anymore. Instead, personalized learning materials will be moved around based on each person's interests and skills. Lastly, learned information is easy to get back because intelligent tools can store a lot of it. Because of this, the lessons taught in schools will focus on building up students' implicit knowledge. Instead of focusing on how well students can remember things, teachers will spend more time teaching them how to be useful and how to handle emergencies in real life.

New Requirements for Schools in the Era of Artificial Intelligence

Faced with the opportunities and challenges of developing education in the age of AI, along with the progress made in education and teaching and the overall growth trend of AI technology, schools will actively look into and promote new requirements for building a school in the age of AI.

Before schools can start using smart technology, they need to hire a group of top-notch teachers who know how to teach in this new age of technology. Teachers are what make education possible and where it all began. For example, create a teacher education innovation base and an innovative teacher training environment. Look for and train teachers who can deal with the challenges of artificial intelligence and other new technologies. Take steps to improve literacy in schools and give outstanding principals and teachers intelligent education leadership training and training in how to teach.

Schools should pay more attention to how fair education is and how well it is done. New standards that are more fair and of better quality will be at the center of goals for educational development. In the age of intelligence, it will be easier for more people to learn new things, more people from disadvantaged backgrounds will be able to get an education, and more people will be able to improve their knowledge. At the same time, schools need to make sure that intelligent education is open to everyone. A big part of fixing the problem of unequal education should be making smart technology more accessible to everyone. This means that smart education shouldn't just be for a select few.

In terms of social ethics, data security, and school governing systems, schools will have to deal with new problems and meet new requirements. A lot of data and algorithms will be created as the intelligent era starts. The progress of artificial intelligence will make it even harder to tell the difference between people, space, and information, which will lead to a number of ethical, legal, and security problems. Teachers should be aware of the possible security risks that AI technology may pose. To do this, they should focus on social value guidance, make sure that prevention and restraint work better in the future, make sure that data is safe and algorithms are fair, and make sure that AI development is safe, reliable, and manageable.

At the scientific research level, schools should do a number of things to help the growth of both the artificial intelligence industry and school education. They should support university scientific research institutions, AI leading businesses, primary and secondary schools, and other groups to work together better and make the best intelligent education technology research and development systems. Schools should also set up a way to spend money in the long term, combine high-quality subject materials with research power, keep up with the latest developments in the AI industry, and find out what their own development needs are. At the same time, we need to speed up the deep integration and creative growth of AI and education. We also need to look into the growth plans, standards, and ways to promote intelligent education.

Summary

Starting with an overview of how artificial intelligence is being used in education right now, this chapter then goes on to talk about how AI can help education and training. In eight different ways, this part suggested that artificial intelligence technology will help change the way schools teach and learn. It also talks about how artificial intelligence is changing teaching materials and the learning setting, as well as teaching methods and learning methods, as well as subject systems, educational content, and how teachers are managed and evaluated. Finally, it provides a summary of the new needs for school growth in the age of AI. In this age of AI, schools should change and improve many things about the school, including the teachers, the students, and how fair the education is so that all students get a better education.

References

Ahmad, S. Z., A. R. A. Bakar, and N. Ahmad. 2018. "An Evaluation of Teaching Methods of Entrepreneurship in Hospitality and Tourism Programs." The International Journal of Management Education 16(1):14-25.

Barret, Mandy, Lisa Branson, Sheryl Carter, Frank DeLeon, Justin Ellis, Cirrus Gundlach, and Dale Lee. 2019. "Using Artificial Intelligence to Enhance Educational Opportunities and Student Services in Higher Education." The Journal of the Virginia Community Colleges 22(1):22.

Chen, Bin. 2019. "Tsinghua University Opens Artificial Intelligence Class." China Science News.

Chen, Kaiquan, Yao He, and Guoqiang Zhong. 2018. "The Transformation of Information Literacy Connotation and the Targeting of AI Education in the Perspective of Artificial Intelligence Also on the Implementation of AI Curriculum and Teaching in Basic Education." Journal of Distance Education 1.

Chen, Le. 2016. "Educational Implications of New American University Minerva." University(Academic) 01:53-61.

Fu, Die. 2019. "Where Is School Education Going in the Era of Artificial Intelligence." Modern Education Management (05):52-57.

Guerrero, Tricia A., and Jennifer Wiley. 2019. "Using 'Idealized Peers' for Automated Evaluation of Student Understanding in an Introductory Psychology Course." Pp. 133-43 in International Conference on Artificial Intelligence in Education. Vol. 11625 LNAI. Springer Verlag.

Guo, Y., and Y. Xiao. 2019. "Artificial Intelligence in Education." In 4th International Conference on Modern Management, Education Technology and Social Science (MMETSS 2019) Atlantis Press.

Hill, Janette R., and Michael J. Hannafin. 2001. "Teaching and Learning in Digital Environments: The Resurgence of Resource-Based Learning." Educational Technology Research and Development 49(3):37-52.

Hinojo-Lucena, F. J., I. Aznar-Diaz, and J. M. Caceres-Reche, M. P., & Romero-Rodriguez. 2019. "Artificial Intelligence in Higher Education: A Bibliometric Study on Its Impact in the Scientific Literature." Education Sciences 9(1):51.

Karsenti, T. 2019. "Artificial Intelligence in Education: The Urgent Need to Prepare Teachers for Tomorrow's Schools." Formation et Profession 27(1):112-16.

Kasinathan, Vinothini, Aida Mustapha, and Imran Medi. 2017. "Adaptive Learning System for Higher Learning." Pp. 960-70 in ICIT2017 - 8th International Conference on Information Technology, Proceedings.

Li, Suang, and Qinhua Zheng. 2019. "Artificial Intelligence + Education: Opportunities and Challenges Coexist." Teacher's Journal 11:14-17.

Li, Yunliang. 2019. "Thoughts on Teaching Reform of Artificial Intelligence Course Based on Innovative Teaching Concept." Digital Communication World 11:247.

Liu, Shufei. 2019. "Analysis on the Application of Face Recognition Technology in Smart Campus." Telecom World 09:44-45.

Luo, Dingshen, Wenxin Li, Zhihong Deng, Yunhai Tong, Jiaying Liu, Jin Chen, and Kunqing Xie. 2019. "Teaching Reform and Practice of Artificial Intelligence Course in Beijing University." Computer Education 10:3-8.

Malik, G., D. K. Tayal, and S. Vij. 2019. "An Analysis of the Role of Artificial Intelligence in Education and Teaching." In Recent Findings in Intelligent Computing Techniques 40717.

Mo, Zhijia. 2017. "Rethinking and Unraveling the Personalized Learning Theory in the 'Artificial Intelligence +' Era." Journal of Distance Education 3(35):22-30.

Murphy, Robert. 2019. Artificial Intelligence Applications to Support K–12 Teachers and Teaching: A Review of Promising Applications, Challenges, and Risks. RAND Corporation.

Park, C. L., C. Crocker, J. Nussey, J. Springate, and D. Hutchings. 2019. "Evaluation of a Teaching Tool-Wiki-in Online Graduate Education." Journal of Information Systems Education 23(3).

Savin-Baden, Maggi, Roy Bhakta, Victoria Mason-Robbie, and David Burden. 2019. "An Evaluation of the Effectiveness of Using Pedagogical Agents for Teaching in Inclusive Ways." Artificial Intelligence and Inclusive Education 117-34.

Takacs, A., G. Eigner, L. Kovacs, I. J. Rudas, and T. Haidegger. 2016. "Teacher's Kit: Development, Usability, and Communities of Modular Robotic Kits for Classroom Education." IEEE Robotics & Automation Magazine 23(2):30-39.

Wang, Jiajia, and Tian Hu. 2019. "Review of the Operation Mechanism of American Virtual Charter Schools." International and Comparative Education 08:29-34.

Wu, Yonghe, Bowen Liu, and Xiaolin Ma. 2017. "Building an 'Artificial Intelligence + Education' Ecosystem." Journal of Distance Education 5:27-39.

Yang, Xixi, Tianyi Gu, and Xiaolong Qian. 2019. "Research on the Characteristics of Artificial Intelligence Talent Training in Stanford University." Journal of Open Learning 05:40-47. Yu, Wei, and Zhongfeng Hu. 2019. "Application of Artificial Intelligence in Foreign Universities and Its Inspiration to China." The Modern Education Journal 06:24-30. Zhang, Baobao, and Allan Dafoe. 2019. "Artificial Intelligence: American Attitudes and Trends." SSRN Electronic Journal.

Zhang, Zhizheng, Linlin Zhang, and Mang Li. 2019. "The Due Analysis of Artificial Intelligence Education Application: The Necessity and Possibility of Teaching Automation." Distance Education in China (01):25-35.

Zhou, Li. 2019. "Artificial Intelligence and Chinese Higher Education: Impact, Application and Countermeasures." Education Modernization 59:185-86.

Zhu, Qiongli, and Minjuan Wang. 2019. "Team-Based Mobile Learning Supported by an Intelligent System: Case Study of STEM Students." Interactive Learning Environments 1-17.

Chapter 5
The Impact of AI on Future Teaching and Learning - United States Perspective

The U.S. Department of Education (Department) wants to see more use of technology in schools to help teachers and students learn better and to encourage new ideas in all schools. This study talks about how important it is to share information and make rules for "artificial intelligence," a group of quickly improving basic skills that are becoming more common in all kinds of educational technology systems and can be used by anyone. We will use the term "educational technology" (edtech) to refer to both (a) technologies that are made to be used in schools and (b) general technologies that are commonly used in schools. This study makes suggestions for how teachers, educational leaders, policymakers, researchers, and people who create and sell educational technology can work together to solve important policy problems that come up when AI is used in schools.

"Automation based on associations" is one way to describe AI. When computers automate reasoning based on data associations (or associations derived from expert knowledge), two fundamental changes happen that take computing beyond traditional edtech: (1) they move from collecting data to finding patterns in data; and (2) they go from giving users access to instructional resources to making decisions about teaching and other educational tasks automatically. Pattern recognition and automatic decision-making are big steps forward in the tasks that can be given to a computer system. It's possible that the process of making an AI system will lead to unfair choices and biased ways of finding patterns. Because of this, AI systems must be controlled by teaching systems. This study talks about the chances of using AI to make education better, the problems that might come up, and makes suggestions for how policies should be made in the future.

Rising Interest in AI in Education

There are still a lot of things that need to be done to make teaching and learning better. Teachers are looking for safe, effective, and scalable ways to use technology to help them deal with these issues. It makes sense that teachers would wonder if the fast changes in technology that affect our daily lives could be helpful. Like the rest of us, teachers use AI-powered services every day. For example, voice assistants in their homes, tools that can fix grammar, finish sentences, and write essays, and apps that can automatically plan their trips on their phones. A lot of teachers are looking into AI tools as soon as they become available to everyone. Educators think that AI-powered features like speech recognition could help students with disabilities, those learning more than one language, and others who could benefit from digital learning tools that are more flexible and tailored to their needs. They are looking into how AI can help them write or make lessons better, as well as how they find, pick, and change materials to use in their lessons.

The people who teach also know about new risks. Powerful and useful features can come with new risks to data privacy and security. Teachers are aware that AI can automatically make product that is wrong or inappropriate. They are worried that the connections or machines that AI makes could make biases stronger. They've seen new ways for students to pass off other people's work as their own. They are very aware of "teachable moments" and teaching methods that a human teacher can use but AI models miss or don't get right. They aren't sure if the suggestions made by a program would be fair. There are many things that worry educators. Everyone who works in education needs to make sure that the good things that AI can do for education are used, and the bad things that could happen because AI is being used in edtech are avoided.

The Department works closely with people in the education field to come up with guidelines for edtech. These groups include educational leaders (teachers, faculty, support staff, and other educators), lawmakers, advocates and funders, technology developers, community members and groups, and most importantly, students and their families or caregivers. The Department has recently seen a sharp rise in interest and worry about AI in its work with constituents. Among other things, a 2021 field scan found that people who make all sorts of technology systems—for student information, classroom teaching, school logistics, parent-teacher communication, and more—plan to add AI features to their work. More than 700 people came to four listening sessions in June and August 2022, and it was clear that constituents think something needs to be done right away to get ahead of the expected rise of AI in education technology. They also want to get their hands dirty and start working together. People learned about new generative AI chatbots in late 2022 and early 2023. They then started to look into how AI could be used to do things like write essays, make lesson plans, make pictures, give kids personalized assignments, and more. The Department learned more about the pros and cons of robots that use AI by reading what people said on social media, at conferences, and in the news. But this report won't focus on a single AI tool, service, or statement, since systems that use AI change so quickly. Lastly, the Department used the educational policy experts that worked for the department and the experts it has ties with in AI policy to shape the report's results and suggestions.

Top Three Reasons to Prioritize AI in Education

To make teaching and learning better, many more things need to be done. To help them deal with these problems, teachers want to use technology in ways that are safe, useful, and easy to expand. The fact that technology changes so quickly in our daily lives makes sense for teachers to wonder if it could be useful. Teachers use services that are driven by AI every day, just like the rest of us. They could have voice helpers in their homes, tools that can fix grammar, finish sentences, and write essays, and apps on their phones that can plan their trips for them. A lot of teachers are excited to get their hands on AI tools as soon as they are made public. Some teachers believe that AI-powered features, such as speech recognition, could help students who have challenges, are learning more than one language, or would benefit from digital learning tools that are more flexible and fit their needs. AI could help them write or improve lessons. They are also looking into how to find, pick, and change things for their lessons.

People who teach also know about new dangers. Users may face new threats to their privacy and security when they add powerful and useful features. Teachers know that AI can make things that are wrong or inappropriate on its own. They are afraid that the biases could get stronger because of the machines or links that AI makes. These people have seen new ways for students to fake their own work. They are very aware of "teachable moments" and ways to teach that an actual teacher can use but AI models miss or get wrong. They aren't sure if the program's ideas are fair. Many things worry people who work in schools. People who work in education need to make sure that AI is used for its good effects and not for its bad effects.

EdTech rules are made with the help of people in the education area who work closely with the Department. Leaders in education (teachers, administrators, support staff, and other teachers), politicians, advocates and funders, tech developers, community members and groups, and, most importantly, students and their families or caregivers. Recently, there has been a sharp rise in interest and worry about AI in the work that the Department does with the public. A 2021 field scan found that people who make many different kinds of technology systems—for student information, teaching, school operations, contact between parents and teachers, and more—plan to add AI features to their work.

Over 700 people showed up to four listening meetings in June and August 2022. It was clear that people want to see action taken right away to prepare for the expected rise of AI in education technology. They also want to work together and get their hands dirty. In late 2022 and early 2023, people learned about AI robots that could learn on their own. Then they looked into how AI could be used to do extra tasks such as write reports, make lesson plans, draw pictures, assign unique tasks to each child, and more. The Department read what people on social media, at workshops, and in the news said about the pros and cons of AI-powered robots to learn more. But because AI systems change so quickly, this report won't just talk about one AI tool, service, or comment. Lastly, the Department used its own educational policy experts and AI policy experts it works with to shape the report's findings and ideas.

Toward Policies for AI in Education

There has been a noticeable increase in investment in AI and more study on ethics, such as issues of fairness and transparency, according to the 2023 AI Index Report from the Stanford Institute for Human-Centered AI. Of course, more study is being done on subjects like ethics because problems are being seen. There will be moral issues in schooling too. In 25 countries, the study found a lot of interest in the number of legislative proposals that include AI. In the US, there are several executive orders that aim to make sure AI is fair and trustworthy. The White House Office of Science and Technology Policy has also released a Blueprint for an AI Bill of Rights (Blueprint) that outlines principles and best practices that can help reach this goal. These plans, along with other AI-related policy work going on in both the executive and parliamentary branches, will shape how AI is used in every part of society. In Europe, the European Commission just put out ethical rules for teachers on how to use artificial intelligence (AI) and data in the classroom.

AI is changing things quickly and bringing about changes in society that need a national policy reaction. Besides general rules that apply to everyone, we also need education-specific rules that take into account federal student privacy laws (like FERPA) and similar state laws. These rules should be able to adapt to new opportunities and problems within the frameworks that are already in place. AI also automatically makes suggestions and does things to help students learn. Because of this, teachers will need to think about how these suggestions and actions can be legal, like the Individuals with Disabilities Education Act (IDEA). In the last part, we talk about specific policies.

Figure 1. Research about AI is growing rapidly. Other indicators, such as dollars invested and number of people employed, show similar trends.

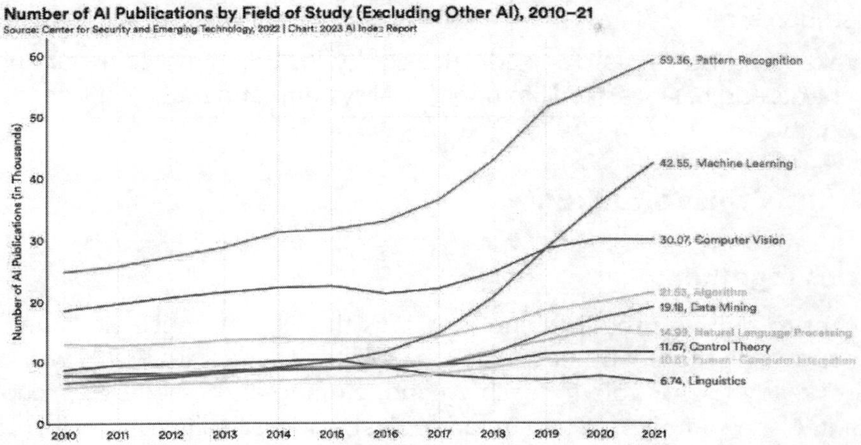

AI is getting better and better all the time (see Figure 1). People can now use powerful new AI features to make pictures and text, which is changing how people make text and images. The progress in AI isn't just happening in study labs; it's also being talked about in the news and in publications aimed at teachers.

A lot of different ideas and frameworks have been put forward by researchers for ethical AI and connected ideas like fair, responsible, and human-centered AI. People who participated in the listening session said that these ideas and frameworks should be built upon, but they also said that more needed to be done. They said that there was an urgent need for safety nets and rules that make the use of AI advances in education safe, especially since AI is being integrated into mainstream technologies at a faster and faster rate. Since making policies takes time, policymakers and people who have an interest in education need to start right away to define the rules, disclosures, requirements, and other frameworks that can help make the future safe and good for everyone, especially students and teachers.

Policies are urgently needed to implement the following:

1. leverage automation to advance learning outcomes while protecting human decision making and judgment;
2. interrogate the underlying data quality in AI models to ensure fair and unbiased pattern recognition and decision making in educational applications, based on accurate information appropriate to the pedagogical situation;

3. enable examination of how particular AI technologies, as part of larger edtech or educational systems, may increase or undermine equity for students; and
4. take steps to safeguard and advance equity, including providing for human checks and balances and limiting any AI systems and tools that undermine equity.

Ensuring Ethics and Equity

Policies Together

We want to build on the listening meetings the Department held to involve and educate all those who have a say in educational decisions. This way, they can get ready for AI's role in teaching and learning and make better choices about it. AI is a complicated and broad subject, and we can't cover it all or solve problems that still need more input from the public. The goal of this report is to be a starting place.

Both the pros and cons of using AI in education are significant in all levels, from K–12 to higher education and the workplace. The examples in this study will only cover K–12 education because they fit within the given scope. The effects are the same at all stages of education, and the Department plans to do more in 2023 to involve people outside of K–12 schools.

Guiding Questions

Now that we know AI makes machines more automated and lets machines do some jobs that people used to do, we can ask two big, important questions:

1. What is our collective vision of a desirable and achievable educational system that leverages automation to advance learning while protecting and centering human agency?
2. How and on what timeline will we be ready with necessary guidelines and guardrails, as well as convincing evidence of positive impacts, so that constituents can ethically and equitably implement this vision widely?

In the report's Learning, Teaching, and Assessment sections, we go into more detail about parts of an educational vision that are based on what students, teachers, and school systems need now. We also talk about key findings and the next steps that need to be taken. Here are four important foundations for understanding these ideas. These roots come from what we know about how to use technology in the classroom to help students get better opportunities, fair treatment, and results. They also have something to do with the new Blueprint.

Foundation 1: Center People (Parents, Educators, and Students)

National, state, and local governments will need to make AI policies that focus on education so that individuals and communities can make smart choices about which technologies to use in schools and classes. Think about what goes on in your daily life. A lot of us use goods with AI because they are often better and easier to use. For instance, not many people want to use paper maps anymore; they think that technology makes it easier and faster to find the best way to get where we want to go. At the same time, many people don't understand how much privacy they give up when they use tools that use AI. AI will pose privacy and other risks that can't be solved by people making their own decisions; more safeguards will be needed.

Clear limits should be put on who can get, use, transfer, and store our personal information. These limits should include limits on targeted ads. Instead of making Americans read a lot of small print, these limits should force platforms to limit how much information they gather.

As new protections are made, we suggest that laws focus on people instead of machines. In order to do this, the first suggestion in this paper is to put more focus on AI while keeping humans involved. People, including teachers and students, need to be able to keep the power to decide what trends mean and what to do next. The idea of putting people in the loop comes from the Blueprint's "Human Alternatives, Consideration, and Fallback" and from ethical ideas used in evaluating AI in general, like protecting human rights. It should be a top policy goal to make sure that humans are always involved in educational applications, even though there are pressures to use AI instead of people to make decisions. Policies shouldn't get in the way of progress and innovation, and they shouldn't be hard to follow. We need an AI policy for education that supports democratic values and protects civil rights in the creation, deployment, and management of automated systems used at all levels of the American school system.

Foundation 2: Advance Equity

"Members of underserved communities—many of whom have endured generations of discrimination and disinvestment—still face significant barriers to realizing the full promise of our great Nation, and the Federal Government has a responsibility to remove these barriers," said President Biden in a recent executive order. The order also said that the Federal Government would "pursue educational equity so that our Nation's schools put every student on a path to success" and "root out bias in the design and use of new technologies, such as artificial intelligence." When policymakers talk about AI in education, they need to have a clear idea of what equity means, like what the Department's new study, Advancing Digital Equity for All, says. Digital equity, according to this chapter, is "the state of having people and communities have the IT skills they need to fully participate in the society and economy of the United States."

At the heart of every listening session we held were issues of fair treatment of people of color and unfair racism. We heard a conversation that became more and more focused on data quality problems and what happens when bad or wrong data is used in AI systems for education. Datasets are used to make AI, and if they aren't representative or have unwanted patterns or connections, the AI models that come from them might find patterns or make decisions in an unfair way. "Algorithmic bias" is when a computer finds patterns or makes choices automatically in a way that isn't fair. Unintentional inequality caused by algorithmic bias could hurt fairness on a large scale. This is not a new conversation, as this document talks about in the part on formative assessment. For decades, people have been right to question whether ratings are fair and unbiased. Just like with tests, it's important for local school leaders to know if an AI model has algorithmic bias or is thought to be fair and reliable before they decide whether to use AI to reach their equality goals.

In the Blueprint, we stress the idea of "algorithmic discrimination." When AI algorithms are built using past data, they are naturally biased, and it can be hard to imagine all the effects of biased data and algorithms when designing a system. The Department thinks that AI algorithms should be fixed if they bring or keep up unfair discriminatory practices in schools. For example, in higher education, algorithms that decide who gets to go to college, pick out students for early intervention, or flag possible exam cheating must be checked for unfair discriminatory bias both when they are first designed and later on when they are widely used.

Foundation 3: Ensure Safety, Ethics, and Effectiveness

The Department's policies are based on the idea that data protection and security are important in systems used by teachers, students, and other people in schools. Access to specific data is needed for the development and use of AI. This data includes more than just student records like rosters and gradebooks. It also includes specific information about what students and teachers do when they use technology to teach and learn. Because AI depends on data so much, data protection, security, and governance need to be looked at again and more carefully (as also suggested in the Blueprint). Most of the time, AI models aren't made with educational use or student privacy in mind. This means that using these models in schools might not be in line with how the school is trying to follow federal or state privacy rules for students, like FERPA.

Figure 2. The Elementary and Secondary Education Act defines four levels of evidence.

Strong	Randomized controlled trial
Moderate	Quasi-experiment
Promising	Correlational study
Demonstrates a Rationale	Logic model informed by research or evaluation

Also, educational leaders are committed to making choices about the use of technology in schools based on proof that it works. This is a key part of the Department's policy. For instance, the Elementary and Secondary Education Act (ESEA), as amended, also says that decisions must be based on evidence. It added four levels of proof (see Figure 2). The Institute of Education Sciences and other research bodies in our country are very important for gathering the evidence we need. The Blueprint asks for proof of success, but the education sector is already there. We need to make sure that AI-enhanced edtech meets ESEA standards too.

Foundation 4: Promote Transparency

Complex AI models are at the heart of technologies that find patterns and automate tasks. This is one big way that AI-enabled apps, goods, and services will be different from mainstream education technology. The Blueprint says that AI models need to be open and honest, which means they need to be disclosed (called "notice") and explained. In education, people who make decisions will need more than just notice. They will also need to know how AI models work in a variety of general educational use cases. This way, they can better predict risks, problems, and limits.

When used in edtech, AI models will be close representations of reality. Because of this, people can always ask these questions: How well do the AI models work? Do they clearly show what's most important? How well do the suggestions that an AI model makes fit with how you want to teach? What are some of the bigger effects of using AI models on a large scale in education?

The parts of this chapter that follow build on what people said and continue the idea of using multiple dimensions to judge the quality of AI systems and tools:

- **About AI**: AI systems and tools must respect data privacy and security. Humans must be in the loop.
- **Learning**: AI systems and tools must align to our collective vision for high-quality learning, including equity.
- **Teaching**: AI systems and tools must be inspectable, explainable, and provide human alternatives to AI-based suggestions; educators will need support to exercise professional judgment and override AI models, when necessary.
- **Formative Assessment**: AI systems and tools must minimize bias, promote fairness, and avoid additional testing time and burden for students and teachers.
- **Research and Development**: AI systems and tools must account for the context of teaching and learning and must work well in educational practice, given variability in students, teachers, and settings.
- **Recommendations**: Use of AI systems and tools must be safe and effective for students. They must include algorithmic discrimination protections, protect data privacy, provide notice and explanation, and provide a recourse to humans when problems arise. The people most affected by the use of AI in education must be part of the development of the AI model, system, or tool, even if this slows the pace of adoption.

We return to the idea that these considerations fit together in a comprehensive perspective on the quality of AI models in the Recommendations section.

Overview of Document

We begin in the next section by elaborating a definition of AI, followed by addressing learning, teaching, assessment, and research and development. Organizing key insights by these topics keeps us focused on exploring implications for improving educational opportunity and outcomes for students throughout the chapter.

Within these topics, three important themes are explored:

1. **Opportunities and Risks**. Policies should focus on the most valuable educational advances while mitigating risks.
2. **Trust and Trustworthiness**. Trust and safeguarding are particularly important in education because we have an obligation to keep students out of harm's way and safeguard their learning experiences.
3. **Quality of AI Models**. The process of developing and then applying a model is at the heart of any AI system. Policies need to support evaluation

of the qualities of AI models and their alignment to goals for teaching and learning during the processes of educational adoption and use.

What is AI?

Our preliminary definition of AI as automation based on associations requires elaboration. Below we address three additional perspectives on what constitutes AI. Educators will find these different perspectives arise in the marketing of AI functionality and are important to understand when evaluating edtech systems that incorporate AI. One useful glossary of AI for Education terms is the CIRCLS Glossary of Artificial Intelligence Terms for Educators.[1]

AI is not a single thing, but rather a broad term for a growing set of modeling skills, as shown in Figure 3.

Figure 3. Components, types, and subfields of AI based on Regona et al (2022).[2]

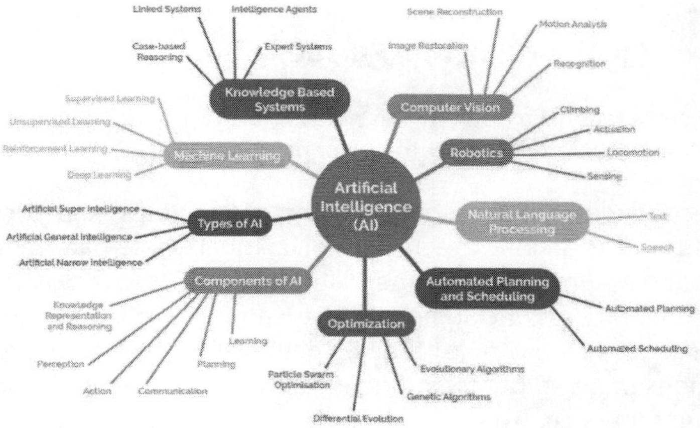

Perspective: Human-Like Reasoning

A lot of people became aware of AI through the 1968 classic movie "2001: A Space Odyssey," in which the "Heuristically-programmed algorithmic" computer, or "HAL," talks to pilot Frank. This is something Frank could not do on his own: HAL helps Frank steer the plane through space. But Frank does leave the spaceship in the end, and HAL takes over. Things do not go well for Frank. Human-like

1 Search for "AI Glossary Educators" to find other useful definitions.

2 Regona, Massimo & Yigitcanlar, Tan & Xia, Bo & Li, R.Y.M. (2022). Opportunities and adoption challenges of AI in the construction industry: A PRISMA review. Journal of Open Innovation Technology Market and Complexity, 8(45). https://doi.org/10.3390/joitmc8010045

actions, like reasoning, talking, and acting, are shown by HAL. Like all AI uses, HAL can help people, but it also comes with risks that were not planned for. This is because AI thinks and acts in different ways and to different limits than humans do.

"Human-like" is a useful word that can be used to quickly sum up the idea that computers today can do a lot of different things than they could do in the early days of edtech. Educational apps will be able to talk to teachers and students, help plan how tasks happen in the classroom, and do things that have a bigger effect on teachers and students. There will be chances to do things much better than we do now, as well as problems that we need to be aware of and deal with.

That being said, the term "human-like" isn't always useful because AI doesn't process knowledge the same way people do. We might make bad rules for AI in schools if we don't take into account the differences between people and computers.

Perspective: An Algorithm that Pursues a Goal

> "Any computational method that is made to act independently towards a goal based on inferences from theory or patterns in data."[1]

This second definition emphasizes that AI systems and tools identify patterns and choose actions to achieve a given goal. These pattern recognition capabilities and automated recommendations will be used in ways that impact the educational process, including student learning and teacher instructional decision making. For example, today's personalized learning systems may recognize signs that a student is struggling and may recommend an alternative instructional sequence. The scope of pattern recognition and automated recommendations will expand.

Correspondingly, humans must determine the types and degree of responsibility we will grant to technology within educational processes, which is not a new dilemma.

In the last few decades, people have argued about the roles of teachers and computers in schools using terms like "personalized learning," "blended instruction," and "computer-aided instruction." Still, how do systems that use both people and algorithms decide which lessons to teach? Today, AI systems

1 Friedman, L., Blair Black, N., Walker, E., & Roschelle, J. (November 8, 2021) Safe AI in education needs you. Association of Computing Machinery blog, https://cacm.acm.org/blogs/blog-cacm/256657-safe-ai-in-education-needs-you/fulltext

and tools already make it possible to tailor lesson plans to each student's needs. This lets teachers give students feedback and help when they need it, like when they are learning a new language or math problems. As AI-enabled systems and tools get better and more common, the debate about how to use AI in the classroom to improve teaching and help students learn will start up again and get more heated.

Now, let's look at another easy case. When a teacher tells an AI system, "Show a map of ancient Greece on the classroom screen," the system may pick one of hundreds of maps by looking at the lesson goals, what has worked well in similar classes, or which maps have features that will help students learn. If an AI system offers a learning resource or gives the teacher a few choices, the teacher may be able to spend less time on less important tasks and more time on more important ones. However, there are types of AI-enabled automation that the teacher may not agree with, such as letting an AI system or tool choose the best reads for the students that are related to a historical event. In this situation, a teacher might decide not to use AI-enabled systems or tools because AI could make up false facts (called "hallucinating") or lead students to wrong internet versions of past events. Every day, teachers will have to weigh these kinds of rewards and risks.

Theories and facts are processed differently by computers than by people. AI works best when it can find connections or relationships in the data that is fed to an algorithm during the model creation process. Some associations may be helpful, but others may be unfair or not right for the situation. It is very dangerous to find bad connections in data, which could lead to automated discrimination. The problem is something every monitor knows about: Someone or a computer could say, "Our data shows that your student should be in this class." The parent or guardian could respond, "No, you are using the wrong data." Because I know my child better, I think they should be put in a different class. You can find this problem with other tools and systems too, but using AI models can make it worse when a computer uses data to make a suggestion. This is because the computer may look more neutral and trustworthy than it really is.

Although this perspective can be useful, it can be misleading. A human view of agency, pursuing goals, and reasoning includes our human abilities to make sense of multiple contexts. For example, a teacher may see three students each make the same mathematical error but recognize that one student has an Individualized Education Program to address vision issues, another misunderstands a mathematical concept, and a third just experienced a frustrating interaction on the playground; the same instructional decision is therefore not appropriate. However, AI systems often lack data and judgement to appropriately include context as they detect patterns and automate decisions. Further, case studies show that technology has the potential to quickly derail from safe to unsafe or from effective to ineffective when the context shifts even slightly. For this and other reasons, people must be involved in goal setting, pattern analysis, and decision-making.[1]

Perspective: Intelligence Augmentation

> "Augmented intelligence is a design pattern for a human-centered partnership model of people and artificial intelligence (AI) working together to enhance cognitive performance, including learning, decision making, and new experiences. "[2]

Foundation #1 (above) keeps humans in the loop and positions AI systems and tools to support human reasoning. "Intelligence Augmentation" (IA)[3] centers "intelligence" and "decision making" in humans but recognizes that people sometimes are overburdened and benefit from assistive tools. AI may help teachers make better decisions because computers notice patterns that teachers can miss. For example, when a teacher and student agree that the student needs reminders, an AI system may provide reminders in whatever form a student likes without adding to the teacher's workload. Intelligence Automation (IA) uses the same basic capabilities of AI, employing associations in data to notice patterns, and, through automation, takes actions based on those patterns. However, IA squarely focuses on helping people in human activities of teaching and learning, whereas AI tends to focus attention on what computers can do.

Definition of "Model"

The above points of view help us understand AI better. But for people to really judge AI, they need to look at individual models and how they are made. The word "model" can mean more than one thing in everyday speech. We explain what we meant, which is something like "mathematical model," below. Also, keep in mind that the word "model" in "AI model" is not the same as in "model school" or "instructional model," since "AI model" is not a single case made by experts to serve as an example.

---

1 Russell, S. (2019). Human compatible: Artificial intelligence and the problem of control. Viking. ISBN 978-0-525-55861-3.

2 Gartner (n.d.) Gartner glossary: Augmented intelligence. Gartner. https://www.gartner.com/en/information- technology/glossary/augmented-intelligence

3 Englebart, D.C. (October 1962). Augmenting human intellect: A conceptual framework. SRI Summary Report AFOSR- 3223. https://www.dougengelbart.org/pubs/augment-3906.html

Like financial models, AI models are close representations of reality that can be used to find patterns, make predictions, or look at different options for making decisions. In most middle school math classes, students use a mathematical model to figure out which of two cell phone plans is better. This kind of model is used by financial managers to help people make plans for their retirement portfolios. At its core, AI is a set of very powerful mathematical tools for making and using models. It's true that well-known chatbots write long articles one word at a time. The AI model suggests which words will probably come after the text that has been written so far. AI chatbots use a very large statistical model to add one likely word at a time, which makes their essays surprisingly coherent.

People start to answer the question "What parts of reality does the model approximate well?" when we ask about the model at the heart of AI. and "how does it fit with the decision that needs to be made?" In the same way, one could ask about algorithms, which are the exact ways that an AI model makes decisions to go from inputs to outputs. Another thing that could be asked is how good the data was that was used to make the model. For example, how representative is that data? It will get hard to keep track of three terms: models, algorithms, and data. We decided to focus on the idea of AI models because the two are closely linked. It's important to know how well the AI model fits the world we care about, where the model will break down, and how. This is what we want to bring to the forefront.

To keep things mysterious, some people don't talk about the details of models. Talking about AI as if it has no limits on what it can do and is very close to reality can get people excited about the possibilities of the future. But the future can be lied about. In the same way, people may stop calling a model AI when it is used a lot, but these systems are still AI models with all the risks we've talked about here. We need to know exactly when and where AI models don't match up with how we want to teach and learn.

Insight: AI Systems Enable New Forms of Interaction

AI models make it possible for computers to make suggestions or plans, and they can also support more normal ways of interacting, like talking to an assistant. People will want educational systems with AI because they can help teachers and students connect with each other in a more natural way. Classic edtech platforms don't let teachers and students connect with edtech in a lot of different ways. You can pick things from a menu or in a multiple-choice question, and so can the teacher. They could type short answers. They can use touch movements or drag things around on the screen. Students and teachers can get outputs from the computer in the form of writing, graphics, and multimedia.

These types of inputs and outputs can be used in many situations, but this style of interaction is not the same as how two people talk to each other; it is unique to human-computer interaction. AI is likely to make interacting with computers more like interacting with other people (see Figure 4). A teacher can talk to an AI helper, and the assistant can talk back. A student could draw something, and the computer could pick out a certain part of the picture. When a teacher or student starts to write, the computer may finish the sentence for them, like how email programs today can finish our thoughts faster than we can type them.

Additionally, the possibilities for automated actions that can be executed by AI tools are expanding. Current personalization tools may automatically adjust the sequence, pace, hints, or trajectory through learning experiences.[1] Actions in the future might look like an AI system or tool that helps a student with homework[2] or a teaching assistant that reduces a teacher's workload by recommending lesson plans that fit a teacher's needs and are similar to lesson plans a teacher previously liked.[3] Further, an AI-enabled assistant may appear as an additional "partner" in a small group of students who are working together on a collaborative assignment.[4] An AI-enabled tool may also help teachers with complex classroom routines.[5] For example, a tool may help teachers with orchestrating[6] the movement of students from a full class discussion into small groups and making sure each group has the materials needed to start their work.

1 Shemshack, A., Spector, J.M. (2020) A systematic literature review of personalized learning terms. Smart Learning Environments, 7(33). https://doi.org/10.1186/s40561-020-00140-9

2 Roschelle, J., Feng, M., Murphy, R. & Mason, C.A. (2016). Online mathematics homework increases student achievement. AERA Open, 2(4), 1-12. DOI: 10.1177/2332858416673968

3 Celik, I., Dindar, M., Muukkonen, H. & Jarvela, S. (2022). The promises and challenges of artificial intelligence for teachers: A systematic review of research. TechTrends, 66, 616-630. https://doi.org/10.1007/s11528-022-00715-y

4 Chen, C., Park, H.W. & Breazeal, C. (2020). Teaching and learning with children: Impact of reciprocal peer learning with a social robot on children's learning and emotive engagement. Computers & Education, 150, https://doi.org/10.1016Zi.compedu.2020.103836

5 Holstein, K., McLaren, B.M., & Aleven, V. (2019). Co-designing a real-time classroom orchestration tool to support teacher-AI complementarity. Journal of Learning Analytics, 6(2). https://doi.org/10.18608/ila.2019.62.3

6 Roschelle, J., Dimitriadis, Y. & Hoppe, U. (2013). Classroom orchestration: Synthesis. Computers & Education, 69, 512-526. https://doi.org/10.1016/j.compedu.2013.04.010

Figure 4. Differences that teachers and students may experience in future technologies.

	Familiar Technology Capabilities	Future Technology Capabilities
Input	• Typing	• Speaking
	• Clicking and dragging	• Drawing
	• Touching and gesturing	• Analyzing images and video
Processing	• Displaying information and tasks	• Assisting students and teachers
	• Sequencing learning activities	• Planning and adapting activities
	• Checking student work	• Revealing patterns in student work
Output	• Text	• Conversations
	• Graphics	• Annotating and highlighting
	• Multimedia	• Suggesting and recommending
	• Dashboards	• Organizing and guiding

Key Recommendation: Human in the Loop AI

A lot of people have been surprised by how technology can suggest what seems like an incredibly personalized product, song, or even word to finish a line in a word processor like the one being used to write this document. We talk about specific ways that AI systems may be useful (or dangerous) in education throughout this addition. We never mean to suggest that AI can take the place of a teacher, a guardian, or an educational leader as the person in charge of a student's education. When we talk about AI models, we talk about their flaws and how people in education need to talk about what they want AI models to have and how they should be used.

This is why our first suggestion is that we work toward a view of AI in which people are involved. So, people are a part of the process of finding patterns in the way schools work and giving those patterns value. It also means that teachers will still make the most important choices about how to teach. This means that teachers have a say in and make decisions about formative exams as well. One loop is the process of finding patterns in what students do and choosing tools or next steps that will help them learn. In other loops, teachers plan lessons and think about what they've taught. This kind of loop is also known as Response to Intervention.

People being involved is an idea that is talked about in a wider range of topics, not just AI in education. People who are interested could find out more about "human-centered AI," "responsible AI," "value-sensitive AI," "AI for social good," and other terms that keep people involved, like "human-centered AI."

Using AI systems and tools with care and judgment is an important part of giving every student the best chance to learn, especially when decisions about school have real-world effects. People are better at making broad judgments about circumstances than AI is. People must still be responsible for our children's health and safety, for all students' success in school and preparation for their careers, and for making society more fair and just.

Learning

The Department's long-standing edtech vision sees students as active learners; students participate in discussions that advance their understanding, use visualizations and simulations to explain concepts as they relate to the real world, and leverage helpful scaffolding and timely feedback as they learn. Constituents want technology to align to and build on these and other research-based understandings of how people learn. Educators can draw upon two books titled How People Learn and How People Learn II by the National Academies of Sciences, Engineering, and Medicine for a broad synthesis of what we know about learning.[1] We should build AI-enhanced educational technology on research-based principles. One main goal should be to improve and support learning for people who have had bad learning experiences, like those caused by the COVID-19 pandemic or larger issues of inequality. And we need to keep a close eye on the ways of learning that will help students the most in their communities and jobs in the future.

The following examples show how AI can help with learning: AI that helps students with math problems (based on cognitive learning theories); AI that adapts to students with special needs (based on the Universal Design for Learning framework and related theories); and AI that helps students work together well (based on theories in the field called "Computer Supported Collaborative Learning").

AI's Impact on Flexible Learning Solutions

Adaptivity has been recognized as a key way in which technology can improve learning.[2] AI can be a set of tools used to make edtech more flexible. AI might

1 National Research Council. 2000. How people learn: Brain, mind, experience, and school. The National Academies Press. https://doi.org/10.17226/9853; National Academies of Sciences, Engineering, and Medicine. 2018. How people learn II: Learners, contexts, and cultures. The National Academies Press. https://doi.org/10.17226/24783

2 Aleven, V., McLaughlin, E. A., Glenn, R. A., & Koedinger, K. R. (2016). Instruction based

help technology meet kids where they are, build on their strengths, and help them learn and get better at things. Because AI can work with natural forms of input and because AI models have basic strengths (which we talked about in the "What is AI?" part), AI can be a very useful tool for giving students more ways to adapt.

Still, adaptability is never as broad and open-ended as a phrase like "meet students where they are." This is especially true when it comes to AI. Core limits come from the way the model at the heart of each AI-powered system is set up. Models are close versions of the real world. When important parts of how people learn are left out of the model or aren't fully developed, the model won't be able to change as well, and the learning supports it creates may be weak or limited. So, this section on Learning is mostly about one main idea: make AI models that fit all of your learning ideas, and don't just focus on what AI can model well right now.

Because of progress in what are sometimes called "foundational models" or "large language models," AI models are getting smarter. These very broad models can only do so much. For instance, generative AI models that are talked about in the news can quickly write convincing articles on a wide range of topics. Other models can draw convincing pictures with just a few instructions. Even though foundational models are getting a lot of attention, experts we talked to during our listening sessions warned that AI models aren't as broad as visions for human learning. It's still very important to keep these limitations in mind when creating learning environments. Also, the models are weak and don't work well when things change. In addition, they don't have the same "common sense" judgment that people have, often responding in ways that are unnatural or incorrect.[1] Given the unexpected ways in which foundational models miss the mark, keeping humans in the loop remains highly important.

Intelligent Tutoring Systems: An Example of AI Models

One long-standing type of AI-enabled technology is an Intelligent Tutoring System (ITS).[2] In an early success, scientists were able to build accurate models

on adaptive learning technologies. In Mayer, R.E. & Alexander, P.A., Handbook of research on learning and instruction, 522-560. ISBN: 113883176X

1 Dieterle, E., Dede, C. & Walker, M. (2022). The cyclical ethical effects of using artificial intelligence in education. AI & Society. https://link.springer.com/article/10.1007/s00146-022-01497-w

2 Mousavinasab, E., Zarifsanaiey, N., R. Niakan Kalhori, S., Rakhshan, M., Keikha, L., & Ghazi Saeedi, M. (2021). Intelligent tutoring systems: A systematic review of characteristics, applications, and evaluation methods. Interactive Learning Environments, 29(1), 142-163. https://psycnet.apa.org/doi/10.1080/10494820.2018.1558257

of how human experts solve mathematical problems. The resulting model was incorporated into a system that would observe student problem solving as they worked on mathematical problems on a computer. Researchers who studied human tutors found that feedback on specific steps (and not just right or wrong solutions) is a likely key to why tutoring is so effective.[3] For example, when a student diverged from the expert model, the system gave feedback to help the student get back on track.[4] Importantly, this feedback went beyond right or wrong, and instead, the model was able to provide feedback on specific steps of a solution process. A significant advancement of AI, therefore, can be its ability to provide adaptivity at the step-by-step level and its ability to do so at scale with modest cost.

As a research and development (R&D) field emerged to advance ITS, the work has gone beyond mathematics problems to additional important issues beyond step-by-step problem solving. In the early work, some limitations can be observed. The kinds of problems that an ITS could support were logical or mathematical, and they were closed tasks, with clear expectations for what a solution and solution process should look like. Also, the "approximation of reality" in early AI models related to cognition and not to other elements of human learning, for example, social or motivational aspects. Over time, these early limitations have been addressed in two ways: by expanding the AI models and by involving humans in the loop, a perspective that is also important now. Today, for example, if an ITS specializes in feedback as a student practices, a human teacher could still be responsible for motivating student engagement and self-regulation along with other aspects of instruction. In other contemporary examples, the computer ITS might focus on problem solving practice, while teachers work with students in small groups. Further, students can be in the loop with AI, as is the case with "open learner models"—a type of AI-enabled system that provides information to support student self-monitoring and reflection.[5]

Although R&D along the lines of an ITS should not limit the view of what's possible, such an example is useful because so much research and evaluation has been done on the ITS approach. Researchers have looked across all the available

3 Van Lehn, K. (2011) The relative effectiveness of human tutoring, intelligent tutoring systems, and other tutoring systems. Educational Psychologist, 46(4), 197-221. https://doi.org/10.1080/00461520.2011.611369

4 Ritter, S., Anderson, J.R., Koedinger, K.R. & Corbett, A. (2007). Cognitive Tutor: Applied research in mathematics education. Psychonomic Bulletin & Review, 14, 249-255/ https://doi.org/10.3758/BF03194060

5 Winne, P.H. (2021). Open learner models working in symbiosis with self-regulating learners: A research agenda. International Journal of Artificial Intelligence in Education, 31(3), 446-459. https://doi.org/10.1007/s40593-020-00212-4

high-quality studies in a meta-analysis and concluded that ITS approaches are effective.[1] Many school systems are looking into high-intensity human teaching as a way to help students who haven't finished what they need to learn. It is hard to find enough good human teachers, and human tutoring is very expensive. For large-scale needs, if an ITS can help human tutors do their jobs, it might be possible to give kids more help than people can.

Important Directions for Expanding AI-Based Adaptivity

Adaptivity is sometimes referred to as "personalization." Although this is a convenient term, many observers have noted how imprecise it is.[2] Different teachers define personalization in different ways. For some, it means giving students "voice and choice." For others, it means that a learning management system suggests a unique "playlist" of tasks for each student. It's important to note that many edtech goods that personalize only do so in a few ways. Most edtech products can be changed by changing two things: the level of challenge and the order of the lesson materials. Still, every teacher knows that helping students learn is more than just changing the level of effort and the order of the materials. A good teacher can, for example, get a student interested by making connections to their own life and can change answers until they really make sense to that student and they have a "aha!" moment with them. People teachers have a much fuller picture of each student than most edtech when we say "meet the learner where they are." The teacher is also not likely to "over personalize," which means acting like a program that only shows the student material that they have shown interest in, limiting their access to new topics. "Teachable moments" that a human teacher can understand are different from those that AI models can understand today.

While we were hearing, we heard a lot of different ways that the core models of an AI system need to be expanded. We'll talk about these below.

1. **From deficit-based to asset-oriented**. Listening session attendees noted that the rhetoric around adaptivity has often been deficit-based; technology tries to pinpoint what a student is lacking and then provides instruction to fill that specific gap. Teachers also orient to students' strengths; they find competencies or "assets" a student has and use those to build up the

---

1 Kulik, J.A., & Fletcher, J.D. (2016). Effectiveness of intelligent tutoring systems: A meta-analytic review. Review of Educational Research, 86(1), 42 -78; Ma, W., Adescope, O.O, Nesbit, J.C. & Liu, Q. (2014). Intelligent tutoring systems and learning outcomes: A meta-analysis. Journal of Educational Psychology, 106(4), 901-918. http://dx.doi.org/10.1037/a0037123

2 Plass, J.L., & Pawar, S. (2020). Toward a taxonomy of adaptivity for learning. Journal of Research on Technology in Education, 52(3), 275-3 00. https://doi.org/10.1080/15391523.2020.1719943;

students' knowledge. AI models cannot be fully equitable while failing to recognize or build upon each student's sources of competency. AI models that are more asset-oriented would be an advance.

2. **From individual cognition to including social and other aspects of learning**. The existing adaptivity rhetoric has also tended to focus on individualized learning and mostly on cognitive elements of learning, with motivational and other elements only brought in to support the cognitive learning goals. Attendees observe that their vision for learning is broader than cognition. Social learning is important, for example, especially for students to learn to reason, explain, and justify. For students who are learning English, customized and adaptive support for improving language skills while learning curricular content is clearly important. Developing self-regulation skills is also important. A modern vision of learning is not individualistic; it recognizes that students learn in groups and communities too.
3. **From neurotypical to neurodiverse learners**. AI models could help in including neurodiverse learners (students who access, process, and interact with the world in less common ways than "neurotypical" students) who could benefit from different learning paths and from forms of display and input that fit their strengths. Constituents want AI models that can support learning for neurodiverse learners and learners with disabilities. Thus, they want AI models that can work with multiple paths to learning and multiple modalities of interaction. Such models should be tested for efficacy, to guard against the possibility that some students could be assigned a "personalized" but inadequate learning resource. In addition, some systems for neurodiverse students are presently underutilized, so designs that support intended use will also be important.
4. **From fixed tasks to active, open, and creative tasks**. As mentioned above, AI models are historically better at closed tasks like solving a math problem or logical tasks like playing a game. In terms of life-wide and lifelong opportunities, we value learning how to succeed at open-ended and creative tasks that require extended engagement from the learner, and these are often not purely mathematical or logical. We want students to learn to invent and create innovative approaches. We want AI models that enable progress on open, creative tasks.
5. **From correct answers to additional goals**. At the heart of many adaptivity approaches now on the market, the model inside the technology counts students' wrong answers and decides whether to speed up, slow down, or offer a different type of learning support. Yet, right and wrong answers are

not the only learning goals. We want students to learn how to self-regulate when they experience difficulties in learning, for example, such as being able to persist in working on a difficult problem or knowing how and when to ask for help. We want learners to become skilled in teamwork and in leading teams. As students grow, we want them to develop more agency and to be able to act on their own to advance toward their own learning goals.

It's not possible for this chapter to list every aspect of expansion that we heard during our listening meetings. In the parts that follow, we'll talk about teaching, testing, and research in more detail. As an example, in Research, we talk about all the ways AI systems have trouble with context—context that people understand and think about easily.

Overall, people who took part in the listening meetings came to the conclusion that we need to have a more positive view of learning in order to prepare students for the future. The people who spoke out were worried about how AI could limit learning. To give you an example, if using AI in schools made teachers pay less attention to students' abilities on creative, open-ended tasks and their ability to lead and work with others, then school districts might not be able to see how far their students have come in becoming the kind of graduates that are sought after in their communities and careers.

People told us that when we think about what we want AI in edtech to do, we need to start with a human-centered view of learning and keep coming back to it.

The Twofold Nature of AI in Learning: Application and Understanding

When AI is used in schools, it can be seen from two main points of view: (1) AI to help students learn, and (2) AI to help people learn about AI and related technologies. So far, we've talked about AI systems and tools that can help students learn and master topics like writing and math. But it's also important for students to learn about AI, think about how it affects society and education, and figure out what role and value it plays in their own lives and jobs. In every part of this chapter, we talk about risks. It is important for students to learn more about the risks of AI, such as the risks of bias and monitoring, because these risks show up in all parts of their lives. In the past few years, schools have helped kids learn things like cybersecurity. Kids need to learn about the new risks that AI will bring.

We are encouraged by efforts we've seen underway that would give students opportunities to learn about how AI works while also giving them opportunities to discuss relevant topics like privacy and security.[1] Other learning goals are noted in the K-12 Computer Science Framework. We've seen that students can begin learning about AI in elementary, middle, and high school. They can use AI to design simulations and products that they find exciting. And we've seen that students want to talk about the ethics of products they experience in their everyday lives and have much to say about the kinds of products they'd like to see or not see in school. (And later, in the Research section, we note the desire for co-design processes that involve students in creating the next generation of AI-enabled edtech). Overall, it's important to balance attention to using AI to support learning and giving students opportunities to learn about AI.

A Challenge: Systems Thinking About AI in Education

As AI moves into the education system, people at our listening session warned us that it will be going into places or parts of the system that don't work right now. It is clear that AI is not a way to fix broken systems. Instead, it needs to be used with even more care when the context of the system is unstable or unclear.

As we've already talked about, AI systems and tools don't fully match with learning goals. Because of this, we need to create educational settings that put AI in the right place so that teachers and other adults can use these tools effectively for teaching and learning. In the ITS example, we saw how AI could improve the process of practicing math problems for learning. In a more comprehensive approach, teachers might be given jobs that focus on mathematical skills like modeling and argumentation. Also, working with others in small groups is likely to stay important. For example, students could use math to guess or explain something while working on a real-life problem in small groups. Right now, the "right place" for people, not AI, is to figure out how to make learning culturally responsive and culturally sustained. This is because AI isn't even close to being ready to connect learning to the strengths in a student's family and community.

Open Questions About AI for Learning

With advances occurring in the foundations for AI, opportunities to use AI in support of learning are rapidly expanding. As we explore these opportunities, the open questions below deserve ongoing attention:

1 Forsyth, S., Dalton, B., Foster, E.H., Walsh, B., Smilack, J., & Yeh, T. (2021, May). Imagine a more ethical AI: Using stories to develop teens' awareness and understanding of artificial intelligence and its societal impacts. In 2021 Conference on Research in Equitable and Sustained Participation in Engineering, Computing, and Technology (RESPECT). IEEE. https://doi.org/10.1109/RESPECT51740.2 021.9620549; Zhang, H., Lee, I., Ali, S., DiPaola, D., Cheng, Y., & Breazeal, C. (2022). Integrating ethics and career futures with technical learning to promote AI literacy for middle school students: An exploratory study. International Journal of Artificial Intelligence in Education, 1-35. https://doi.org/10.1007/s40593-022- 00293-3

- To what extent is AI enabling adaptation to students' strengths and not just deficits? Is AI enabling improved support for learners with disabilities and English language learners?
- How are youth voices involved in choosing and using AI for learning?
- Is AI leading to narrower student activities (e.g., procedural math problems), or the fuller range of activities highlighted in the National Educational Technology Plan (NETP), which emphasizes features such as personalized learning, project-based learning, learning from visualizations, simulations, and virtual reality, as well as learning across school, community, and familial settings?
- Is AI supporting the whole learner, including social dimensions of learning such as enabling students to be active participants in small group and collaborative learning? For example, does AI contribute to aspects of student collaboration we value like shared attention, mutual engagement, peer help, self-regulation, and building on each other's contributions?
- When AI is used, are students' privacy and data protected? Are students and their guardians informed about what happens with their data?
- How strong are the processes or systems for monitoring student use of AI for barriers, bias, or other undesirable consequences of AI use by learners? How are emergent issues addressed?
- Is high-quality research or evaluations about the impacts of using the AI system for student learning available? Do we know not only whether the system works but for whom and under what conditions?

Key Recommendation

A lot of focus has been paid to how advances in AI are important for adaptivity and how adaptivity is limited by the model's nature. We saw that the word "personalized" was used in different ways in the first wave of edtech, and it was important to make sure that everyone knew what it meant for each product or service. So, our main suggestion is to figure out the pros and cons of the AI models that will be used in new educational technology and to focus on AI models that are very close to how we want people to learn. A lot of progress has been made in AI lately. We should tell the difference between goods that have basic AI-like features and those that have more complex AI models.

We can see a lot of work and push being put into getting around these problems when we look at what's going on in research and development. We said that people who make decisions should be careful about choosing AI models that might limit their ability to learn, since there is no such thing as general AI. Also, AI models will never be as accurate as real-life experience, so we need to keep using systems thinking, where people are involved and the pros and cons of each school system are taken into account. We believe that the learning system as a whole is bigger than just AI.

Teaching

Teachers have long thought about the many ways that technology could improve their classes, their students, and themselves. However, the recent pandemic has made them think of changes that technology could bring about. Today, almost all teachers have seen how tools can be used in ways that no one thought possible. Some of those events were good, while others were bad. As we think more about teaching and technology, all of these events give us important background information.

We need to prioritize solving the problems teachers face right away. Teachers should be able to do the great work they always do with less trouble. Also, let's keep in mind why people become teachers and make sure they can do the important work. This part talks about some ways AI helps teachers and teaching, such as AI assistants that make routine tasks easier for teachers, AI that helps teachers figure out what their students need and do more work with them, and AI that helps teachers think about, plan, and improve their practice.

Always Center Educators in Instructional Loops

To make AI work as a learning and teaching tool, we must always put educators first (ACE). To put "ACE in AI" into practice, you need to keep a humanistic view of teaching at the top of your mind. When asked, "Will AI replace teachers?" the Department can safely say "no" thanks to ACE. ACE doesn't just make things easy for teachers; it also lets them do what most of them want to do. That means, for example, getting to know their kids better and having more time to think of creative ways to teach when the chance arises.

To bring more precision to how and where we should center educators, we return to our advocacy for human in the loop AI and ask, what are the loops in which teachers should be centered? Figure 5 suggests three key loops (inspired by research on adaptivity loops[1]):

1. The loop in which teachers make moment-to-moment decisions as they do the immediate work of teaching.

1 Aleven, V., McLaughlin, E.A., Glenn, R.A., & Koedinger, K.R. (2016). Instruction based on adaptive learning technologies. In Mayer, R.E. & Alexander, P.A., Handbook of research on learning and instruction, 522-560. ISBN: 113883176X

2. The loop in which teachers prepare for, plan, and reflect on teaching, which includes professional development.
3. The loop in which teachers participate in decisions about the design of AI-enabled technologies, participate in selecting the technologies, and shape the evaluation of technologies—thus setting a context for not only their own classroom but those of fellow teachers as well.

Figure 5. Three ways to center educators as we conceptualize human in the loop AI

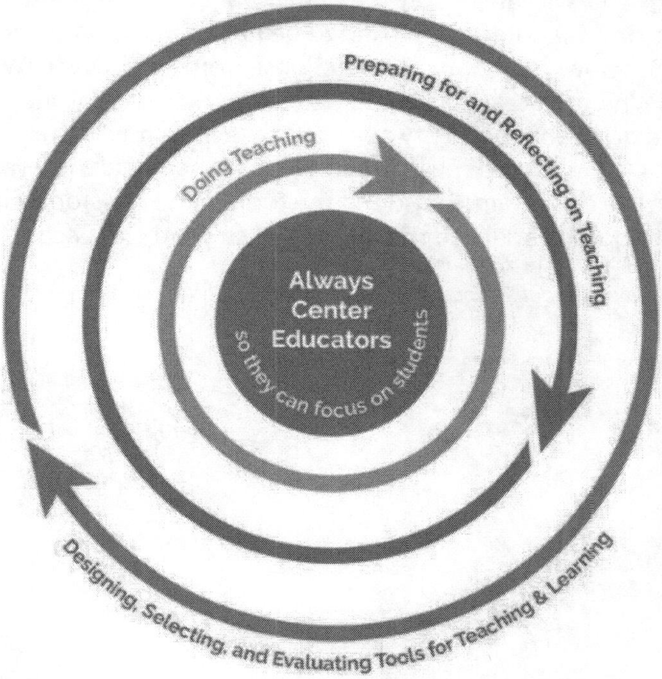

Please note that we will also talk about teachers' important part in feedback loops that help students and help schools get better in the next section, which is about formative assessment. Teachers will also find it useful to read about the ideas of "bias" and "fairness" in that part.

Insight: Using AI to Improve Teaching Jobs

As everyone knows, being a teacher is a very hard job. Every day, teachers have to make thousands of decisions. Teachers take part in what goes on in the classroom, in relationships with students outside of class, in work with other teachers, and in running the school. They are also a part of their communities, which means they should connect with family and caregivers.

> If the teacher is able to efficiently predict and understand the range of other answers given by students in the class, it becomes possible to think creatively about the novel answer and figure how and why the student might have generated it.[1]

We feel grateful for how much easier some daily jobs have become. It's possible to ask for and get alerts and notices about events. No longer do we have to go through several steps to choose the music we want to hear (even with digital music). Now we can just say the name of the song we want to hear, and it will play. Similarly, planning a trip used to be hard because you had to look at a lot of maps. But now, cell phones let us choose from a number of ways to get to our location. Why can't teachers be helped to see how their students' needs are changing and given the tools they need to use technology in their lessons? Why is it so hard for them to plan the learning paths of their students? Things change all the time in the classroom. Why don't the tools in the classroom make it easier for teachers to quickly adapt to the needs and strengths of each student?

Figure 6. Teachers work about 50 hours a week, spending less than half the time in direct interaction with students.

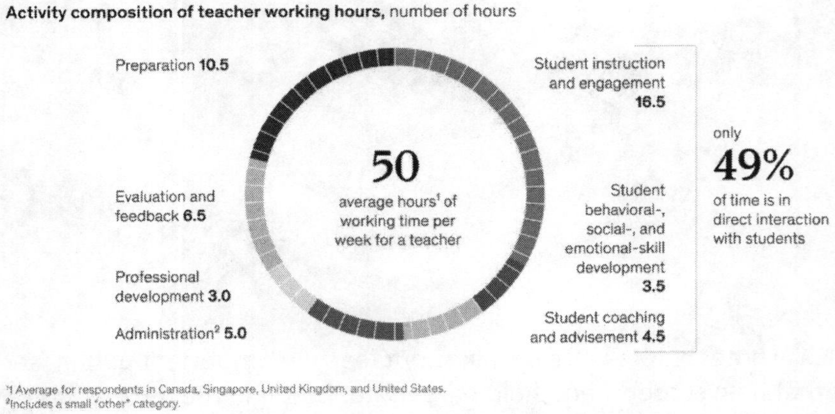

Source: McKinsey Global Teacher and Student Survey

A McKinsey study first said that AI might help by making teaching jobs better by easing up on low-level administrative or clerical work (Figure 6). The chapter also says that the time saved by technology that allows AI should be used for better teaching, especially to reach goals like cutting the average of 11 hours of weekly preparation down to just six. We'll talk about these possibilities and two more below.

1 Hammerness, K., Darling-Hammond, L., & Bransford, J. (2005). Preparing teachers for a changing world: What teachers should learn and be able to do. Jossey-Bass. ISBN: 0787996343

1. **Handling low-level details to ease teaching burdens and increase focus on students.** A good teacher must master all levels of details, big and small. When working with a particular student, the teacher may wish to later send that student a helpful learning resource. How will they remember to send it? A voice assistant or other forms of an AI assistant could make it easier to stay organized by categorizing simple voice notes for teachers to follow up on after a classroom session ends. We are beginning to see AI- enabled voice assistants in the market, and they could do many simple tasks so that the teachers can stay focused on students. These tasks can include record-keeping, starting and stopping activities, controlling displays, speakers, and other technologies in the classroom, and providing reminders. Many workers may eventually use assistants to make their jobs easier, and teachers are the most deserving of efforts to ease their jobs now.
2. **Extending beyond the teacher's availability with their students but continuing to deliver on the teacher's intent**. Teachers almost always want to do more with each student than they can, given the limited number of hours before the next school day. A teacher may wish to sit with the student as they practice 10 more math problems, giving them ongoing support and feedback. If the teacher can sit with the student for only three problems, perhaps they could delegate to an AI-enabled learning system to help with the rest. Teachers cannot be at their best if on call at all hours to help with homework, but perhaps they can indicate what types of supports, hints, and feedback they want students to receive while studying after school hours. An AI assistant can ensure that students have that support wherever and whenever they do homework or practice skills on their own. Teachers may wish to provide more extensive personal notes to families/caregivers, and perhaps an AI assistant could help with drafts based on students' recent classroom work. Then, the teacher could review the AI-generated comments and quickly edit where needed before returning it to the student for another draft. AI tools might also help teachers with language translation so they can work with all parents and caregivers of their students. AI tools might also help teachers with awareness. For example, in the next section, Formative Assessment, we note that teachers can't always know what's going on for each student and in each small group of students; emerging products might signal to the teacher when a student or teacher may need some more personal attention.
3. **Making teacher professional development more productive and fruitful**. Emerging products already enable a teacher to record her classroom and allow an AI algorithm to suggest highlights of the classroom

discussion worth reviewing with a professional development coach.[1] AI can compute metrics, such as whether students have been talking more or less, which are difficult for a teacher to calculate during a lesson.[2] For teachers who want to increase student engagement, these metrics can be a valuable tool. Classroom simulation tools are also emerging and can enable teachers to practice their skills in realistic situations.[3] Simulators can include examples of teaching from a real classroom while changing the faces and voices of the participants so that teaching situations can be shared and discussed among teachers without revealing identities.

Note the emphasis above on what listening-session panelist Sarah Hampton said about the human touch. Teachers will feel that AI is helping them teach with a focus on their human connection to their students when the necessary (but less meaningful) burdens of teaching are lessened. In Figure 7, below, see concerns that teachers raised about AI during listening sessions.

Figure 7. Concerns raised during the listening session about teaching with AI

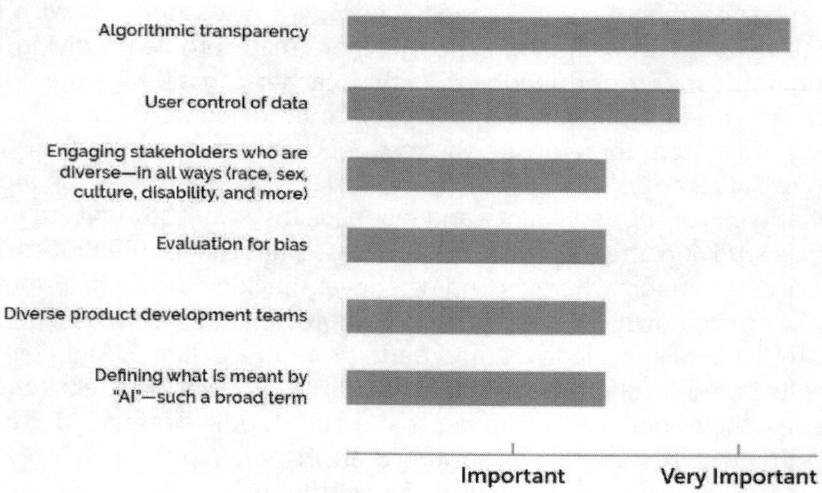

1 Chen, G., Clarke, S., & Resnick, L.B. (2015). Classroom Discourse Analyzer (CDA): A discourse analytic tool for teachers. Technology, Instruction, Cognition and Learning, 10(2), 85-105

2 Jensen, E., Dale, M., Donnelly, P.J., Stone, C., Kelly, S., Godley, A. & D'Mello, S.K. (2020). Toward automated feedback on teacher discourse to enhance teacher learning. In Proceedings of the 2020 CHI Conference on Human Factors in Computing Systems (CHI '20). https://doi.org/10.1145/3313831.3376418

3 Ersozlu, Z., Ledger, S., Ersozlu, A., Mayne, F., & Wildy, H. (2021). Mixed-reality learning environments in teacher education: An analysis of TeachLivETM Research. SAGE Open, 11(3). https://doi.org/10.1177/2158244 0211032155.

Preparing and Supporting Teachers in Planning and Reflecting

ACE also means getting teachers ready to use opportunities like the ones above and more. In the Research section, we talk about how pre-service education still tries to separate technology into different areas and not talk about it enough. That part makes it sound like money should be spent on study into how to fully incorporate technology into programs that train people to become teachers. Teachers who are already working will also need to get more training in order to take advantage of the chances that AI can offer, such as the ones described in the Teaching part. As part of teachers' professional growth, we will need to talk about both opportunities and new risks, while also giving them tools to avoid the problems that come with AI.

By its very nature, teaching takes a lot of time to plan for all the different needs of the students they are responsible for, especially those who are in inclusive classrooms or have IEPs or 504 plans. AI could help teachers by giving them suggestions based on their position and the way they teach, as well as help with changing found materials to fit the needs of their classroom. To help students with an IEP find the right parts to add to their lesson plans that meet all standards and goals and also meet the specific needs of each student, AI could be used. AI could help customize standard resources to better meet specific needs, such as by providing a voice assistant that lets a student who has trouble seeing hear and respond to material or by letting a group of students present their project using American Sign Language (ASL), which could be voiced for other students using an AI ASL-to-Spoken-English translation feature. In fact, arranging IEPs takes a lot of time and could use some help from helpful automation and personalized interaction that AI can offer.

Thought is also important. With all the noise and activity in the classroom, it can be hard to fully understand what a student is saying or why they are acting a certain way. Once more, context is very important. At the time, teachers might not know about events going on outside of school that could change how they see their students acting in class. Tools that find patterns and suggest ways to share knowledge could help teachers and students talk more about what they need and what they are good at.

Designing, Selecting, and Evaluating AI Tools

The most important loop for teachers to be a part of is the one that decides what tools can be used in the classroom and is open to everyone. Teachers already help make choices about what tools to use. Teachers can give their opinions on what is useful and possible. Teachers look at proof that something works and tell other school leaders what they find. Teachers already talk about what they think is needed to use technology well.

These worries will still be there, but AI will also bring up new ones. As an example, the next part on Formative Assessment brings up concerns about unfairness and bias that can lead to discrimination by algorithms. These worries aren't just about data privacy and security; they also bring up the issue of how technologies may wrongly direct or limit some students' chances to learn. An important thing to remember is that teachers will need time and help to keep up with both old and new problems that are coming up and to fully take part in the planning, choosing, and judging processes that lower risks.

Challenge: Balancing Human and Computer Decision-Making

One of the biggest problems teachers face with AI-enabled tools is that AI can let a computer do things on its own, so when a teacher gives work to an AI-enabled tool, it may do some of it on its own. Professor Inge Molenaar has thought about the difficulties of keeping things under control in a mixed classroom: When should the teacher be in charge? What tasks can be given to a computer system? How can a teacher keep an eye on the AI system and change its mind or take back control if needed?

Figure 8. The tension between human and AI decision making: Who is in control?

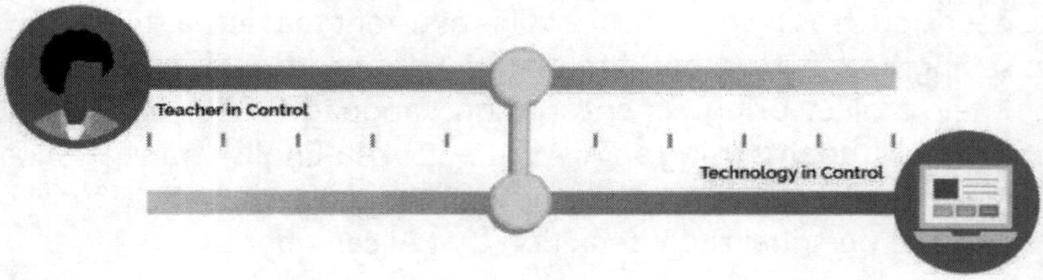

Figure 8 shows how tense things are around power. In the picture on the left, the teacher is in charge and AI is not used in the classroom. To the right, the technology is in charge and there is no teacher present, which is usually not a good thing. There are many options in the middle ground, which is not a flat area. Molenaar looked at the goods and came up with some ideas:

- The technology only offers information and recommendations to the teacher.
- The teacher delegates specific types of tasks to the technology, for example, giving feedback on a particular math assignment or sending out reminders to students before an assignment is due.
- The teacher delegates more broadly to the technology, with clear protocols for alerts, for monitoring, and for when the teacher takes back control.

We need to have open conversations about these and other options. For example, we might want to spell out the different kinds of instructional decisions that can have different kinds of effects on a student. We should also be very careful about giving other people power over decisions that have very big effects, like recommending a student for a new course of study or for discipline. For human in the loop to really work, AI technologies need to let teachers watch over students, have ways to let teachers know when their opinion is needed, and let teachers reverse choices made for their students at the classroom, school, or district level. We can't forget that if a technology gives a teacher choices, which it should, it will take a lot of time for them to think about and set up all of them, so it will take longer at first.

Challenge: Making Teaching Jobs Easier While Avoiding Surveillance

We're also aware that the tools that make work easier could also open up new ways to spy on people (Figure 9). As an everyday example, if we turn on a voice helper in the kitchen, it could help us do simple things around the house like setting a timer for cooking. That being said, the same voice assistant could hear things we meant to keep secret. This kind of problem will come up in the classroom and for teachers. If they let an AI-helper record what they say, what teaching resources they look for, and other actions, the assistant could use that information to make resources and suggestions more relevant to the teacher. But the same information could also be used to keep an eye on the teacher, which could have effects on the teacher. It will be very hard to make AI that teachers can trust that makes their jobs easier if they are watched more closely.

Figure 9. Highly customized assistance vs. increased teacher surveillance

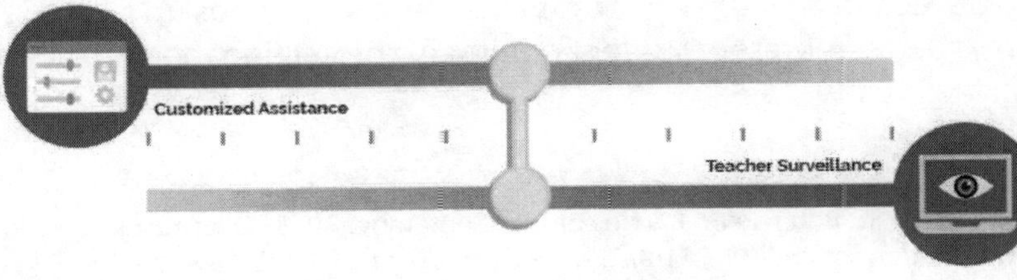

One more issue is that asking teachers to be "in the loop" could make their jobs harder if it's not done right. Being in the loop might be at odds with making teachers' jobs easier. There is also the conflict between not trusting AI enough (to get help) and trusting it too much (and losing privacy or being watched). For example, researchers have documented that people will follow instructions from a robot during a simulated fire emergency even when (a) they are told the robot is broken and (b) the advice is obviously wrong.[1] We anticipate teachers will need training and support to understand how and when they will need to exercise human judgement.

Challenge: Responding to Students' Strengths While Protecting Their Privacy

Educators seek to tackle inequities in learning, no matter how they manifest locally (e.g. in access to educational opportunities, resources, or supports). In culturally responsive[2] and culturally sustaining[3] approaches, educators design materials to build on the "assets"—individual, community, and cultural strengths that students bring to learning. Along with considering assets, of course, educators must meet students where they are, including both strengths and needs. AI could assist in this process by helping teachers with customizing curricular resources, for example. But to do so, the data inputted in an AI-enabled system would have to provide more information about the students. This information could be, but need not be, demographic details. It could also be information about students' preferences, outside interests, relationships, or experiences.[4] Concerns about what is done with this data, how it is removed, and who sees it are very high among teachers. If teachers are thinking about using AI-enabled technologies to help fix educational inequality, they need to know if the data they share with or store in an AI-enabled system is protected by federal or state privacy rules like FERPA. Also, teachers need to think about whether the interactions between students and AI systems make legal records that need to be kept safe. For example, when an AI chatbot or tutor writes or speaks with a student, this could be considered legal documentation. The choices made by AI technologies and the reasons for those choices that are made by algorithms may also be records that the law needs to protect. This brings up a third tension: the need to better represent students while also protecting their privacy (Figure 10).

---

1 Wagner, A.R., Borenstein, J. & Howard, A. (September 2018). Overtrust in the robotics age. Communications of the ACM, 61(9),22-24. https://doi.org/10.1145/3241365

2 Gay, G. (2018). Culturally responsive teaching: Theory, research, and practice. Teachers College Press. ISBN: 978-0807758762

3 Paris, D., & Alim, H.S. (Eds.). (2017). Culturally sustaining pedagogies: Teaching and learning for justice in a changing world. Teachers College Press. ISBN: 978-0807758342

4 Zacamy, J. & Roschelle, J. (2022). Navigating the tensions: How could equity-relevant research also be agile, open, and scalable? Digital Promise. http://hdl.handle.net/20.500.12265/159; Baker, R.S., Esbenshade, L., Vitale, J., & Karumbaiah, S. (2022). Using demographic data as predictor variables: A questionable choice. https://doi.org/10.35542/osf.io/y4wvj

Figure 10. Responding to students' strengths while fully protecting student privacy

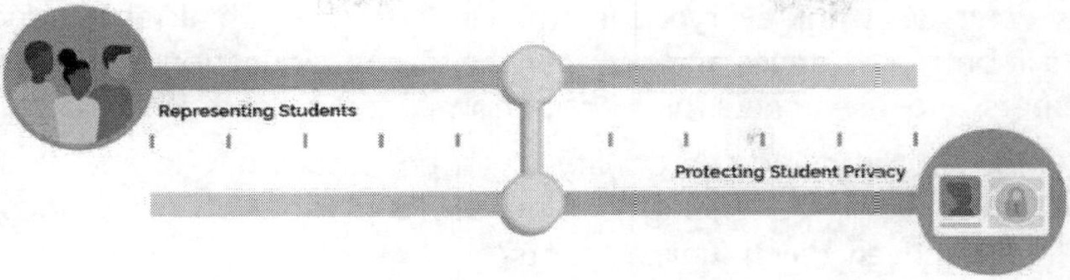

Having a voice would also only be the beginning of an answer. As we've already talked about, AI can lead to artificial discrimination if the data, code, or models used in AI-enhanced education technology are biased. Engineers use current data to build AI models that can find patterns. The data they use might not be representative or might have connections that go against policy goals. Also, engineers design the automations that AI uses when it finds trends, and the automations might not work for every group of students with a variety of needs. Most of the time, the people who make AI aren't as varied as the people they work with. Because of this, they might not think about how pattern recognition and automation could hurt a community, group, or person.

Using what the teacher knows about each student's needs and strengths, AI could help teachers make things more relevant and useful for those students. Customizing curriculum materials takes time, and teachers are already looking into how AI chatbots can help them make more materials for their kids. An elementary school teacher could get a lot of help changing the pictures in a storybook to make it more interesting for their students, changing words that don't fit with the way people speak in their area, or even changing the stories to include other parts of their lesson. We talked about how AI could help find a learner's strengths in the part on learning. For instance, a math teacher might not know how a student is making sense of motion graphs and tables while they are in the physics classroom of another teacher. This teacher might also not know that using the same motion graphs could help them with their lesson on linear functions. When teachers try to make or change lessons to fit the needs of each student, AI might help. But, to avoid algorithmic discrimination while increasing community and cultural responsiveness, we need to focus on the four foundations we talked about earlier: human in the loop, equity, safety and effectiveness, and evaluation of AI models. We can't expect AI models to be sensitive to different cultures. Concerns raised by the Department include the fact that educators and other responsible adults are best able to address issues of equity and that these issues can never be solved simply through computer programming.

Questions Worth Asking About AI for Teaching

This is what we want everyone in the ecosystem to think about more as leaders in both pre-service and post-service teacher education and lawmakers, developers, and researchers think about how AI can make teaching better:

- Is AI improving the quality of an educator's day-to-day work? Are teachers experiencing less burden and more ability to focus and effectively teach their students?
- As AI reduces one type of teaching burden, are we preventing new responsibilities or additional workloads being shifted and assigned to teachers in a manner that negates the potential benefits of AI?
- Is classroom AI use providing teachers with more detailed insights into their students and their strengths while protecting their privacy?
- Do teachers have oversight of AI systems used with their learners? Are they exercising control in the use of AI-enabled tools and systems appropriately or inappropriately yielding decision-making to these systems and tools?
- When AI systems are being used to support teachers or to enhance instruction, are the protections against surveillance adequate?
- To what extent are teachers able to exercise voice and decision-making to improve equity, reduce bias, and increase cultural responsiveness in the use of AI-enabled tools and systems?

Key Recommendation: Inspectable, Explainable, Overridable AI

In the Introduction, we discuss the notion that when AI is incorporated into a system, the core of the AI is a model. In the Learning section, we discuss that we need to be careful that models align to the learning we envision (e.g., that they aren't too narrow). Now, based on the needs of teachers (as well as students and their families/caregivers), we add another layer to our criteria for good AI models: the need for explainability.[1] Some AI models can see patterns in the world and take the right action, but they can't explain why (for example, how they found the link between the pattern and the action). This lack of being able to be explained won't work for teaching; teachers will need to know how an AI model looked at one of their students' work and why it suggested a certain lesson, resource, or next step to that student.

---

1 Khosravi, H., Shum, S.B., Chen, G, Conati, C., Tsai,Y-S., Kay, J., Knight, S., Martinez-Maldonado, R., Sadiq, S., Gasevic, D. (2022). Explainable artificial intelligence in education. Computers and Education: Artificial Intelligence, 3. https://doi.org/10.1016/j.caeai.2022.100074

So, being able to explain an AI system's choice is important for a teacher to be able to judge that choice. This kind of explainability helps teachers figure out how much to trust and doubt AI, especially when it comes to figuring out where the AI model tends to make bad choices. It's also important for teachers to be able to tell when an AI system is acting unfairly because it has the wrong knowledge, which means it is biased. We talk more about fairness and bias in the next part, "Assessment."

Teachers need to be able to look at what an AI model is doing, which goes along with the idea of explainability. For instance, what kinds of suggestions are being made for how to teach and to which students? For which kids is the assignment of extra work never ending? Which ones are getting better? Some of this information is shown on dashboards in current products, but with AI, teachers may want to learn more about which decisions are being made and for whom, as well as the student-specific factors that an AI model considered (and possibly which factors were most important) when making a decision. Some of today's adaptive classroom products, for instance, use limited suggestion models that only look at how well a student did on their last three math problems. They don't look at other factors that a teacher would know to look at, like whether a student has an IEP Plan or other needs.

In order to follow through on our call to think about fairness when judging AI models, we need to know how discriminatory bias might show up in certain AI systems and what the authors have done to fix it. To do this, it's important for everyone to know how the tools use information to get results and what data they have access to or that a teacher could use in her decision-making but the system doesn't (IEP status is an example above).

Teachers will also need to be able to see automated choices and make their own decisions about them. For example, they will need to be able to see which set of math problems a student should work on next and decide for themselves what to do. They need to be able to intervene and override decisions when they disagree with the logic behind an instructional recommendation.[1] Teachers need protection against adverse ramifications when they assert human judgement over an AI system's decision.

Formative Assessment

Formative assessment is traditionally a key use of edtech because feedback

1 Ruiz, P. & Fusco, J. (2022). Teachers partnering with artificial intelligence: Augmentation and automation. Digital Promise. https://digitalpromise.org/2022/07/06/teachers-partnering-with-artificial-intelligence-augmentation-and-automation/

loops are vital to improving teaching and learning.[1] As we have emphasized throughout this chapter, a top priority with AI is to keep humans in the loop and in control, which includes focusing on the people engaged with formative assessments: students, teachers, school leaders, families/caregivers, and others who support learners. In the definition below, please note the overlap between definitions of AI and formative assessment; both have to do with detecting patterns and choosing a future course of action (that adapts to learner strengths and needs).

> Assessment refers to all those activities undertaken by teachers, and by the students in assessing themselves, which provide information to be used as feedback to modify the teaching and learning activities in which they are engaged. Such assessment becomes "formative assessment" when the evidence is actually used to adapt the teaching to meet the needs.[2]

Building on Best Practices

A number of dimensions hold potential for shaping the future of formative assessments, and many have ready extensions to the field of AI-enabled systems and tools. For example, the 2017 NETP discussed how technology can lead to improved formative assessments along seven dimensions, listed below:

1. **Enabling Enhanced Question Types**: to give students more ways to show what they know and can do.
2. **Measurement of Complex Competencies**: to better elicit growth in important skills that go beyond typical subject matter standards, for example, in measuring practices, social skills like teamwork, self-regulation, and work-relevant skills (e.g., making presentations or leading teams).
3. **Providing Real-Time Feedback**: to maintain and increase student engagement and to support effective learning, providing timely and helpful responses and suggestions to each learner.
4. **Increasing Accessibility**: to include neurodiverse learners and to engage learners' best communication capabilities as they share what they know and can do.
5. **Adapting to Learner Ability and Knowledge**: to make assessments more precise and efficient.

---

1 Shute, V.J. (2008). Focus on formative feedback. Review of Educational Research, 78(1), 153-189. https://doi.org/10.3102/0034654307313795

2 Black, P. & Wiliam, D. (1998). Inside the black box: Raising standards through classroom assessment. Phi Delta Kappan, 92(1), 81-90. https://kappanonline.org/inside-the-black-box-raising-standards-through-classroom-assessment/

6. **Embedded Assessment in the Learning Process**: to emphasize an assessment's role in improving teaching and learning (this chapter does not focus on assessment for accountability purposes).
7. **Assess for Ongoing Learning**: to reveal progress over time and not just predetermined milestones.

AI models and AI-enabled systems may have potential to strengthen formative assessments. In one example, a question type that invites students to draw a graph or create a model can be analyzed with AI algorithms,[1] and similar student models might be grouped for the teacher to interpret. Enhanced formative assessment may enable teachers to better respond to students' understanding of a concept like "rate of change" in a complex, real-world situation. AI can also give learners feedback on complex skills, such as learning American Sign Language[2] or speaking a foreign language[3] and in other practice situations where no person is available to provide immediate feedback.

In general, an AI assistant might be able to make it easier for teachers to grade simpler parts of student answers. This would free up the teacher to focus on more important parts of a whole essay or a complicated project. We might also be able to give better comments when it comes to accessibility. An AI-enabled learning tool might be able to talk to a student about their answer to an essay question, asking questions that help the student make their point more clear without them having to read a screen or type on a keyboard. In the examples given earlier in the Learning section, we saw that AI can be built into the learning process so that it gives students input as they work to solve a problem, rather than only after they've gotten it wrong. When formative assessment is more embedded, it can better support learning, and timely feedback is critical.[4]

There are many connections between AI and formative assessments, like these. However, our listening sessions also showed that people wanted to fix some problems with formative assessment, like how time-consuming and sometimes difficult tests, quizzes, and other assessments are, and how teachers and students don't see much value in the feedback loop.

---

1 Zhai, X., He, P., Krajcik, J. (2022). Applying machine learning to automatically assess scientific models. Journal of Research in Science Teaching. https://doi.org/10.1002/tea.21773

2 Shao, Q., Sniffen, A., Blanchet, J., Hillis, M.E., Shi, X., Haris, T.K., & Balkcom, D. (2020). Teaching american sign language in mixed reality. Proceedings of the ACM on Interactive, Mobile, Wearable and Ubiquitous Technologies, 4(4), 1-27. https://doi.org/10.1145/3432211

3 Godwin-Jones, R. (2021). Big data and language learning: Opportunities and challenges. Language Learning & Technology, 25(1), 4-19. http://hdl.handle.net/10125/44747

4 Wiggins, G. (2015). Seven keys to effective feedback. ACSD. https://www.ascd.org/el/articles/seven-keys-to-effective- feedback

Implications for Teaching and Learning

Real-time feedback during teaching can be helpful if it helps both students and teachers get better. Too often, though, students and teachers don't like being tested, which creates an interesting conflict between the possible benefits of collecting data through formative assessments and the practical effects of giving more tests in schools and classrooms.

Some AI-enabled systems and tools seek to address this potential conflict. For example, one AI- enabled reading tutor listens to students as they read aloud and provides on-the-spot feedback to improve their reading.[1] Students reportedly enjoyed reading aloud, and the approach was effective. Researchers have also embedded formative assessments in games so that students can show how well they understand Newtonian physics as they play increasingly difficult levels of a game.[2] If a student can more easily ask for and receive help when they feel frustrated or confused, reducing those feelings can feel encouraging. Student feelings of safety, confidence, and trust in the feedback generated by these AI-enabled systems and tools are essential to showcase their learning. That focus on learning growth and gains is optimal (absent negative consequences or a high-stakes environment).[3]

Formative exams that use AI might be able to save teachers time (for example, time spent grading), so the teacher can spend more time helping students. AI-enhanced tests may also help teachers if they give teachers detailed information about students' strengths and needs that they might not be able to see and if they help teachers change or improve their lessons by offering a small set of evidence-based ways to help students learn the material. These kinds of tests might also be useful outside of school if they can give feedback when the teacher isn't around, like when students are doing their chores or practicing an idea during study hall. Putting teachers at the center of system design is an important part of using AI-based formative testing, as we talked about in the Teaching section.

---

1 Mostow, J., Aist, G., Burkhead, P., Corbett, A., Cuneo, A., Eitelman, S., Huang, C., Junker, B., Sklar, M.B., & Tobin, B. (2003). Evaluation of an automated reading tutor that listens: Comparison to human tutoring and classroom instruction. Journal of Educational Computing Research, 29(1), 61-117. https://doi.org/10.2190/06AX-QW99-EQ5G-RDCF

2 Shute, VJ., Ventura, M., & Kim, Y.J. (2013). Assessment and learning of qualitative physics in Newton's Playground. The Journal of Educational Research, 106(6), 423-430. https://doi.org/10.1080/00220671.2013.832970

3 Shute, V J. (2008). Focus on formative feedback. Review of Educational Research, 78(1), 153-189. https://doi.org/10.3102/0034654307313795

Insight: AI Can Enhance Feedback Loops

The term "formative assessment" does not singularly mean a test or a measurement. Assessment becomes formative when it results in useful reflections and changes to the course of teaching, learning, or both.[1] The phrase "feedback loops" makes it clear that measuring is just one part of the process. The best results for students come from feedback loops that lead to better education, such as changes in how students are taught and how they are taught.

There are also more than one kind of important feedback loop, so we use the word "feedback loops" as a plural noun. Giving students feedback can help them when they work alone, in a small group, or during a class talk. Feedback loops are useful "right now," like when a student is practicing a skill. Another good time to use feedback loops is when you want to cover a lot of work and think about it, like when you're finishing a project or term paper. Additionally, feedback loops can help teachers by, for example, making them more aware of the ways they usually react to student ideas. Also, feedback loops are very important for making sure that goods and programs keep getting better.

Because feedback loops are so important, formative assessment could be one of the first areas where schools look for strong ways to use AI to help them teach and learn. Teachers can build on the ways that their long-held ideas about formative testing and the new tools that AI has to offer are similar. Also, the group of professional assessors brings a set of tools for asking and answering questions about things like fairness and bias. The psychometric toolkit of methods is a good place to start asking and answering the questions that need to be asked and answered. It already has ways to measure fairness and bias, as well as ways to compare the quality of formative tests in general. However, as we've talked about, AI can only improve feedback loops if we pay close attention to its flaws and how it raises new issues.

An Example: Automated Essay Scoring

One instructive example is Automated Essay Scoring (AES). To become strong writers, which is a valuable life skill, students need regular and specific feedback. However, reviewing and providing feedback on essays is very time consuming for humans. Hence, Ellis Page provided a first vision for computer programs that could review and provide feedback on student essays in 1966[2],

1 Black, P., & Wiliam, D. (2009). Developing the theory of formative assessment. Educational Assessment, Evaluation and Accountability, 21(1), 5-31. https://doi.org/10.1007/s11092-008-9068-5

2 Page, E.B. (1966). The imminence of grading essays by computer. Phi Delta Kappan, 47(5), 238-243

and much effort has gone into AES technologies in the intervening 56 years. Many research review articles are available to summarize the progress, which has been impressive.[1] Also, readers will already know some of the ways that AES technologies are used today, like Grammarly, Turnitin, and the different essay analysis tools that publishers and testing companies use. Also, keep in mind that older versions of AES were mostly about rating or scoring essays, while newer products that use AI are more about giving students helpful feedback and helping them improve their writing skills. Writing is an important life skill that will help you in college and in your job, and writers who are still improving need a lot of feedback. If developers could add AI feedback to human feedback for emerging writers at a low cost, it might be possible for everyone to get more help with learning to write.

And yet, AES is an instructive example because researchers have analyzed limitations, too.[2] AES technologies in AI can analyze some features of student essays but can also be misled by the length of an essay, by a student who places appropriate keywords in sentences that don't make sense, and other flaws that a human reader would easily notice. In a telling quote, one team that reviewed the state of the art wrote this:

The authors further note that while human and AI judgements of essays may correlate, people and computers are not noticing the same things in student writing. Due to these limitations, we must continue to emphasize a human in the loop foundation for AI-enhanced formative assessment. AI may support but not replace high-quality, human-led processes and practices of formative assessment in schools.

Key Opportunities for AI in Formative Assessment

Based on the listening sessions we held, we see three key areas of opportunity in supporting formative assessment using AI systems and models.

First, we recommend a strong focus on measuring what matters[3] and particularly those things that have not been easily measured before and that

1 Ke, Z., & Ng, V. (2019). Automated essay scoring: A survey of the state of the art. In Proceedings of the Twenty-Eighth International Joint Conference on Artificial Intelligence, 6300-6308. https://doi.org/10.24963/ijcai.2019/879

2 Doewes, A. & Pechenizkiy, M. (2021). On the limitations of human-computer agreement in automated essay scoring. In Proceedings of the 14th International Conference on Educational Data Mining (EDM21). https://educationaldatamining.org/EDM2021/virtual/static/pdf/EDM21 paper 243.pdf

3 Merrill, S. (2020). In schools, are we measuring what matters? Edutopia. https://www.edutopia.org/article/schools-are-we- measuring-what-matters

many constituents would like to include in feedback loops. The above case, AES, was picked because writing is still an important skill for school, work, and everyday life. When we look at community goals through the lens of what they want their high school graduates to be like, we can see that families and caregivers, students, and community leaders all want graduates who can solve problems in new ways, communicate and work together well, and keep going even when things get tough. "What matters" today is more than just the core academic material that is tested on large-scale summative assessments. It's also about giving students and teachers feedback that they can use to improve the skills they need to succeed and thrive in life. In addition, AI could help us give comments on the more realistic and difficult parts of core academic subjects like math, science, history, literature, and so on.

Second, we'd like to see a strong focus on improving help-seeking and help-giving.[1] Asking for and giving help is crucial to learning[2] and practicing a growth-mindset and central to the notion of human feedback loops. Students may not always know when they need help. In one example, computer algorithms can detect a student who is "wheel spinning" (working hard on mastering content but not making progress).[3] A student who is working hard may not feel like they need help, and the teacher may not be aware that the student is struggling if he or she appears to be "on task." AI may also be helpful by highlighting for students and teachers what forms of assistance have been most useful to the student in the recent past so that an educator can expand access to specific assistance that works for that individual student. Finally, educators may learn things from AI-enabled systems and tools that give feedback and hints during the completion of homework, utilizing that feedback to later reinforce concepts in direct instruction and strengthen the one-on-one support provided to students.[4] AI-enabled systems and tools can provide teachers with additional information about the students' recent work, so their instructor has a greater contextual sense as they begin to provide help.

---

1 Roll, I., Aleven, V., McLaren, B.M., Koedinger, K.R. (2011). Improving students' help-seeking skills using metacognitive feedback in an intelligent tutoring system, Learning and Instruction, 21(2), 267-280. https://doi.org/10.1016/j.learninstruc.2010.07.004.

2 Webb, N.M., & Farivar, S. (1994). Promoting helping behavior in cooperative small groups in middle school mathematics. American Educational Research Journal, 31(2), 369-395. https://doi.org/10.3102/00028312031002369

3 Kai, S., Almeda, M.V., Baker, R. S., Heffernan, C., & Heffernan, N. (2018). Decision tree modeling of wheel-spinning and productive persistence in skill builders. Journal of Educational Data Mining, 10(1), 36-71.
https://doi.org/10.5281/zenodo.3344810

4 Walker, E., Rummel, N. & Koedinger, K.R. (2015). Adaptive intelligent support to improve peer tutoring in algebra. International Journal of Artificial Intelligence in Education, 24, 33-61 https://doi.org/10.1007/s40593-013-0001-9

Third, we advocate for teachers and students to be strongly involved in designing feedback loops as developers produce AI-enhanced formative assessments so they can directly voice what would make assessments less onerous and more convenient and valuable to them.[1] We talked about how important it is for teachers to be involved in creating, choosing, and evaluating technologies that use AI earlier in the Teaching section. Students also need to be in the middle. In their daily lives, they use AI, and they have strong opinions about what is safe and useful. People give and get feedback in different ways depending on where they live and their culture, so it's important to make sure that feedback fits with community values.

Key Recommendation: Harness Assessment Expertise to Reduce Bias

Bias and fairness are important issues in assessment design and administration,[2] and they hold relevance for the area of AI-enabled assessment. In traditional assessment, a test item might be biased if unnecessary details are included that differentially advantage some students (e.g., a story-based item that references a sport that only boys play regularly may be less helpful to girls). As discussed earlier, with AI, we now must worry about algorithmic discrimination which can arise due to the manner in which AI algorithms are developed and improved from large datasets of parameters and values that may not represent all cohorts of learners.

Algorithmic discrimination isn't just about the testing part of formative assessment; it's also about the feedback loop and the changes and help that can be given to students based on the results of formative assessments. There are concerns about both how easy it is to get these kinds of interventions and how good they are or whether they are even proper. It's important to make sure that when an algorithm gives a student hints, next steps, or tools, it's not unfair, because if one group doesn't get useful help, that's unfair. Fairness is more than just not being biased. In AI-enabled formative assessment, both the opportunity to learn through feedback loops, as well as the quality of learning in and outside of such loops, should be addressed. Issues of bias and fairness have arisen in traditional assessments, and the field of psychometrics has already developed valuable tools to challenge and address these issues.[3] As a field, assessment may

1 Swiecki, Z., Khosravi, H., Chen, G., Martinez-Maldonado, R., Lodge, J.M., Milligan, S., Selwyn, B. & Gasevic,D. (2022). Assessment in the age of artificial intelligence. Computers and Education: Artificial Intelligence, 3. k https://doi.org/10.1016/_i.caeai.2022.100075

2 Reynolds, C.R., & Suzuki, L.A. (2012). Bias in psychological assessment: An empirical review and recommendations. Handbook of Psychology, Second Edition. https://doi.org/10.1002/9781118133880.hop210004

3 Kaplan, R.M., & Saccuzzo, D.P. (2017). Psychological testing: Principles, applications, and

already be doing a lot to fight bias and unfairness in AI used in schools. But the problems get worse with AI, so the work is still not done. As new developmental tests are made, they need to pay close and careful attention to bias and fairness.

Related Questions

As was already said, AI is growing in the area of formative assessment along a continuum that can be led by plans that are already in place, like the 2017 NETP. This is an area where AI is likely to grow, especially now that it can power more feedback loops in the learning process. During this time of growth, we recommend that you keep the following questions in mind:

- Is formative assessment bringing benefits to the student learning experience and to the efficacy of classroom instruction?
- Are humans being centered in AI-enabled formative assessment and feedback loops?
- Are we providing empowering professional development to teachers so they can leverage feedback loops and safeguard against concerns?
- To what extent are the developers and implementers of AI-enabled systems and tools tackling new sources of algorithmic bias and continuing to make assessment fairer?
- Are governance policies regarding who owns, controls, and can view or use AI-enabled formative assessment data appropriate and adequate?
- Do we have sufficient guardrails against misuse of formative assessment data or automatically generated interpretations of student achievement and learning, such as on dashboards?
- Is trust in an AI-enabled assessment system, feedback loops, and data generated by such assessments growing or diminishing?

Research and Development

Research-based knowledge is used to make policy, and feedback loops that look at real-world facts are used to make practice better. So, the NETP of 2010 listed a number of "grand challenges," or "R&D problems that could be funded and coordinated at the national level." One of the NETP grand challenges for 2010 was to make individual learning systems that get better over time:

> "Design and validate an integrated system that provides real-time access to learning experiences tuned to the levels of difficulty and assistance

issues. Cengage Learning.

> that optimize learning for all learners and that incorporates selfimproving features that enable it to become increasingly effective through interaction with learners. "[1]

A lot of research and development has been done on this problem since 2010. There are now a lot more conferences on learning analytics, educational data mining, and learning at scale. Platforms have been made that use algorithms and the study of large amounts of data to improve the way people learn. The challenge still needs to be fully met, and more work needs to be done on it right now.

Insight: Research Can Strengthen the Role of Context in AI

Even though 2010's grand challenges are still important, it's clear that the R&D group wants to focus on other things right now. It was said that the troubles in 2010 were technical. Researchers today want to look into context in more depth, and tech companies today want to make tools that can adapt to learners' traits and situations in a wider range of ways, not just in terms of specific cognitive traits. There is a push to change R&D to deal with context awareness. We hope that the word "adaptive" will be used in ways that are broader than they have been in the past ten years. Because people learn best when they are with other people, "adaptive" should not always mean "individualized." So, researchers are expanding the meaning of "adaptivity" to include helping students do what they need to do when they learn in groups, which is a common way for students all over the U.S. to learn.

The focus on context is not an accident. Context is a traditional challenge in AI.[2] Thus, researchers and developers are wise to prioritizing context. Unless we invest more in AI that is context-sensitive, it is quite likely that AI will break and fail to achieve educational goals.

Agreeing to prioritize context won't be easy. As illustrated above in Figure 11, there will be a tension between depth of context and pace of technological advances in AI R&D. On the one hand, AI is sometimes presented as a race to be the first to advance new techniques or scale new applications—innovation is sometimes portrayed as rapidly going to scale with a minimally viable product, failing fast, and only after failure, dealing with context. On the other hand, researchers and developers see that achieving good innovations with AI

---

1 U.S. Department of Education, Office of Educational Technology. (2010). Transforming American Education: Learning Powered by Technology. U.S. Department of Education. p. 78

2 Boden, M.A. (2018). Artificial intelligence: A very short introduction. Oxford. ISBN: 978-0199602919

in education will clearly require bringing more context into the process early and often. For example, researchers highlight that humans must be continually adjusting the goals for technology and have noted that when we set forth goals, we often don't yet fully understand context; and as we learn about context, the goals must change.[1] This suggests that context must be prioritized early and habitually in R&D; we don't want to win a race to the wrong finish line.

Figure 11. The tension between depth of context andpace of technological advances in AI

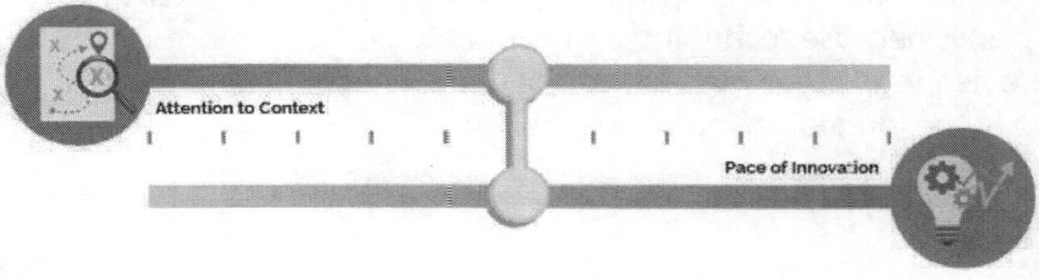

This work will also be different if the attention is shifted even more to context. In R&D, there won't be just one kind of change because context can mean more than one thing. People who came to our listening groups talked about four types of context that will be important in the future.

We'll talk more about each of these four types of context in its own part after the list. These four types were brought up to get people to think differently about R&D, but they are by no means the only important ways to look into context.

1. **Focus on the Long Tail**: How could we use big data and AI to pay more attention to the "long tail" of edtech use—going beyond a few "most typical" ways of using emerging technology and instead solving for digital equity and inclusion?
2. **Partnership in Design-Based Research**: How can we change who is involved and influential in designing the future of AI in education to more centrally include students, teachers, and other educational constituents?
3. **Connect with Public Policy**: How can work on AI in education build on general advances in AI ethics, safety, and regulation and contribute additional advances specific to educational policy?
4. **Rethink Teacher Professional Development**: How can we solve for new systems of teacher professional development (both pre-service and in-service) that align to the increasingly core role of technology in the teaching profession?

1 Russell, S. (2019). Human compatible: Artificial intelligence and the problem of control. Penguin. ISBN: 9780525558637

"We can't necessarily always apply traditional research methodologies to this topic because educational technology changes so quickly. "—Kristina Ishmael, Office of Educational Technology

Attention to the Long Tail of Learner Variability

Builders of new AI tools for schools will spend a lot of time making models that work with the data they have access to. There are a lot of different places where the data comes from and includes different ways that people teach and learn in those places because technology is becoming more and more common. When we were hearing, researchers talked about how AI could help with "context" by looking at the long tail of learner variability.

Figure 12. The long tail of learner variability

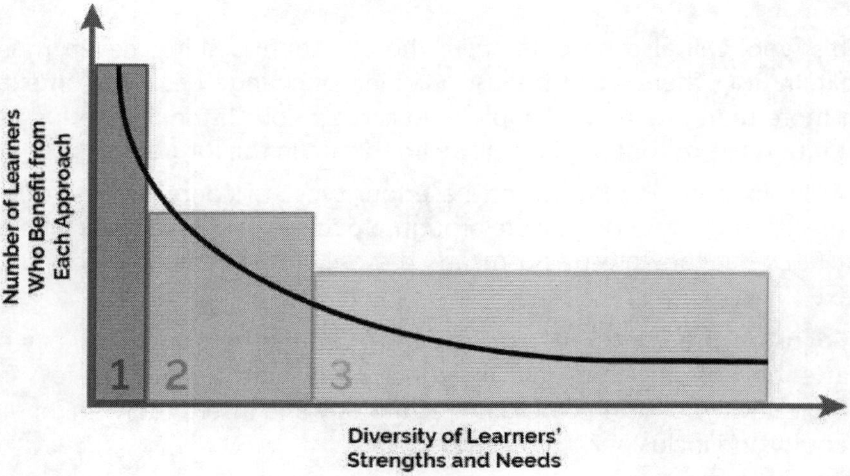

Figure 12 shows that learners have different needs and skills. The mix of strength and needs that happens most often (also called "teaching to the middle") is on the left, and the mixes that happen less often are moving to the right. The amount of students who benefit from a certain learning design, pathway, or approach is shown by the line going up. We say that AI can help with a bigger range of strengths and needs, but only if developers and innovators pay attention to the "long tail" instead of just "teaching to the middle."

Just to make a point, the picture shows three zones. There is a first zone where most of the curriculum materials are standard, with one or two areas where they can be changed. For instance, a lot of current goods change based on how well students answer, and they might also let you read or hear text in a second language. On the other hand, the main way of teaching is very normal. A second zone has a better mix between the amount of standardization and the amount of flexibility that students can use. Universal Design for Learning (UDL) is one set of recommendations for providing learning opportunities in multiple formats and for accommodating different learning progressions.[1] UDL can enable accommodating more ways in which learners vary, and as teachers know, there are many more important ways to adapt to students than found in today's edtech products.

The students' brains are different. From what they've learned at home, in their neighborhoods, and in their cultures, they bring different skills to the table. Their goals and hobbies are different. And they learn in different places—schools and classrooms are not the same, and kids who learn at home do so in less formal settings that could help them learn in school. All of these parts of "context" are important. Zone 3 is for highly flexible learning. This is where standardization doesn't work as well, and we need to find more ways to keep students interested and learning effectively. During our listening sessions, researchers talked about the potential of Zone 3. They said that AI can see patterns in data that go beyond the most common patterns and can create personalized content that goes beyond what humans can properly create on their own.

Keep in mind that the Zone 1 bar isn't actually the highest. That's just how it looks. There are actually more students in Zones 2 and 3, which is where AI can help them the most. Because of this, it's important to know where AI developers and experts are focusing their efforts. When we say that a model "fits," do we mean that teachers and students can use it in the most common ways? More of this kind of R&D can be done. While machine learning and AI can adapt a model to more common situations, they can also make it fit situations that are more culturally unique. So, how can members build knowledge across disciplines to get researchers and developers to pay more attention to the long tail? If we do that, what we do for those in that tail might be more flexible and adjusted to the situation. And for it to work best, it will need to combine technical, content, and environmental knowledge.

People in the long-tail challenge are trying to figure out how to find study insights that are both broad and specific. When study comes up with very broad ideas about how people learn, it doesn't always tell developers how to make their learning environments better. On the other hand, when research creates

1 Rose, D. (2000). Universal design for learning. Journal of Special Education Technology, 15(4), 47-51. https://doi.org/10.1177/016264340001500407

a specific adaptive program that works on one educational platform, it can be hard to use on other platforms. This is because the research can be too detailed. Researchers are also thinking about forming new partnerships that could bring in more data and different points of view. This is what the next piece is about.

It's important to look at the long tail of learner variability if we want to answer a key study question that has been around for a long time: "Do new AI-enhanced approaches work to improve learning, and for whom and under what conditions?"

Partnership in Design-Based Research

Of course, teachers must be included in rethinking their own professional development. This thought leads to another priority aspect of context: partnership in design-based research. With regard to inclusive design, attendees in our listening sessions brought up a variety of co-design[1] and other participatory processes and goals that can be used in R&D.[2] By co-design, they mean sharing power with non-researchers and non-developers through all the phases of design and development, which would result in more influence by teachers, students, and other constituents in the shape of AI-enabled edtech. The shift toward co-design was palpable throughout our listening sessions, but as researchers and developers have not standardized on one particular co-design method, we share some representative examples.

- Youth can powerfully participate in design when researcher methods include participant co-design. Such research can investigate how to improve edtech while educating students. A listening session attendee asked about developing students' awareness of what data are being collected and how data are being used by developers.
- There is a near future need to go beyond representation so that co-designed solutions consider more generous contexts for broader possibilities, according to attendees.
- The shift of power dynamics is another research-worthy interest of the panel and attendees to understand the balance between a teacher's agency and a machine's suggestions.
- Likewise, such longitudinal research will require both the infrastructure

1 Roschelle, J., Penuel, W., & Shechtman, N. (2006). Co-design of innovations with teachers: definition and dynamics. In Proceedings of the 7th International Conference on Learning Sciences, Bloomington, IN. https://doi.dx.org/10.22318/icls2006.606

2 Center for Integrative Research in Computing and Learning Sciences (CIRCLS). (2022, Feb.). From Broadening to Empowering: Reflecting on the CIRCLS'21 Convening. https://circls.org/circls21report

and institutional support to fund necessary experimentation and requisite failures to elicit positive results and safe innovation.

- There is a desire for rapid cycle evaluations with inclusive feedback loops that return to the educators themselves as essential relative to traditional research approaches.
- Many researchers also mentioned a focus on explainable AI as essential to enable participation in the design and evaluation of emerging AI approaches in education.

The talks brought up this question: how can co-design give people a way to participate in design that gives them power, and in this way help reach digital inclusion goals? Digital inclusion can happen at many levels of design, such as including different voices in the creation of data policies, the design of AI systems' adaptability and other user experiences, the creation of plans to teach people how to use AI on new platforms, and finally, the creation of plans to test the systems.

Re-thinking Teacher Professional Development

Concerning teachers as professionals, researchers and other teachers who came to our listening sessions were very worried about the difference between how teachers are trained and how they are supposed to use new technology. When we talk about learning, teachers play a big role. Because of this, the ways in which they are trained are very important for their ability to do great work in new and current technology settings.

People thought that teacher professional development, professional learning, and leadership (PD or PL) for new technologies needed to be rethought in a big way, and study could help. Today, most people who are in an established pre-service program to become teachers don't learn about how to use technology effectively in schools and classrooms. Those who do learn about technology rarely think about the structures that affect how it is used in the classroom and by educational leaders. There is a worrisome divide between a small group of researchers who focus on educational technology in their studies of teaching and a larger group of teachers who see educational technology as a general tool for teaching. The task is big because professional development for teachers will still look very different depending on where they work. However, a lot of study on teacher professional development doesn't pay enough attention to teachers as leaders in the use and development of useful educational technology.

As an answer, one could be to look into how to help all teachers learn more about AI. AI knowledge is important to keep teachers and students safe from possible harm, and it's also useful to help teachers find new ways to use AI's good qualities. One of the panelists told the group that this work has implications for how we teach teachers about AI and how to use it. A study said that trust is one of the most important things for all teachers and students, and that more openness and real conversation can help build it.

This doesn't mean that learning about AI is a cure or even an easy fix. Researchers want to know what it really means for teachers to be professionals. This is especially important as new technologies become more common in schools and classes, which are where teachers do their jobs. Researchers want to change how we think about teachers as professionals in a broad sense and stop seeing technology as an extra part of professional growth.

Connecting with Public Policy

Adopting a human-centered concept and foundation for making rules about how AI can be used and applied in society as a whole is needed to define human-centered AI for education. For instance, the same kinds of power struggles that happen between businesses and customers in everyday life over things like who owns data will also happen in the education environment. Also, the public discourse in which people talk about ethics, bias, responsibility, and many other important ideas will happen at the same time in both public policy and school ecosystems.

During our listening meetings, it became clear that improving AI literacy in schools could be important and good for society as a whole. One speaker, for example, said that if people want to have a say in how AI technologies are made, there needs to be a broad goal of making people smarter about AI. Another researcher was interested in how edtech can create spaces where students can have tough conversations with people of different points of view, which is a problem that exists in our society right now. A third researcher pointed out that previous attempts to deal with algorithmic bias, ethics, and inclusion were not enough because of how complicated the social interactions are in a classroom.

Researchers want to take a lead in going beyond checkbox approaches to take these issues seriously. And they also acknowledge that engaging with policy is often a new form of context for edtech and AI researchers, many of whom don't have long experiences in policy arenas. Likewise, developers often do have experience with some policy issues, such as data privacy and security, but are now needing to become part of new conversations about ethics, bias, transparency, and more, a problem that the EdSAFE AI Alliance is addressing through multisector working groups and policy advocacy.[1]

Key Recommendation: Focus R&D on Addressing Context

People who came to the listening groups that led up to this chapter made it very clear that they thought future R&D would move away from narrow technical questions and toward more in-depth contextual questions. The people who came to the listening session thought that this broad shift toward context, which is explained below, was essential for moving R&D forward. The following were listed by attendees as background dimensions:

- learner variability, e.g., in disabilities, languages spoken, and other relevant characteristics;
- interactions with peers, teachers, and others in the learning settings;
- relationships across home, school, and community settings, including cultural assets;
- instructional resources available while learning;
- teacher preparation; and
- policies and systems that structure teaching and learning.

These and other aspects of text will need to be included in AI models in order to better reflect the context of teaching and learning. Researchers will need to work together to figure out which context aspects are most important to teaching and learning and how to make them useful.

Ongoing Questions for Researchers

People are good at understanding context, but AI isn't so good at it. So, putting money into research and development for context-rich education technology could help more than one country, since improving how it handles context would be a big step forward in AI. In fact, these kinds of questions come up in all areas of AI use in society, and education is a great place to start looking into them:

- Are AI systems moving beyond the tall portions of the "long tail" to adapt to a greater range of conditions, factors, and variations in how people learn?

1 Nentrup, E. (2022). How Policymakers Can Support Educators and Technology Vendors Towards SAFE AI. EdSAFE AI Alliance. https://www.edsafeai.org/post/how-policymakers-can-support-aied

- To what extent are AI technologies enhancing rather than replacing human control and judgment of student learning?
- How will users understand the legal and ethical implications of sharing data with AI enabled technologies and how to mitigate privacy risks?
- To what extent does technology account for the complex social dynamics of how people work and learn together, or is technology leading humans to narrow or oversimplify?
- How can we more clearly define what we mean by a context-sensitive technology in terms that are both concrete and broad enough? How can we measure it?
- To what extent are technical indicators and human observations of bias or unfairness working together with human observations? How can concerns about ethics and equity in AI technologies become actionable both in R&D, and later, when AI is widely used?
- Are we learning for whom and under what conditions AI systems produce desired benefits and impacts and avoid undesirable discrimination, bias, or negative outcomes?

Desired National R&D Objectives

Attendees sought immediate progress on some key R&D issues, such as these:

- Clarifying and achieving a consensus on the terms that go beyond data privacy and data security, including ideas like human-centered, value-sensitive, responsible, ethical, and safe so constituents can advocate for their needs meaningfully and consistently
- Creating and studying effective programs for AI literacy for students, teachers, and educational constituents in general, including literacy with regard to the ethics and equity issues specific to AI in educational settings
- Advancing research and development to increase fairness, accountability, transparency, and safety in AI systems used in educational settings
- Defining participatory or co-designed research processes that include educators in the development and conduct of research related to the development, use, and efficacy of AI- enabled systems and tools
- Highlighting and advancing R&D efforts that empower the participation and voices of youth regarding research, data, and design of AI applications for teaching and learning

Longer term desires for a national R&D program include some of the following objectives:

- Funding sustainable partnerships that uncover what context means and how it can be addressed over longer periods of time
- Better connecting goals for "broadening participation" (for example, in STEM learning pathways) to strategies for addressing learner variability and diversity
- Prioritizing research to revitalize support for instructors in light of the increasingly technological nature of K-12, higher education, and workplace learning settings
- Creating infrastructure and new ways of working together beyond individual field- initiated grants so that R&D with big data and leveraging emerging AI capabilities becomes safer and more productive

Recommendations

Earlier, we asked two guiding questions:

1. What is our collective vision of a desirable and achievable educational system that leverages automation while protecting and centering human agency?
2. On what timeline will we be ready with necessary guidelines and guardrails along with convincing evidence of positive impacts, so that we can ethically and equitably implement this vision widely?

The Learning, Teaching, Assessment, and Research areas all have answers to the first question. This part goes on to give education leaders advice and a call to action. The Department's main point of view is that education will need leadership that is unique to our field. There has been a lot of good work done in edtech in the past, like protecting student privacy and school data. Leaders should build on this work, as well as on broad guidelines for safe AI, like the Blueprint for an AI Bill of Rights. Leadership needs to look beyond these achievements and frameworks to address new risks and opportunities that come with AI's new features and uses in education.

Insight: Aligning AI to Policy Objectives

There were different parts of this policy report that talked about learning, training, assessment, and research. These ideas, gathered from many meetings and conversations with stakeholders, show that improvements in AI can open up ways to help the Department reach its policy goals:

- In support of our objective of attracting and retaining teachers, our nation could focus on AI assistants that make teaching jobs better and provide teachers with the information they need to work closely and empathically with students. An emphasis on teachers in the loop could ensure that AI-enabled classroom technologies keep teachers in the know, in touch with their students, and in control of important instructional decisions. Keeping the teacher in the loop is important to managing risks, as well.
- In support of equitable learning, especially for those most affected by the pandemic, AI could shift edtech from a current deficit-based model to a strengths-based alternative. In addition to finding student weaknesses and assigning fixes, edtech could make recommendations based on strengths that students bring to learning and how adapting to the whole student—a cognitive, social, and self-regulating person—could enable more powerful learning. Adapting to the whole student should include supporting students with disabilities as well as English learners. With regard to equity, we must remain highly attuned to the challenges of bias (which are inherent to how AI systems are developed) and take firm action to ensure fairness.
- With regard to growth trajectories to successful careers, AI-enabled assessments could provide students and teachers with formative guidance on a wider range of valuable skills, focusing on providing information that enhances learning. Aligned with the human-centric view, we should take a systems view of assessments where students, teachers, and others remain at the center of instructional decision making.
- With regard to equity, as research advances and brings more context into AI, we will be better able to use AI to support goals that require customization of learning resources, such as enabling teachers to more easily transform materials to support neurodiverse learners and increase responsiveness to local communities and cultures.

From now on, educational leaders should bring these and their own policy priorities to every AI talk. This way, people's priorities will be at the center of the conversation, not just their excitement about what new technology might do. AI's main goal is to handle tasks that help it reach its goals, but AI itself should never set goals. The goals must come from how teachers see teaching and learning and from what they know about the needs and skills of each student.

Calling Education Leaders to Action

We put together a list of seven policy suggestions. These suggestions are for people in charge of schooling. In the opening, we talk about how important it is to include people who work in education in making decisions about AI policies. During our listening sessions, we also saw that people with a wide range of jobs in education all have a lot to offer in terms of passion, knowledge, and new ideas. We believe that people from all walks of life can be school leaders. We don't want to say that one member role is more important than another in order to move any of the recommendations forward, but we do point out specific actions that need to be taken in some of the recommendations when they are needed.

Recommendation #1: Emphasize Humans in the Loop

We begin with a main suggestion that will run through this whole chapter. It was clear that constituents liked this suggestion the most. Indeed, among the more than 700 people who came to our listening meetings, the main topic of conversation was how to get people to agree on a vision for AI-enabled education technology that puts people at the center. In the same way, the Blueprint for an AI Bill of Rights says that people should be able to get human help and a second chance if an automated system fails, makes a mistake, or someone wants to protest or fight its effects. Based on this agreement, we urge everyone to make "humans in the loop" a very important rule for using AI in education.

We see a world where technology is more like an electric bike and less like robot vacuums. A person riding an electric bike is fully aware and in charge, but their load is lighter and their effort is multiplied by a complementary technology improvement. Robot vacuums do their job, so a person doesn't have to do it or keep an eye on it.

Teachers shouldn't be the only people in loops, but Figure 5 shows three types of teacher loops that are important to education and can be used to show what it means to have a "human in the loop." Here, we'll use an AI robot to show what the loops mean in more detail. First, as students deal with AI chatbots for longer periods of time, teachers will need to teach them how to use AI safely, keep an eye on how they use it, and make sure that students know what to do if something goes wrong. Second, teachers are starting to use chatbots to plan personalized lessons for their students. To learn how to use effective prompts and check AI-generated lesson plans for errors, teachers will need to be in loops with other teachers. This will help them avoid the human tendency to trust AI systems too much and not use their own judgment enough. Third, teachers should be involved in making AI systems and testing them before they are used in schools and again when it is clear that they need to be improved. As an example, teachers who know a lot about the cognitive, motivational, and social supports their students need will be able to help AI writers make homework help chatbots that will help students with their schoolwork.

"Human in the loop" AI is a key recommendation in this chapter's discussion of AI in education. This is because the phrase easily communicates a standard that everyone can use to decide which AI-enabled systems and tools are proper for use in teaching and learning. Human in the loop is a friendly and humane criterion in an area that is mostly technical. This term doesn't mean that AI-enabled systems and tools should replace teachers. Instead, it emphasizes the important role of educators as leaders in the classroom and as people who make decisions about how to teach. It also stresses that teachers have the responsibility to use their own judgment and control when AI is used in the classroom. It fits with the important idea of feedback loops, which are a big part of how we learn and teach. It also fits with the ideas of AI that can be inspected, explained, cut off, and overridden.

The Department agrees with the people who spoke at the listening session that teachers shouldn't be the only humans in the loop. They also want parents, families, students, policymakers, and system leaders to look at the "loops" they are responsible for, think about how AI is becoming more and more involved in those loops, and figure out what they need to do to support the idea that human judgment should be the most important thing in educational systems.

Recommendation #2: Align AI Models to a Shared Vision for Education

As we've talked about in every part of this chapter, AI technologies are based on models, and these models are always missing some information. People are the ones who set educational goals and decide how well models work and are useful, or not work and could be dangerous. It may seem clear to judge how well different tools help with educational goals, but the allure of technology can make us say, "Let's see what the tech can do," which can take our attention away from our goals and lead us to use models that don't work well with our priorities.

At this point, we want people in charge of education at the local, state, and federal levels to use their power to make sure that goals, educational strategies, and decisions about adopting new technology are all in line with putting students' needs first, rather than the excitement about new AI capabilities. We want them to pay more attention to the state, county, and school rules that govern the use and adoption of technology in education. These rules include the four levels of evidence in ESSA, the privacy rules in FERPA, and new rules that will be made. Leaders in local education know best what their most important educational goals are right now. When we talk about AI (or any other new technology), we should always start by putting the students' needs and priorities first. Then, when we talk about how to measure success, we should go back to those needs and priorities. Naturally, equity is a matter that needs constant attention, especially now that AI models might be biased and cause bad things to happen.

It is especially important for leaders not to fall in love with AI or only focus on its potential uses or results. Instead, they should carefully consider how AI-powered teaching systems and tools work. We tell leaders not to believe broad promises and to ask the following six types of questions. This part went into more detail about which aspects of using AI models in education are the most important to look at to make sure they fit with the educational goals that were set. Figure 13 is a summary of what we've learned about AI models and how they can be used in training systems and tools to help leaders.

Figure 13. Recommendation for desired qualities of AI tools and systems in education

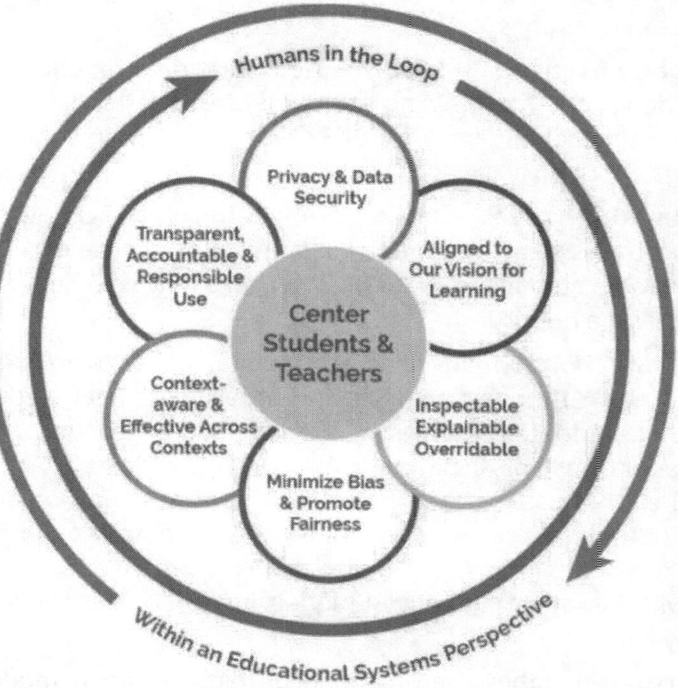

This graph puts teaching and learning at the center of all the things we think about when deciding if an AI model is good for use in education. People will continue to define, improve, and use AI models. Using ideas from the Blueprint for an AI Bill of Rights and adapting them to fit the needs of educational systems, we list the six qualities that AI models for education should have:

1. **Alignment of the AI Model to Educators' Vision for Learning**: When choosing to use AI in educational systems, decision makers prioritize educational goals, the fit to all we know about how people learn, and alignment to evidence-based best practices in education.
2. **Data Privacy**: Ensuring security and privacy of student, teacher, and other human data in AI systems is essential.
3. **Notice and Explanation**: Educators can inspect edtech to determine whether and how AI is being incorporated within edtech systems. Educators' push for AI models can explain the basis for detecting patterns and/or for making recommendations, and people retain control over these suggestions.
4. **Algorithmic Discrimination Protections**: Developers and implementers of AI in education take strong steps to minimizing bias and promoting fairness in AI models.
5. **Safe and Effective Systems**: The use of AI models in education is based on evidence of efficacy (using standards already established in education for this purpose) and work for diverse learners and in varied educational settings.
6. **Human Alternatives, Consideration and Feedback**: AI models that support transparent, accountable, and responsible use of AI in education by involving humans in the loop to ensure that educational values and principles are prioritized.

We first talk about our advice to educational leaders who use technology to look into how AI models are used in schools, but other leaders also play important roles. Adoption choices are also affected by teachers, students, and their families or caretakers in big ways. Also, parents and leaders should back up teachers when they use their professional judgment to question or overrule an AI model. Technology developers should be open about the models they use, and lawmakers might need to make disclosure requirements so that the market can work with information about AI models instead of just claims about how helpful they are.

We also stress that the government needs to play a part. AI models are made by people and aren't exactly like the real world. So, we need rules that make sure the AI models built into schools are clear and allow people to check them out, explain them, and change them if necessary. During our listening sessions, people asked the government to do more to make developers answer for not telling us what kinds of AI models they use in big goods and what safety features are built into them. It is possible for government leaders to help create market conditions that help build trust as AI systems are bought and used in schools. In suggestion #4, which is about building trust, we talk more about these rules.

Recommendation #3: Design Using Modern Learning Principles

We want the R&D sector to make sure that the ideas of their products are based on the best and newest ways to teach and learn. In the first ten years of adaptivity in edtech, many important ideas were used. For example, how to give students feedback and how to organize learning events. Still, the idea behind it was often based on deficits. The system looked at what was wrong with the student and picked learning materials that were already out there that might help fix that problem. In the future, we need to use AI's ability to figure out what learners are good at and build on that. Also, the last ten years of approaches have been focused on the person, even though we know that people are social by nature and that learning is strongly social. Moving forward, we need to improve AI in ways that work with collaboration and social learning ideas and value each student's knowledge as well as all of their other skills. In the future, we should also try to make AI systems that are culturally responsive and culturally sustaining. To do this, we can use the growing body of written techniques. Also, most of the first AI systems didn't have many features that helped students with disabilities or who were learning English. From now on, we need to make sure that AI-enabled learning materials are designed to include these kids. Edtech hasn't yet been made that builds on each student's ability to make decisions and keep themselves in check in settings that are getting more complicated. It's time to make edtech that helps students learn in more creative ways and improves their speaking, writing, and leading skills.

Also, we want teachers to say no to AI uses that are based only on machine learning from data, without integration based on learning theory and knowledge from practice. To make educational systems work well and fairly, we need to do more than just process "big data." We also want to get insights from data, but people still need to understand it. We don't agree with the idea that technological determinism means that data trends can tell us what to do on their own. When AI is used in education, it should be based on current, well-established learning principles and the knowledge of people who work in education. It should also use the knowledge of people who work in the educational testing community to find bias and make tests more fair.

Recommendation #4: Prioritize Strengthening Trust

We have to trust technology in order for it to help us reach our educational goals. Still, our listening meetings showed us how common it is to not trust edtech and AI. People don't trust new tools for a number of reasons. They may have had their privacy invaded. It's possible that the user experience will be harder than expected. Promised improvements in how well students learn might not be backed up by studies on efficacy. They may have had effects they didn't expect. Costs may come up out of the blue. People may not trust complexity. Trust needs to include things like safety, usefulness, and effectiveness.

The Department is strong in its belief that people want AI that helps teachers and don't want AI to replace teachers. Still, teachers, students, and the people who care for them need help building trust in the processes that affect their work. In the bigger picture, building trust in AI is seen as a problem with many sides. We worry that distrust will get in the way of innovation that serves the public good, which AI could help make possible, if every step forward doesn't include strong parts of building trust.

We think that groups and clubs will play a big part in building trust. Leaders in edtech are helped by groups like the State Educational Technology Directors Association and the Consortium for School Network. Leaders in higher education are helped by groups like EDUCAUSE. There are other groups and associations that work with teachers, school leaders, and people who train school workers. Networks in an industry, like the EdSAFE AI Alliance, can bring together leaders in that industry to work together to build trust. More groups bring together researchers. There are enough members of these groups for all parts of the educational ecosystem to be involved in talks about trust, and they can also speak for their members in policy discussions that affect many areas.

Recommendation #5: Inform and Involve Educators

The people we listened to were also asked for more specific advice on what school leaders should do (see Figure 14). The most common answers fell into three groups: the need for rules and guidelines, making teachers' jobs safer, and changing the goal of research and development. People are asking for these things to be done, and they could help build trust. These wishes are met by the suggestions that follow.

Figure 14. Listening session attendees prioritized involving practitioners, research, and evaluation and the need for guidelines and guardrails.

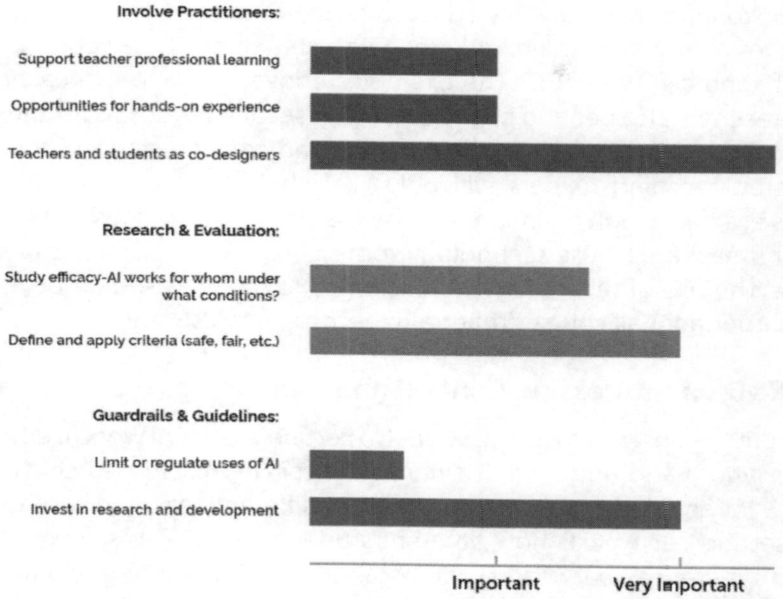

One worry that came up a lot during our listening meetings was that AI might make people not respect teachers as much or value their skills as much. Across the country, fewer people want to become teachers or stay in the field, so we are now reacting. Now is the time to show educators how much we respect and value them by keeping them informed and involving them in every step of designing, building, testing, improving, adopting, and managing edtech that uses AI. This includes getting teachers involved in reviewing current AI-enabled systems, tools, and data use in schools, coming up with new AI uses based on what teachers say, testing out proposed new teaching tools in small groups, working with developers to make the system more reliable, and bringing up concerns about risks and unintended outcomes as the system is put in place.

We've already seen educators step up to the task of making general rules, planning specific ways to use AI-enabled tools and systems, and finding problems. But we can't just assume that teachers will have an impact on the future of AI-powered products; instead, people need laws that back it up. Could we get top educators from every state and area to work together as a national corps to provide leadership? Could we promise to create the career development tools that are needed? Can we find ways to pay teachers so that they can be at the head of planning how schools will work in the future? Our rules should let teachers have a big say in how AI-powered learning tools are made.

We understand that all levels of national and school government need to do their part to inform and involve educators. However, the Office of Educational Technology can play a major role in doing this through its reports, events, outreach, and a future NETP. The examples above are for K–12 teachers, but college teachers also need to be included. Our second request is for the edtech business to include teachers in the planning and creation stages. For instance, AI-powered teaching helpers will only likely help teachers do their jobs if teachers are fully involved in making the assistants. Our request is for schools that train teachers to use technology more consistently in their courses. For example, the use of technology in teaching and learning should be a central theme throughout all courses that train teachers, not just one.

Focus R&D on Addressing Context and Enhancing Trust and Safety

Finding out the answer to the question "Do certain uses of AI work in education? If so, for whom and under what circumstances?" requires research that looks into how AI-enabled systems can adapt to different teaching methods and school settings, as well as how different students learn? This saying in quotes refers to differences between students and between learning environments. Researchers should focus their efforts on making AI better in the long tail of learning diversity, where a lot of students would benefit from having their learning tailored to their needs. We also want R&D to take the lead in figuring out how to build trust in AI-enabled systems. This builds on the Blueprint's call for safe and effective systems while also including education-specific needs, such as how teachers can be involved in the design stages as well as the implementation and evaluation phases.

There are a lot of adaptive products on the market today, but some only change based on one or a few variables, like how well students solve problems. They know there are many more important ways to meet the needs and strengths of each kid. The students are neurodiverse, and some of them may have problems. They bring different skills from what they've learned at home, in their neighborhoods, and in their cultures. Their goals and hobbies are different. They are at different points in their English learning journeys. They also learn in a variety of places. Schools and classrooms are not the same thing. At home, kids learn in more casual ways that could help them at school. We suggest paying attention to "context" as a way to talk about the many things that need to be thought about when expanding on the phrase "for whom and under what conditions." We also recognize the importance of researchers' work in conducting reviews, which must now look at more than just how well something works. They must also look into where harm might happen and the system issues that can happen when people don't trust AI systems enough or too much.

Research and development (R&D) needs to make AI models more aware of their surroundings and make sure they are safe, reliable, and useful for a wide range of students in a variety of settings. In contrast to humans, AI can find patterns in a lot more variables than just the ones we usually think about. However, AI is not as good as humans at understanding and using context. Over time, learning sciences have become less focused on individualistic cognitive concepts and more on social learning and the many context-related factors that affect learning. When we use AI for teaching purposes, we need to keep going in this direction toward context.

People who came to the listening session said that teams will need time and freedom to figure out how to best handle the tension between how quickly technology is changing and how much more we need to know about the bigger picture for trust and safety. They will need time and freedom to come up with new ways to involve teachers and students more as co-designers, while also making sure that power is shared fairly. And they will have to stop focusing on older ways of setting priorities, like achievement gaps, and start focusing on new ways of setting priorities for digital equality. We ask people who fund research into new ideas to pay attention to the long tail of student variability, the need for AI-enabled systems that better take context into account, and the time it takes to get these things right. In their work to improve AI, we urge researchers and writers to put context, trust, and safety issues at the top of their lists.

Develop Education-Specific Guidelines and Guardrails

Our last suggestion is very important for lawmakers. The American school system puts a lot of weight on making decisions at the neighborhood level. It's getting harder for local leaders to make smart choices about how to use artificial intelligence because technology is getting more complicated so quickly. There are more problems than just data privacy and security, which we've already talked about. These problems include bias, openness, and responsibility. This changing, complicated set of criteria will make it harder to judge how well potential edtech platforms that use AI systems work.

The Family Educational Rights and Privacy Act (FERPA), the Children's Internet Privacy Act (CIPA), and the Children's Online Privacy Protection Act (COPPA) all protect student and family data. Because of new technologies in schools, these laws need to be looked at again and given more thought. As new situations appear with AI-powered learning tools, laws like the Individuals with

Disabilities Education Act (IDEA) may also be taken into account. We've talked a lot about how the Blueprint for an AI Bill of Rights is an important context for this work.

People at all levels of the school system are encouraged to work together by the Department. Along with the important federal laws we just talked about, many states have also passed privacy laws that control how educational technology and edtech platforms are used in schools. People who have a stake in this issue can also expect that general frameworks for responsible AI in related fields like health, safety, and consumer goods will be useful, but not enough to meet the needs of education. Leaders at every level need to be aware of how this work affects more than just privacy and security. For example, they need to be aware of how this work could lead to bias and unfairness. They also need to be ready to deal with the next level of problems.

Next Steps

We're glad that people are talking more about the role of AI in schooling across the board. As people talk about these three types of questions, we can see growth that we can build on: What are the most important risks and opportunities? How can we make teaching AI that we can trust? How can we learn about the models that are at the heart of AI applications and make sure they have the right traits for educational goals?

The Department wrote this chapter knowing that a lot of different kinds of groups and organizations could make inputs. We know that the European Union, the United Nations, and other places around the world are all working on AI at the same time. We know that groups like UNESCO, the EdSAFE AI Alliance, and study groups in many countries are leading the way in making progress. We are going to keep working with other federal agencies, like the Office of Science and Technology Policy, to make sure that we can take the next steps outlined in the Blueprint for an AI Bill of Rights. We see a broad and rich background for the next steps that need to be taken:

The Department will think about specific rules and policies so that teachers can make the most of the benefits of AI in education technology while reducing the risks. For instance, the Department is making a list of possible uses for AI to improve the process of reviewing and improving rules and laws. The rules and guidelines in the Blueprint for an AI Bill of Rights will be used to make sure that the situations reduce important risks and harms.

We will create more resources and events to help people who will be most affected by AI understand it better. These people include education leaders, teachers, faculty, support staff, and other educators; researchers; policymakers;

funders; technology developers; community members and organizations; and most importantly, learners and their families and caregivers.

We will revise and update the NETP to help everyone move toward safe, fair, and effective AI in education in the US, in line with our overall educational goals. We will do this by working together across sectors, such as education, innovation, research, and policy.

References

Akgun, S., Greenhow, C. (2022). Artificial intelligence in education: Addressing ethical challenges in K-12 settings. AIEthics, 2, 431-440. https://doi.org/10.1007/s43681-021- 00096-7

Aleven, V., McLaughlin, E. A., Glenn, R. A., & Koedinger, K. R. (2016). Instruct on based on adaptive learning technologies. In Mayer, R.E. & Alexander, P.A., Handbook of research on learning and instruction, 522-560. ISBN: 113883176X

Baker, R.S., Esbenshade, L., Vitale, J., & Karumbaiah, S. (2022). Using demographic data as predictor variables: A questionable choice. https://doi.org/10.35542/osf.io/y4wvj

Black, P. & Wiliam, D. (1998). Inside the black box: Raising standards through classroom assessment. Phi Delta Kappan, 92(1), 81-90. https://kappanonline.org/inside-the-black-box-raising-standards-through-classroom-assessment/

Black, P., & Wiliam, D. (2009). Developing the theory of formative assessment. Educational Assessment, Evaluation and Accountability, 21(1), 5-31. https://doi.org/10.1007/s11092-008-9068-5

Boden, M.A. (2018). Artificial intelligence: A very short introduction. Oxford. ISBN: 978-0199602919 Bryant, J., Heitz,C., Sanghvi, S., & Wagle, D. (2020, January 14). How artificial intelligence will impact K-12 teachers. McKinsey. https://www.mckinsey.com/industries/education/our-insights/how-artificial-intelligence-will-impact-k-12-teachers

Celik, I., Dindar, M., Muukkonen, H. & Jarvela, S. (2022). The promises and challenges of artificial intelligence for teachers: A systematic review of research. TechTrends, 66, 616630. https://doi.org/10.1007/s11528-022-00715-y

Center for Integrative Research in Computing and Learning Sciences (CIRCLS). (2022, Feb.). From Broadening to empowering: Reflecting on the CIRCLS'21 Convening. https://circls.org/circls21report

Chen, C., Park, H.W. & Breazeal, C. (2020). Teaching and learning with children: Impact of reciprocal peer learning with a social robot on children's learning and emotive engagement. Computers & Education, 150, https://doi.org/10.1016/j.compedu.2020.103836 Chen, G., Clarke, S., & Resnick, L.B. (2015). Classroom Discourse Analyzer (CDA): A discourse analytic tool for teachers. Technology, Instruction, Cognition and Learning, 10(2), 85-105 Dieterle, E., Dede, C. & Walker, M. (2022). The cyclical ethical effects of using artificial intelligence in education. AI & Society. https://link.springer.com/article/10.1007/s00146- 022-01497-w

Doewes, A. & Pechenizkiy, M. (2021). On the limitations of human-computer agreement in automated essay scoring. In Proceedings of the 14th International Conference on Educational Data Mining (EDM21). https://educationaldatamining.org/EDM2021/virtual/static/pdf/EDM21_paper_243.pdf

Englebart, D.C. (October 1962). Augmenting human intellect: A conceptual framework. SRI Summary Report AFOSR-3223. https://www.dougengelbart.org/pubs/augment-3906.html

Ersozlu, Z., Ledger, S., Ersozlu, A., Mayne, F., & Wildy, H. (2021). Mixed-reality learning environments in teacher education: An analysis of TeachLivETM Research. SAGE Open, 11(3). https://doi.org/10.1177/21582440211032155.

European Commission, Directorate-General for Education, Youth, Sport and Culture. (2022). Ethical guidelines on the use of artificial intelligence (AI) and data in teaching and learning for educators. Publications Office of the European Union. https://data.europa.eu/doi/10.2766/153756

Forsyth, S., Dalton, B., Foster, E.H., Walsh, B., Smilack, J., & Yeh, T. (2021, May). Imagine a more ethical AI: Using stories to develop teens' awareness and understanding of artificial intelligence and its societal impacts. In 2021 Conference on Research in Equitable and Sustained Participation in Engineering, Computing, and Technology (RESPECT). IEEE. https://doi.org/10.1109/RESPECT51740.2021.9620549

Friedman, L., Blair Black, N., Walker, E., & Roschelle, J. (November 8, 2021) Safe AI in education needs you. Association of Computing Machinery BLOG@ACM, https://cacm.acm.org/blogs/blog-cacm/256657-safe-ai-in-education-needs-you/fulltext

Gardner, J., O'Leary, M. & Yuan, L. (2021). Artificial intelligence in educational assessment: "Breakthrough? Or buncombe and ballyhoo?" Journal of Computer Assisted Learning, 37(5), 1207-1216. https://doi.org/10.1111/jcal.12577

Gartner (n.d.) Gartner glossary: Augmented intelligence. Gartner. https://www.gartner.com/en/information-technology/glossary/augmented-intelligence

Gay, G. (2018). Culturally responsive teaching: Theory, research, and practice. Teachers College Press. ISBN: 978-08 07758762

Godwin-Jones, R. (2021). Big data and language learning: Opportunities and challenges. Language Learning & Technology, 25(1), 4-19. http://hdl.handle.net/10125/44747 Hammerness, K., Darling-Hammond, L., & Bransford, J. (2005). Preparing teachers for a changing world: What teachers should learn and be able to do. Jossey-Bass. ISBN: 0787996343 Holmes, W. & Porayska-Pomsta, K. (Eds.) (2022). The ethics of artificial intelligence in education. Routledge. ISBN 978-0367349721

Holstein, K., McLaren, B.M., & Aleven, V. (2019). Co-designing a real-time classroom orchestration tool to support teacher-AI complementarity. Journal of Learning Analytics, 6(2). https://doi.org/10.18608/jla.2019.62.3

IEEE-USA Board of Directors. (February 10, 2017). Artificial intelligence research, development and regulation. IEEE http://globalpolicy.ieee.org/wp-content/uploads/2017/10/IEEE17003.pdf Jensen, E., Dale, M., Donnelly, P.J., Stone, C., Kelly, S., Godley, A. & D'Mello, S.K. (2020). Toward automated feedback on teacher discourse to enhance teacher learning. In Proceedings of the 2020 CHI Conference on Human Factors in Computing Systems (CHI '20). https://doi.org/10.1145/3313831.3376418

Kai, S., Almeda, M.V., Baker, R. S., Heffernan, C., & Heffernan, N. (2018). Decision tree modeling of wheel-spinning and productive persistence in skill builders. Journal of Educational Data Mining, 10(1), 36-71. https://doi.org/10.5281/zenodo.3344810

Kaplan, R.M., & Saccuzzo, D.P. (2017). Psychological testing: Principles, applications, and issues. Cengage Learning.

Ke, Z., & Ng, V. (2019). Automated essay scoring: A survey of the state of the art. In Proceedings of the Twenty-Eighth International Joint Conference on Artificial Intelligence, 6300-6308. https://doi.org/10.24963/ijcai.2019/879

Khosravi, H., Shum, S.B., Chen, G, Conati, C., Tsai,Y-S., Kay, J., Knight, S., Martinez-Maldonado, R., Sadiq, S., Gasevic, D. (2022). Explainable artificial intelligence in education. Computers and Education: Artificial Intelligence, 3. https://doi.org/10.1016Zj.caeai.2022.100074

Kulik, J.A., & Fletcher, J.D. (2016). Effectiveness of intelligent tutoring systems: A meta-analytic review. Review of Educational Research, 86(1), 42-78

Ma, W., Adescope, O.O, Nesbit, J.C. & Liu, Q. (2014). Intelligent tutoring systems and learning outcomes: A meta-analysis. Journal of Educational Psychology, 106(4), 901-918. http://dx.doi.org/10.1037/a0037123

Maslej, N., Fattorini, L., Brynjolfsson E., Etchemendy, J., Ligett, K., Lyons, T., Manyika, J., Ngo, H., Niebles, J.C., Parli, V., Shoham, Y., Wald, R., Clark, J. and Perrault, R., (2023). The AI index 2023 annual report. Stanford University: AI Index Steering Committee, Institute for Human-Centered AI.

Merrill, S. (2020). In schools, are we measuring what matters? Edutopia. https://www.edutopia.org/article/schools-are-we-measuring-what-matters

Molenaar, I. (2022). Towards hybrid human-AI learning technologies. European Journal of Education, 00,1-14. https://doi.org/10.1111/ejed.12527

Mostow, J., Aist, G., Burkhead, P., Corbett, A., Cuneo, A., Eitelman, S., Huang, C., Junker, B., Sklar, M.B., & Tobin, B. (2003). Evaluation of an automated reading tutor that listens: Comparison to human tutoring and classroom instruction. Journal of Educational Computing Research, 29(1), 61-117. https://doi.org/10.2190/06AX-QW99-EQ5G-RDCF Mousavinasab, E., Zarifsanaiey, N., R. Niakan Kalhori, S., Rakhshan, M., Keikha, L., & Ghazi Saeedi, M. (2021). Intelligent tutoring systems: A systematic review of characteristics, applications, and evaluation methods. Interactive Learning Environments, 29(1), 142-163. https://psycnet.apa.org/doi/10.1080/10494820.2018.1558257

National Academies of Sciences, Engineering, and Medicine. 2018. How people learn II: Learners, contexts, and cultures. The National Academies Press. https://doi.org/10.17226/24783

National Research Council. 2000. How people learn: Brain, mind, experience, and school. The National Academies Press. https://doi.org/10.17226/9853

Nentrup, E. (2022). How Policymakers Can Support Educators and Technology Vendors Towards SAFE AI. EdSAFE AI Alliance. https://www.edsafeai.org/post/how-policymakers-can-support-aied

Page, E.B. (1966). The imminence of grading essays by computer. Phi Delta Kappan, 47(5), 238243

Paris, D., & Alim, H.S. (Eds.). (2017). Culturally sustaining pedagogies: Teaching and learning for justice in a changing world. Teachers College Press. ISBN: 978-0807758342

Plass, J.L., & Pawar, S. (2020). Toward a taxonomy of adaptivity for learning. Journal of Research on Technology in Education, 52(3), 275-300. https://doi.org/10.1080/15391523.2020.1719943 Regona, Massimo & Yigitcanlar, Tan & Xia, Bo & Li, R.Y.M. (2022). Opportunities and adoption challenges of AI in the construction industry: A PRISMA review. Journal of Open Innovation Technology Market and Complexity, 8(45). https://doi.org/10.3390/joitmc8010045 Reynolds, C.R., & Suzuki, L.A. (2012). Bias in psychological assessment: An empirical review and recommendations. Handbook of Psychology, Second Edition. https://doi.org/10.1002/9781118133880.hop210004

Ritter, S., Anderson, J.R., Koedinger, K.R. & Corbett, A. (2007). Cognitive Tutor: Applied research in mathematics education. Psychonomic Bulletin & Review, 14, 249-255/ https://doi.org/10.3758/BF03194060

Roll, I., Aleven, V., McLaren, B.M., Koedinger, K.R. (2011). Improving students' help-seeking skills using metacognitive feedback in an intelligent tutoring system, Learning and Instruction, 21(2), 267-280. https://doi.org/10.1016/jdearninstruc.2010.07.004.

Roschelle, J., Dimitriadis, Y. & Hoppe, U. (2013). Classroom orchestration: Synthesis. Computers & Education, 69, 512-526. https://doi.org/10.1016/j.compedu.2013.04.010

Roschelle, J., Feng, M., Murphy, R. & Mason, C.A. (2016). Online mathematics homework increases student achievement. AERA Open, 2(4), 1-12. DOI: 10.1177/2332858416673968 Roschelle, J., Penuel, W., & Shechtman, N. (2006). Co-design of innovations with teachers: definition and dynamics. In Proceedings of the 7th International Conference on Learning Sciences, Bloomington, IN. https://doi.dx.org/10.22318/icls2006.606

Rose, D. (2000). Universal design for learning. Journal of Special Education Technology, 15(4), 47-51. https://doi.org/10.1177/016264340001500407

Ruiz, P. & Fusco, J. (2022). Teachers partnering with artificial intelligence: Augmentation and automation. Digital Promise. https://digitalpromise.org/2022/07/06/teachers-partnering-with- artificial-intelligence-augmentation- and-automation/

Russell, S. (2019). Human compatible: Artificial intelligence and the problem of control. Viking. ISBN 978-0-525-55861-3.

Shao, Q., Sniffen, A., Blanchet, J., Hillis, M.E., Shi, X., Haris, T.K., & Balkcom, D. (2020). Teaching american sign language in mixed reality. Proceedings of the ACM on Interactive, Mobile, Wearable and Ubiquitous Technologies, 4(4), 1-27. https://doi.org/10.1145/3432211 Sharples, M. & Perez y Perez, R. (2022). Story machines: How computers have become creative writers. Routledge. ISBN 9780367751951

Shemshack, A., Spector, J.M. (2020) A systematic literature review of personalized learning terms. Smart Learning Environments, 7(33). https://doi.org/10.1186/s40561-020-00140-9 Shute, V J. (2008). Focus on formative feedback. Review of Educational Research, 78(1), 153-189. https://doi.org/10.3102/0034654307313795

Shute, V. J., Ventura, M., & Kim, Y. J. (2013). Assessment and learning of qualitative physics in Newton's Playground. The Journal of Educational Research, 106(6), 423-430. https://doi.org/10.1080/00220671.2013.832970

Swiecki, Z., Khosravi, H., Chen, G., Martinez-Maldonado, R., Lodge, J.M., Milligan, S., Selwyn, B. & Gasevic,D. (2022). Assessment in the age of artificial intelligence. Computers and Education: Artificial Intelligence, 3. https://doi.org/10.1016Zj.caeai.2022.100075

The White House (February 17, 2023). Executive order on further advancing racial equity and support for underserved communities through the federal government. https://www.whitehouse.gov/briefing-room/presidential-actions/2023/02/16/executive- order- on-further- advancing-racial-equity

The White House (September 8, 2022). Readout of White House listening session on tech platform accountability. https://www.whitehouse.gov/briefing-room/statements-releases/2022/09/08/readout-of-white-house-listening-session-on-tech-platform-accountability/

U.S. Department of Education, Office of Educational Technology (2022). Advancing digital equity for all: Community-based recommendations for developing effective digital equity plans to close the digital divide and enable technology-empowered learning. Us Department of Education.

U.S. Department of Education, Office of Educational Technology. (2010). Transforming American Education: Learning Powered by Technology. U.S. Department of Education. p. 78

Van Lehn, K. (2011) The relative effectiveness of human tutoring, intelligent tutoring systems, and other tutoring systems. Educational Psychologist, 46(4), 197-221. https://doi.org/10.1080/00461520.2011.611369

Wagner, A.R., Borenstein, J. & Howard, A. (September 2018). Overtrust in the robotics age. Communications of the ACM, 61(9), 22-24. https://doi.org/10.1145/3241365

Walker, E., Rummel, N. & Koedinger, K.R. (2015). Adaptive intelligent support to improve peer tutoring in algebra. International Journal of Artificial Intelligence in Education, 24, 33-61 https://doi.org/10.1007/s40593-013-0001-9

Walton Family Foundation (March 1, 2023). Teachers and students embrace ChatGPTfor education. https://www.waltonfamilyfoundation.org/learning/teachers - and- students - embrace - chatgpt- for- education

Webb, N.M., & Farivar, S. (1994). Promoting helping behavior in cooperative small groups in middle school mathematics. American Educational Research Journal, 31(2), 369-395. https://doi.org/10.3102/00028312031002369

White House Office of Science and Technology Policy (October 2022), Blueprint for an AI bill of rights: Making automated systems work for the American people. The White House Office of Science and Technology Policy. https://www.whitehouse.gov/ostp/ai-bill-of-rights/ Wiggins, G. (2015). Seven keys to effective feedback. ACSD. https://www.ascd.org/el/articles/seven-keys - to - effective - feedback

Winne, P.H. (2021). Open learner models working in symbiosis with self-regulating learners: A research agenda. International Journal of Artificial Intelligence in Education, 31(3), 446-459. https://doi.org/10.1007/s40593-020-00212-4

Zacamy, J. & Roschelle, J. (2022). Navigating the tensions: How could equity-relevant research also be agile, open, and scalable? Digital Promise. http://hdl.handle.net/20.500.12265/159 Zhai, X., He, P., Krajcik, J. (2022). Applying machine learning to automatically assess scientific models. Journal of Research in Science Teaching. https://doi.org/10.1002/tea.21773

Zhang, H., Lee, I., Ali, S., DiPaola, D., Cheng, Y., & Breazeal, C. (2022). Integrating ethics and career futures with technical learning to promote AI literacy for middle school students: An exploratory study. International Journal of Artificial Intelligence in Education, 1-35. https://doi.org/10.1007/s40593-022-00293-3

Chapter 6
AIED: Analyzing the Implications and Addressing the Challenges

Introduction

Henry Ford made the point that innovation doesn't mean that people should stick to what has always been done. For example, finding ways to make horses faster is an example of innovation. Sometimes it's important to go beyond what's usual and come up with new ways to do things. Our goal should not be to make horses faster, but to make cars faster so that people can get from A to B more quickly. Also, instead of figuring out how to make charcoal less smokey, you should figure out how to get rid of charcoal as a way to heat something and make a stove that uses pure heat instead. It will work better and be safer. These ideas and methods have helped speed up the progress in technology over the past few years, especially in the schooling field. The same ideas can be used in education. Instead of trying to find ways for teachers to grade more papers correctly, why not use computerized technology to do the boring work of teaching and free up teachers to do more creative tasks where they can teach in a more effective and efficient way? That is, why can't we use the power of smart computers to make tests, grade exams, and give students general feedback, just like teachers do?

To put it simply, Artificial Intelligence (AI) is the study of how machines can act intelligently. The goal is to give computers freedom and intelligence by using algorithms that can learn from what people do and spot patterns. In 1956, the area was first introduced to academics in an official way. When computers first came out, people had very simple ideas about what they could do with AI. At that time, some scientists thought computers might be able to solve algebra questions. The main goal of current AI research is to teach computers how to talk to people in a natural way, solve hard problems, make accurate predictions, and do many jobs that used to be done by hand automatically.

In every part of life, artificial intelligence (AI) is becoming more and more useful. Since AI has become more flexible, everyday life has changed. A lot of work is being done by researchers and AI scientists to make people's lives easier and more technologically advanced using AI tools and methods. The IDC study says that companies could spend around $342 billion on AI hardware, software, and services. The latest edition of IDC's Worldwide Semiannual Artificial Intelligence Tracker says that the market for AI will grow faster in 2022, with growth of 18.8%. It will still be on track to reach more than $500 billion by 2024. From 2021 to 2025, Figure 1 shows how much money AI startups got in millions of dollars.

Figure 1. Worldwide AI Software Forecast 2021-2025 3

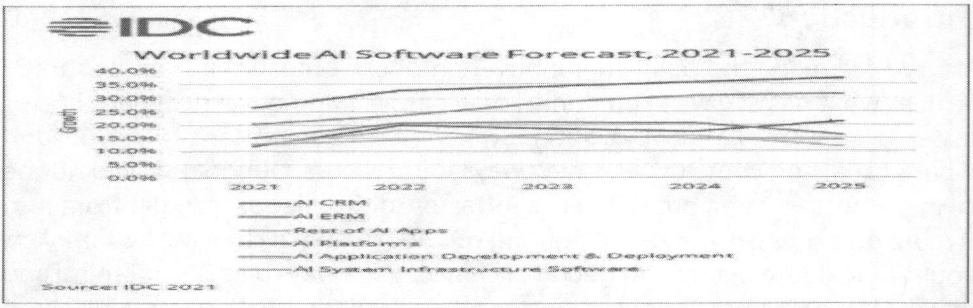

It's been about fifty years since researchers first looked into how artificial intelligence could be used in schools. Amazon, Google, and Facebook are just a few of the big tech companies that have recently spent millions of dollars on AIED research and development. Knewton and Carnegie Learning are two other well-funded AIED startups. At the same time, the $15 million Global Learning XPrize is looking for software that helps students take care of their own learning. This is pretty much the same thing as AIED. While this is going on, AI is being added as a new subject to some regular schools, it is being studied as a way to improve teacher training, and it is being used to make online tutoring better. To sum up, the market for artificial intelligence (AI) in education is expected to grow at a rate of 32% per year until 2024, when it will reach $6 billion.

Information and Communication Technology (ICT) landscapes are used in education. AI is one of the most common ICT models used in education. ICT has been used a lot in the education field. For example, France's elementary schools are required to teach kids how to use computers in real life. Learning Management Systems (LMS) are also being used by more and more schools around the world. Massive Online Open Courses (MOOCs) have become very popular over the past ten years, which shows that people are okay with the idea of learning online. Students can learn new technologies through these MOOCs, and they can also improve their resumes by getting a certificate, a Nanodegree, or even a diploma. MOOCs and huge online teaching sites like Preply, Khan Academy, Code Hero, and many more show that more and more people want to learn online.

Many of us may have a basic idea or experience of AI in everyday life or through the media, but many of us still don't know how it can be used in schools. The process of thinking creates a lot of questions that need to be answered. What, exactly, does artificial intelligence (AI) do in schools? How does it work? How can the privacy of students be protected when AI is used, since it needs a lot of data? How will artificial intelligence change the jobs of teachers in the long term? Are people who support AIED making more claims than they can possibly keep? How does AI affect how well kids do in school? When AI is used in schooling, are there social effects that happen?

The goal of this chapter is to look into how artificial intelligence (AI) can be used to help people learn and teach better. This article shows how AI technology can help school systems use current tools to make learning more fair and better. This chapter gives examples of how AI is being used in schools in the real world. The latest chapter has a lot of good points. This chapter will help many people in the education field. It will help with more study and the development of theory, knowledge, and real-world findings that show and argue about the many ways AI affects education. It will help researchers, professionals, and lawmakers by encouraging decision-making and management and leadership in the education sector that is based on evidence. This includes administrators, management, and leadership of educational institutions. The results add to what other study has found and will help shape government policies and programs that aim to encourage the useful use of technology, especially artificial intelligence (AI), in education. Educators and the government can work together to create policies, strategies, and programs that support the positive effects of AI on education while reducing the possible negative effects. This can be done once everyone knows what the effects of AI on education are and how they work, such as making lessons and learning more effective.

Artificial Intelligence: A Clear Definition

With the help of improvements in computer and data transmission methods over the years, artificial intelligence has been made possible. This was possible because technology kept getting better. Basically, artificial intelligence is just programming computers to think and act like humans do. The first meaning has four parts: think humanely, act humanely, think logically, and act logically.

AI System That Think Humanly

Haugeland says that AI is the exciting new quest to make computers think or to make robots that really do have brains. Automation of jobs that require human thought, like learning, making decisions, and solving problems, is another way to describe it.

AI System That Acts Humanly

AI, which stands for "imitating human action," is the field of creating machines that can do things that humans would normally do that require intelligence. The study of how to make computers do things that people are better at right now is another way to describe AI. To put it another way, AI is the study of how to get computers to do things.

AI System That Think Rationally

AI is the study of mental abilities through the use of computer models, according to Winston. From a logical point of view, AI is the study of the computations that allow people to see, think, and act.

AI System That Act Humanly

Ginu said that AI is the study of making intelligent beings, while Nilsson said that it is the study of making things intelligent. From the above definitions, we can say that artificial intelligence is when computers and intelligent agents give tools the ability to think smart enough to perceive, reason, and act like humans in many situations, such as making decisions, solving problems, learning, and automating boring or repetitive tasks.

Artificial Intelligence Definition

AIED is the act of using computers and other gadgets to mimic how humans think, make decisions, and do other things in order to complete a job. AI is the way that robots match up complicated patterns and learn as they go. There are different ways to understand what AI is. Two examples AI with evaluation methods based on rules and AI with evaluation methods based on machine learning are two examples. The first one uses decision-making rules to come up with an idea or a solution. This is the most basic shape in this sense. This kind of technology can be seen in an intelligent teaching system (ITS), which can give students thorough and relevant feedback. AI that is built on machine learning is more powerful (especially scary) because machines can really learn and get better over time.

Ai-based, step-by-step personalized learning and dialogue systems, AI-supported exploratory learning, the study of student writing, intelligent agents in game-based environments, and student help are all parts of AIED. In addition, it includes students working with computers one-on-one, methods that involve the whole school, students using cell phones outside of school, and the list goes on. Aside from that, AIED could also put light on different ways of teaching and learning.

Leveraging AI towards Improving the Learning Process

The next part talks about how AI can be used in the classroom to improve learning and make education more fair. This part is mostly about two main topics: using AI to make personalization better (pedagogical scale) and school management information systems (system management scale).

Promoting Personalized Learning

In the past ten years, there have been many questions about how well traditional schooling works. College dropout rates are at an all-time high, which shows that students are not interested in going to college and have low confidence. Experts in the field say that the "one-size-fits-all" approach is the main reason why the school hasn't been able to keep students excited. Good news is that progress has already been made in AI technology, especially in Big Data and Machine Learning. Several companies have made tools that help students learn in a way that is more fun and fits their needs better. This is mostly done by giving each student a unique learning experience that is based on their skills and interests. Personalized learning means that each student's learning is based on their own unique needs. Personalized learning lets you change things about the way you teach, the materials you use, the speed at which you teach, the series you use, the technologies you use, the quality of the lessons, the way you teach, the materials you use, and other things to fit the needs and goals of each kid.

Adapting learning to meet the needs of each student has been a problem for teachers for a long time. AI could offer a level of variety that teachers with 30 students in a class could never imagine. A number of companies, such as Content Technologies and Carnegie Learning, are working on intelligent instructional design and digital platforms that use AI to help students from pre-K to college level learn, test, and get feedback. These platforms will be able to see where students are lacking knowledge and guide them to new topics when necessary. As AI gets better, it might be possible for a computer to read a student's face to see if they are trying to learn something and then change the lesson to fit that. It's not possible to make lessons fit the needs of every student right now, but it will be possible for robots driven by AI.

Collaborative learning can be made better with the help of AI. One of the most innovative things about computer-supported group learning is that it can be used when people are not in the same room. When and where students want to learn is flexible because of this. For computer-supported collaborative learning to work, online talk groups that meet at different times are very important. AI systems use AI techniques like machine learning and shallow text processing to keep an eye on online discussion groups. These systems give teachers information about what students are talking about and help them stay interested and learn. AI could help personalized learning in a number of ways. AI can help make the environment more professional so that students who are having trouble can be helped. Teachers spend a lot of time at school doing routine and administrative tasks, such as making projects and answering questions that are asked often. A dual-teacher method has a teacher and a virtual teaching assistant who can do routine tasks for the teacher. This gives teachers more time to focus on supervising students and talking to them one-on-one. AI helpers are already being used by teachers to help them get the best results for their students.

Artificial intelligence (AI) helps adaptive learning systems create scientific profiles of each student. Big data, which has a lot of information, also helps create a pedagogical profile for each student. A personalized path can help you reach your goal of achieving a certain learning result. When students use adaptive learning platforms that are helped by AI, they can go at their own pace and move on to the next idea when they understand it well.

Computer Assisted Learning (CAL) is the field that creates digital and AI-based tools to help people learn. An AI solution might help make a map of each student's unique learning paths and plans, including their skills and weaknesses, topics that are harder to learn or incorporate, and the activities and learning styles they prefer. AI can tailor learning and give students more chances by using algorithms to help them find different ways to follow the curriculum. New studies show that Intelligent Tutoring Systems are one of the new technological ways that poor countries can improve their students' education.

Improving in Teachers' Collaboration

AI has been used in education before, mostly in tools for learning new skills and systems for testing students. AI educational solutions will get better over time so that it can fill in gaps in learning and teaching. This will help schools and teachers do more than ever before. AI could make things more efficient and personalized, as well as cut down on routine tasks. This would give teachers more time and freedom to teach understanding and adaptability, which are human traits that robots don't have. The goal of AI in education is for tools and teachers to work together to get the best results for kids by combining the best parts of both. We need to get kids ready for a world with AI because they will have to work in it.

Automatic Routine Tasks

You might be interested in how automated software for special education works if you are a teacher or school leader. Robotic Process Automation, or RPA, doesn't mean that robots will teach instead of people. In reality, automation is not the same as a process. Instead, technology makes a process better. In simple words, robotic process automation (RPA) is another way to make work processes more efficient by using software robots (Bots) and algorithms that can do tasks without any help from a person: In some way, every computer device uses algorithms. An algorithm is a set of exact instructions that tell a device how to do a job or handle data. They are used in automated software for special education.

Figure 2. Teachers' Administrative Tasks 23

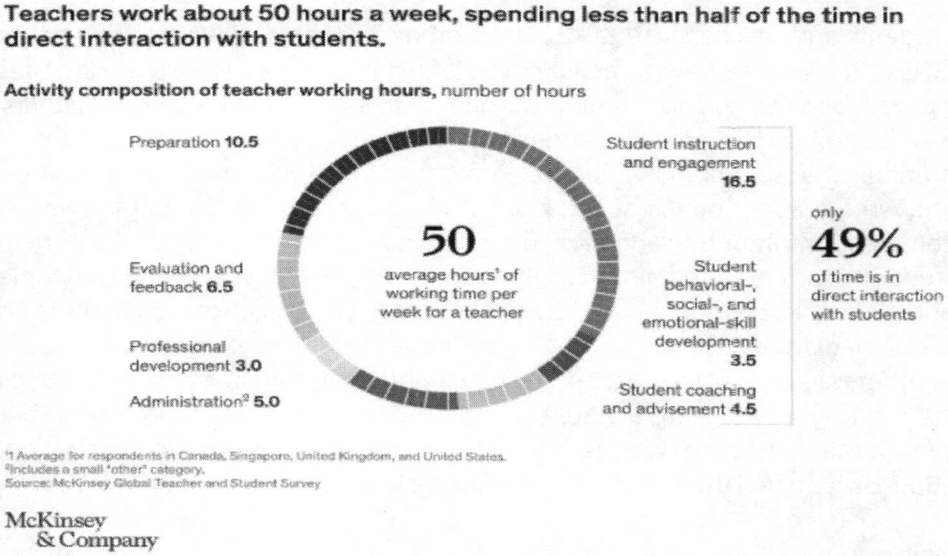

A global study by McKinsey & Company found that teachers were spending less time on direct teaching and more time on things like planning, grading, and running the school. At the same time, technology has been shown to help teachers spend 20 to 30 percent more time on student learning. Using AI in the classroom will help teachers be more productive and spend less time on tasks that are done over and over again. It will also allow them to connect with their students more deeply. If teachers had more time and energy to build a stronger bond with their students, those students would probably learn more and have a better chance of succeeding.

Teachers work fifty hours a week, but they only talk to kids for about fifty hours of that time.

An AI system could keep track of information about each student's individualized education program (IEP) and offer automatic help to teachers so they can make the right changes for each student. In a learning management system, for example, if a student needs more time to finish a task, the system could either make a list to send to the teacher or change the due date for that student's work by hand. This chapter talks about how important it is for AI systems to be able to talk to or be a part of other systems. The system also needs to make sure that all of the kids' private information is always safe. In addition to text-to-speech and speech-to-text, an AI system might also be able to read to kids with special needs in a way that is tailored to their needs.

Social Networking Sites and Chatbots

Students and teachers can talk to each other through social networking sites (SNSs). Researchers have stressed how useful it is to use social networking sites like Facebook to spread learning outside of school, keep an eye on students' well-being, and improve relationships between students and teachers. A number of academics have looked into the role of social media in education and written about how it affects both student and teacher learning as well as conversation among academics. They say that using social media may help students learn how to learn actively, work together, and connect with people outside of school. Thanks to different AI systems, you can also find chatbots on social media sites. They're also called dialogue systems or conversational bots. Chatbots are helpful because they can respond easily and in a way that sounds like a question. At Georgia State University, for example, a text-based chatbot system called "Pounce" was used to help students with things like registration, admission, financial aid, and other routine tasks.

Using AI with Big Data

Big data and artificial intelligence (AI) technologies are changing all parts of society very quickly. These changes are being felt in the business, politics, science, education, and more. Thanks in large part to these changes, many of our social events can go on during the COVID-19 pandemic. Using digital tools, platforms, apps, and talking to each other has created huge amounts of data (called "big data") spread out in many places. Big data tools try to use the power of very large amounts of data, whether it's real-time or not. Big data analytics usually includes getting large datasets, analyzing them, and judging them. One of the main benefits of the "big data" revolution is that it makes it easier to find useful information and trends in large amounts of data. A few of the technologies and tools that are used in big data analytics are text analytics, social network analysis, signal processing, machine learning, and statistical analysis. Digital systems make an amazing 2.5 quintillion bytes of new data every day. Companies have been collecting data for years to become more efficient and productive. This data is often kept in "big data silos" where it is easy for customers to access. "Artificial intelligence lets data owners turn a resource that isn't being used into a powerful tool for development."

As time goes on, computers can learn and get better, which makes AI based on machine learning more powerful, especially when it comes to big, complicated datasets. AI technologies built on machine learning can be used in education for many things, like keeping an eye on how students behave and making models that can accurately predict how they will do in school. AI that is built on machine learning is still in its early stages, but it has already shown great results when given hard tasks that aren't limited by rules, like grading students' written answers or looking at large, complicated datasets. There are other big differences in AI that mostly have to do with how it is used technically. One branch is natural language processing, which is the use of computers to understand what people write.

Predictive analytics and tools that can recognize faces Face recognition software records and keeps an eye on the students' facial reactions. Through these methods, teachers can see how their students are behaving while they are learning, which lets them act or step in and help create learner-centered practices that get students more involved. Most of the time, predictive analytics algorithm systems are used to find and identify trends in learners based on statistical analysis. For instance, these tools could be used to find college students who are about to fail or already have failed a course. Teachers can step in and help students who need it by using these recognition sheets.

Challenges Faced by AI in Educational Settings

When schools start using AI for different tasks, they will probably find that there are still a lot of issues that need to be fixed. The best way for schools to teach kids about the new technology-based society and the many disruptive technologies that will change how people work is probably the most important problem to solve. As time goes on, students need to understand that jobs that are done over and over again will finally be done by robots, AI, and automation. But there will always be jobs that need people who are smart, creative, and emotionally intelligent. These days, a lot of schools don't teach kids the kinds of skills that will and won't help them in their future jobs.

Privacy Concerns

When AI tools are used in schools, privacy is very important. People usually have privacy problems when they share too much personal information on the internet. Even though there are rules and laws in place to protect private information, people are more worried about their privacy when AI-based tech companies break those rules when it comes to data access and security. Both Akgun and Greenhow. Most of the time, AI uses formulas, which are fed by personal data, to solve problems. "These algorithms don't just appear out of thin air; they are shaped and changed by cultural, social, institutional, and political forces and structures that are always changing." One example is that fitness trackers create information about people that didn't exist before but could now be considered personal information. But this raises big regulatory worries about "trustworthy AI," such as data privacy and security, as well as the possibility of bad data and uses that are biased against people or groups. There is also a worry about monitoring and tracking with AI because the technologies would get detailed information about how students and teachers behave and what they like. AI tracking systems use algorithms and machine-learning models to not only watch how people behave, but also to guess what they will like and do in the future. AI's predictive systems might use surveillance methods to guess how well students are learning, what their skills and weaknesses are, and how they learn best. Studies show that teachers who use social networking sites (SNSs) for teaching have a number of concerns, such as worries about privacy limits, friendship authority, duty, and availability. How do the privacy of these tools keep people safe? How can schools make sure that both kids and parents are on board when they introduce them? Should experts and other outsiders be able to see data that has been anonymized?

The proposed AI system also raises privacy issues, but it also helps teachers do what they do best by making sure their students get the help they need and then keeping track of that help. There are risks in using these kinds of systems, and AI systems that work with student IEP data need to follow the tightest rules for keeping data safe and keeping an eye on them. As was already said, teachers need to be involved. For example, the teacher is responsible for giving feedback, but the system may give the teacher thoughts on how to do it better. If teachers aren't kept up to date, bad things could happen to the kids. Teachers need to be careful and not just take every change an AI system suggests as the right or best choice.

Lack of Emotional Bonds

You should also think about how important social and emotional ties are, as well as how education is a very human experience. In simple terms, AI will not take the place of teachers. Bias is another problem with AI experts that has been brought up. Scores that are made by machines will be based on how thousands of tests went. However, as this topic short says, test scores may show a lack of chances rather than a lack of skill. Machine scores won't be able to tell the difference between these things.

Jobs

AI has the potential to make teaching and learning better by automating tasks. However, the use of AI in education raises important ethical questions and presents major challenges. For example, when money is tight, managers might be tempted to replace lessons with automated AI solutions that make more money. Teachers, teaching aids, counselors for students, and people who work in administration may be worried that smart tutors, expert systems, and chatbots will eventually take their jobs. AI can make learning analytics more useful, but these systems need a lot of data, including private data about students and teachers. This raises serious privacy and data protection issues. Some organizations, like the Institute for Ethical AI, were just started not long ago.

Disruptive Technology

This study shows that AI can be used in many different ways. However, it may also be a disruptive technology that makes differences and divides worse because the disadvantaged and marginalized are more likely to be left out of AI-powered education. Because of this, there is a new kind of digital divide: one in how people use data-based knowledge to make smart choices. When it comes to using AI in schools, the hardest part is planning and budgeting for the money. Most of the time, making budget predictions is fairly hard. For instance, the amount of power used might go up if all schools can have a robot helper. After that, governments would have to pay for a big budget to meet the costs. Another bad thing about this problem is that electricity is not a resource that can be used over and over again. To get around this problem, students need to know about the AI-based learning tools that are out there and how they can help them. Recent studies have given an outline of the problems that come up when AI is used in schooling in developing countries. The most important ones are these: 1-Accessibility of ICT hardware; 2-Electrical accessibility; 3-Reliability of the internet; 4-Data costs; 5-Students' basic ICT skills; 6-Language; and 7-Lack of material that is culturally important. Further research on the use of big data in developing countries has found that the lack of basic infrastructures creates a new digital gap that makes it hard to use data-based knowledge to make smart decisions.

Technology Addiction

Kids used to have to put away their phones and computers and open their old textbooks when they went to school. The fact that kids use technology in every class makes it impossible for them to picture what life will be like without it. Because of this, in a few decades there will be a lot of people who are hooked on technology but don't know how to interact with others. This is because AI can make people more dependent on technology.

Promoting Bias

The ethical problems and dangers that AI systems pose seem to go against marketing campaigns that try to show algorithms as objective and value-free tools. In a way, algorithms reflect the values of the people who made them, who are in charge. People who make algorithms also create a set of data that reflects the past and systemic biases of society. These biases become algorithmic biases over time. There is no intention for bias to be built into the algorithmic model, but we may still find a range of gender and racial biases in different AI-based systems.

Less Flexibility

AI robots can be very smart, but they can't help a student learn as much as a teacher can. Teachers can teach different ways to solve problems, but AI doesn't have a lot of different ways to teach. AI also works on the principle of "trash in, garbage out." Even though it can find problems, it can't fix them. AI will still do the research even if a person types in the wrong data. But the end result will show that mistakes were made. This wastes time and means the process has to be done again.

Conclusion

Some people have too high of hopes for what artificial intelligence (AI) can do for us, but it is likely to be the most important technological development of the first few decades of this century. It will change almost every business, if not all human efforts in general. Businesses and governments all over the world are putting huge amounts of money into a wide range of projects, and hundreds of new businesses are getting billions of dollars to get started. It is not reasonable to think that AI will not have an effect on education, since traditional education needs to be changed a lot to fit the world we live in now.

Because they are excited about one or more technologies, people are sometimes drawn to one part of those technologies without thinking about the others. While this might work for some things, it won't work for AI because it has so much potential that people don't want to even learn about its basic features. AI will likely be around for a long time because the idea that it will make our lives easier by getting rid of boring tasks is appealing. AI is a technology that is getting stronger all the time. It has uses outside of business and academia, and it will definitely have an impact on people all over the world.

The many platforms and trends that the future of AI growth in education could bring are very appealing, but they may not be possible in some situations. But computer-based learning methods probably won't take the place of all human teachers in schools. In certain situations, is it okay to use and participate in AI in Africa and Latin America? Yes, because these kinds of technologies are necessary for long-term growth in the area. They boost efficiency and competitiveness, which can lead to a real transformation with new and better opportunities in the global market.

In conclusion, AI applications can improve the learning experiences of both students and teachers and help them solve problems and issues that come up during teaching. AI, on the other hand, can't replace talking to other people. Every student learns in a unique way and with a set of needs. AI can save teachers time and help them think more clearly, but it's not the only thing they can use. So, for teachers and students to get the most out of AI apps in education while keeping costs low, they need to know the limits, possible risks, and moral issues that come with using them.

References

Zhang, K. & Aslan, A. B. AI technologies for education: Recent research & future directions. Computers and Education: Artificial Intelligence 2, 100025 (2021).

Lauritsen, S. M. et al. Explainable artificial intelligence model to predict acute critical illness from electronic health records. Nat Commun 11, 3852 (2020).

Wiggers, K. IDC: AI spending will reach $342B in 2021. VentureBeat https ://venture-beat.com/business/idc-ai-spending-will-reach-342b-in-2021/ (2021).

Cumming, G. & Mcdougall, A. Mainstreaming AIED into Education? International Journal of Artificial Intelligence in Education 11, 197 (2000).

Vallanc, C. & McMahon, Li. Amazon takes on Microsoft as it invests billions in Anthropic. BBC News (2023).

Holmes, W., Bialik, M. & Fadel, C. Artificial intelligence in education. in In: Data ethics : building trust: how digital technologies can serve humanity. (pp. 621-653). Globethics Publications (2023) 621-653 (Globethics Publications, 2023).

Wogu, I. A. P. et al. Artificial Intelligence, Smart Classrooms and Online Education in the 21st Century: Implications for Human Development. JCIT 21, 66-79 (2019).

Dawson, D. et al. Artificial Intelligence: Australia's ethics framework - a discussion paper. (2019).

Renz, A. & Hilbig, R. Prerequisites for artificial intelligence in further education: identification of drivers, barriers, and business models of educational technology companies. International Journal of Educational Technology in Higher Education 17, 14 (2020).

Haugeland, J. Artificial Intelligence: The Very Idea. (MIT Press, 1989).

Kurzweil, R. & Schneider, M. L. The age of intelligent machines. vol. 580 (Cambridge :MIT Press).

Charniak, M. Introduction to artificial intelligence. (Pearson Education India, 1985).

Qomarlyah, N. Artificial Intelligence Definition. Computer Science https://international.binus.ac.id/computer-science/2020/11/09/artificial-intelligence-definition/ (2020).

George, G. & Thomas, M. Integration of Artificial Intelligence in Human Resource. International Journal of Innovative Technology and Exploring Engineering 9, 22783075 (2019).

Nilsson, N. Artificial Intelligence - 1st Edition. (Elsevier, 1998).

Bell, H. AI For Personalized Learning: Potential And Challenges. eLearning Industry https://elearningindustry.com/ai-for-personalized-learning-potential-and-challenges (2021).

K, M. How AI Is Personalizing Education For Every Student. eLearning Industry https://elearningindustry.com/how-ai-is-personalizing-education-for-every-student (2023).

Bernard Marr. How Is AI Used In Education -- Real World Examples Of Today And A Peek Into The Future | Bernard Marr. https://bernardmarr.com/how-is-ai-used-in-education-real-world-examples-of-today-and-a-peek-into-the-future/ (2021).

Francesc, P., Subosa, M., Axe, R. & Valverde, P. Artificial intelligence in education: challenges and opportunities for sustainable development - UNESCO Digital Library. https://unesdoc.unesco.org/ark748223/pf0000366994 (2019).

Impelsys. Powering Personalized Learning with Artificial Intelligence (AI). https://www.impelsys.com/blog/powering-personalized-learning-with-artificial-intel- ligence (2021).

Tapalova, O., Zhiyenbayeva, N. & Gura, D. Artificial Intelligence in Education: AIEd for Personalised Learning Pathways. Electronic Journal of e-Learning 20, 639-653 (2022).

Microsoft Educatino Team. How data and AI are changing the world of education. Microsoft Education Blog https://educationblog.microsoft.com/en-us/2022/04/how-data- and-ai-are-changing-the-world-of-education (2022).

Bryant, J., Heitz, C. & Wagle, D. Artificial intelligence in education: How will it impact K-12 teachers | McKinsey. https://www.mckinsey.com/industries/education/our-insights/how-artificial-intelligence-will-impact-k-12-teachers (2020).

Burns, E., Laskowski, N. & Tucci, L. What is artificial intelligence (AI)? - AI definition and how it works. Enterprise AI https://www.techtarget.com/searchenterpriseai/defini- tion/AI-Artificial-Intelligence.

Allam, H. et al. Artificial Intelligence in Education: An Argument of Chat-GPT Use in Education. in 2023 9th International Conference on Information Technology Trends (ITT) 151-156 (2023). doi:10.1109/ITT59889.2023.10184267.

Allam, H. et al. A Proposed AI Method for Tracking College Students' Academic Progress. in 2023 9th International Conference on Information Technology Trends (ITT) 215-219 (2023). doi:10.1109/ITT59889.2023.10184256.

Akgun, S. & Greenhow, C. Artificial intelligence in education: Addressing ethical challenges in K-12 settings. AI Ethics 2, 431-440 (2022).

Daniel, B. K. Big Data and data science: A critical review of issues for educational research. British Journal of Educational Technology 50, 101-113 (2019).

Bell, D., Lycett, M., Marshan, A. & Monaghan, A. Exploring future challenges for big data in the humanitarian domain. Journal of Business Research 131, 453-468 (2021).

Jimenez, L. & Boser, U. Future of Testing in Education: Artificial Intelligence - Center for American Progress. https://www.americanprogress.org/article/future-testing-edu- cation-artificial-intelligence/.

Rainie, L. The Future of Jobs and Jobs Training. Pew Research Center: Internet, Science & Tech https://www.pewresearch.org/internet/2017/05/03/the-future-of-jobs-and- jobs-training/ (2017).

Allam, H., Ahamed, J., Spiteri, L. & Pandya, B. Students' Acceptance of Learning Management Systems in Higher Education: A UAE Case Study. in 2022 8th International Conference on Information Technology Trends (ITT) 150-153 (2022). doi:10.1109/ITT56123.2022.9863969.

Seo, K., Tang, J., Roll, I., Fels, S. & Yoon, D. The impact of artificial intelligence on learner-instructor interaction in online learning. International Journal of Educational Technology in Higher Education 18, 54 (2021).

Future of Testing in Education: Artificial Intelligence. Center for American Progress https://www.americanprogress.org/article/future-testing-education-artificial-intelli- gence/ (2021).

Hilbert, M. Big Data for Development: A Review of Promises and Challenges. Development Policy Review 34, 135-174 (2016).

Alharbi, S. & Drew, S. Using the Technology Acceptance Model in Understanding Academics' Behavioural Intention to Use Learning Management Systems. International Journal of Advanced Computer Science and Applications (IJACSA) 5, (2014).

Kandamby, I. (10) CHALLENGES AND RISKS OF APPLYING AI IN SCHOOL EDUCATION | LinkedIn. https://www.linkedin.com/pulse/challenges-risks-applying-ai-school-education-imalsha-kandamby/?trk=articles_directory (2021).

Galvis, N. Advantages and Challenges of AI in Education for Teachers and Schools. https://www.robotlab.com/blog/advantages-and-challenges-of-ai-in-education-for- teachers-and-schools.

Dempere, J., Modugu, K., Allam, H. & Ramasamy, L. The impact of ChatGPT on higher education. Frontiers in Education 8, 1-13 (2023).

Ocana-Fernan Use of AI in Education Delivery and Assessment dez, Y., Valenzuela-Fernandez, L. A. & Garro-Aburto, L. L. Artificial Intelligence and Its Implications in Higher Education. Journal of Educational Psychology - Propositos y Representaciones 7, 553-568 (2019).

Chapter 7
Equity and AIEd: Evaluating the Effects on Educational Inequality

Introduction

People are becoming more aware of the negative effects that algorithmic bias and automation can have on society. As a result, researchers are paying more attention to issues of fairness, accountability, and openness in data-driven AI systems in a number of high-stakes areas, such as healthcare, loan-granting, and hiring. There has been some discussion in the academic field of AI in Education about how to make systems more open and responsible. However, there has not been as much discussion about how to make educational AI (AIEd) systems fair and equal.

AIEd systems were often created because they could help make education more fair and close the achievement gaps between different groups of students. For example, they could do this by making one-on-one tutoring more accessible to more students or by filling in gaps in current educational services. With these good goals, why could AIEd systems have effects that aren't fair?

The question we ask in this chapter is whether AIEd systems will eventually make educational inequality worse or whether they will help to make things more fair. We talk about four ways to look at how and why AIEd systems might make current unfair situations worse: (1) things that are built into the sociotechnical system as a whole; (2) the use of datasets that show unfair pasts; (3) things that are built into the algorithms that power machine learning and automated decision-making; and (4) things that come up when automated and human decision-making interact in a complicated way. Using these as starting points, we then talk about some possible ways for AIEd to have a more fair future, pointing out the problems with each one. We hope that this will start new talks about how to make AIEd more fair and move forward conversations that are already going on in the field.

Pathways toward Inequity in AIED

First, we give you four ways to look at how AIEd systems might make current unfair situations worse or even make new ones. Each view looks at the ways that unfairness happens in AIEd in a different way, but they are all pointing to the same sociotechnical system. Figure 1 shows a broad view of the larger social and technological systems that AIEd systems are a part of, along with some of the parts we will talk about in the four lenses. The designs of these systems are shaped by the choices made by designers, researchers, policymakers, and other stakeholders over time. On-the-ground stakeholders, like students, teachers, or school administrators, may not only use or be affected by AIEd systems, but they may also help shape their designs. This can happen directly, through participatory design processes, or indirectly, by creating training data while interacting with an AIEd interface. Then, choices about what data is used to create an AIEd system (for example, when it is used as training data for machine learning methods) can affect how its algorithms work (for example, the rules it follows when learning from data). This connection usually goes both ways: the AIED system's automated behavior also shapes and limits the data that users then create by interacting with it.

Figure 1. High-level overview of AIEd systems and the broader socio-technical systems in which they are embedded.

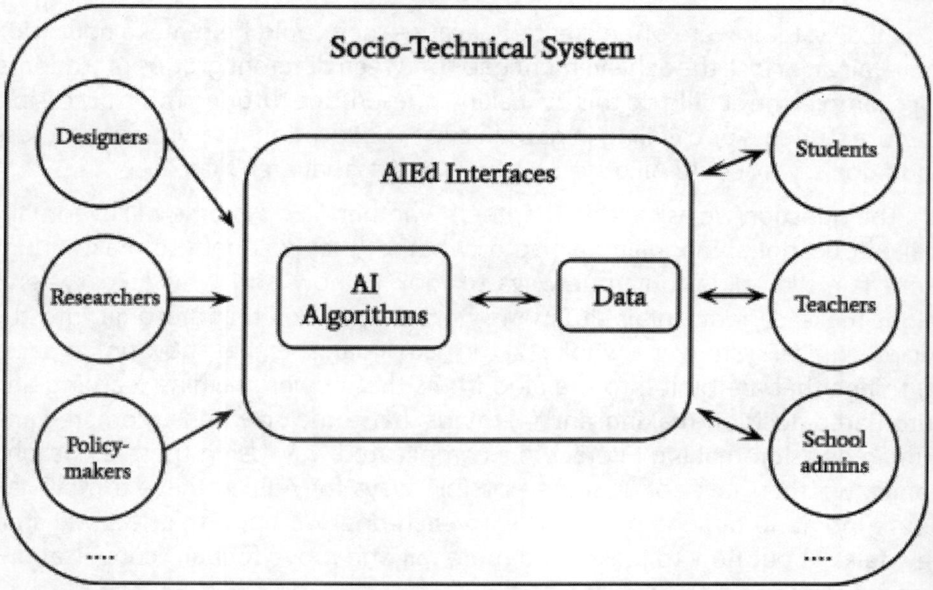

In order to make AIEd tools that are more fair, you need to be able to think about more than one level of abstraction at a time. But sometimes looking at these problems through different views can help you find new ways to solve them. So, the main difference between these four lenses is where they focus, with each giving more detail to a different part of the sociotechnical system as a whole. Actually, different study groups, both inside and outside of education, have looked at issues of fairness and equity in AI systems in rather different ways. In the past, AI and machine learning communities have mostly looked at these problems through the second (Data) and third (Algorithmic) lenses. On the other hand, human-computer interaction (HCI) and the learning sciences have mostly looked at them through the first (System) and fourth (Human-Algorithm) lenses. As we'll talk about below, making AIEd systems more fair will probably require integrating all four lenses in a useful way.

Lens 1 (System): Factors Inherent to the Overall Socio-Technical System Design

We begin by talking about things about the creation of AIEd technologies besides the use of AI algorithms that might make education less fair. Figure 2 draws attention to these factors. They include parts of a technology that don't directly use AI, like the user interface, the learning theories and pedagogical principles that the system is based on, and how subject knowledge is stored in the system. This view also looks at the bigger sociotechnical system that the technology is part of. This includes different people who have a stake in the technology, their values and beliefs, business models, the situation in which the system is used, and more.

In this way of thinking, one of the main reasons why AIEd technologies aren't fair is that some groups of students can get to them more easily than others. For instance, schools or families with more money may be more likely to buy more expensive tools. The price of computers, including mobile devices like phones, has gone down a lot, but not everyone has access to computers. A poll from 2015 found that 15% of US families with kids under 18 do not have an internet connection and 5% do not have a desktop, laptop, or mobile computer in their home. Also, these numbers are smaller for families of underrepresented minorities than for families of White and Asian people. Even though there aren't that many families who don't have any kind of Internet access, Rideout and Katz (2016) found that many low- and moderate-income families who did have some Internet access were still not fully connected in at least one way. This could be because of slow Internet access, sharing computers, mobile-only access, or limited data plans. Lack of connectivity can then affect how much kids use digital tools for learning. For example, Rideout and Katz (2016) discovered that only 35% of kids who only had access to the Internet on their phones would often use it for interest-driven learning, while 52% of those who had access to a desktop or laptop would do so.

Figure 2. Lens 1 (System) focuses on the overall socio-technical system design, rather than the actual AI or data-driven aspects of an AIEd system. In this figure and in subsequent figures, the components highlighted in blue show the focus of the current lens, while those greyed out are out-of-focus.

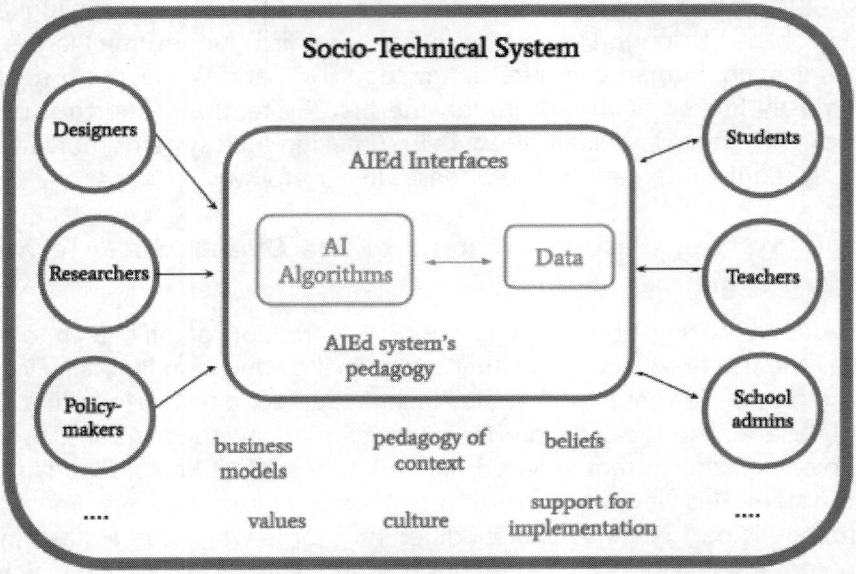

But even if all of the students can physically get to a certain tool, there may still be differences in how they can use it. For instance, an AIEd system that only gives help (like on-demand hints or scaffolding questions) in English will make it harder for people who don't understand English to use, and it may even make non-native English speakers worse off than native English speakers. In AIEd systems, kids from minority groups who speak a different dialect at home may be at a disadvantage because those systems expect them to use a mainstream dialect. As an example, Finkelstein et al. (2013) found that African American students were better at scientific thinking when they were taught by a virtual avatar that spoke only African American Vernacular English (AAVE) instead of Mainstream American English (MAE). These kinds of differences can also happen when teaching materials are clearly geared toward certain cultures. Chipman et al. (1991) discovered that how well you did on math word problems depended on how familiar you were with the situations they described, even if the basic math format stayed the same. Also, unless AIEd technologies are specifically made with accessibility in mind, they could speed up learning for some groups of students while slowing it down for others. For example, this could happen if a school uses the technology to replace an activity that was previously accessible with one that is less accessible.

Inequalities caused by the general sociotechnical system design go beyond differences in who can access what. Reich and Ito (2017) put together a lot of research that shows that "new technologies tend to be used and accessed in unequal ways, and they may even make inequality worse," even when schools and individual students have equal access. It's possible for schools and teachers to use the same technologies in different ways, for example because they have different ideas and attitudes about how to use technology in the classroom. Rafalow (2020), for example, found that teachers in schools with different racial and ethnic groups had different views toward their students' digital literacy skills and expressions because they had preconceived ideas about those groups. One interesting fact is that schools with more resources and kids from better-off families tend to use technology in more creative ways. It's not just a technical problem; people who make AIEd technologies should be aware that there are systematic differences in how they are used or adopted, and they should think about how to measure, respond to, and plan for these differences. Sims (2014) found that different social groups might have "differentiating practices" when it comes to using technology, which could make social differences worse. This can happen even if kids in the same school have similar levels of access and digital literacy. Reich and Ito (2017) also pointed out that just because educational resources are open to everyone (like massive open online classes), that doesn't mean that everyone will benefit from them in the same way. MOOCs are mostly used by students from wealthy families, and many of them already have advanced degrees. This might be because of cultural and social barriers that keep people from using some tools, even when they are free. But Kizilcec et al. (2017) showed that simple interventions based on social belonging and value-affirmation could make students from less developed countries more likely to stick with and finish MOOCs. This could close the completion gap between students from less developed countries and those from more developed countries. As a similar example, people who make AIEd tools should think about how to get more people to use them. It's not enough to just make entry better.

The "social distance between developers and those they seek to serve" is a major factor that may lead to inequality in education that is supported by Al-Quran. Even when teams design technologies to help underserved groups, the technologies may not meet the needs of those groups or may even make equity gaps worse (as we'll talk more about in the next section). This can happen if the design process is not led by respected voices from those groups.

We've mostly talked about things that are true for all educational tools so far, not just AIEd systems. There are, however, some design elements that are similar to AIEd systems that may make them less fair to use. For example, a lot of AIEd systems, like intelligent teaching systems, are made so that a student can talk to them one-on-one. Both the way these systems are designed to interact with people one-on-one and the AI algorithms they use to adapt and personalize teaching are based on this idea. It's possible for the system to make choices that aren't the best for students if it's not used in the right way. However, studies have shown that in some cultural settings, students are more likely to work together than alone with these tools.

Another reason is that AIEd systems are not very flexible or adaptable. Because AIEd technologies are usually complicated systems with lots of parts that work together, end users can't change them much. In particular, AIEd systems don't usually have flexible customization choices that would let teachers change the systems to fit their own needs. Simpler teaching technologies that don't rely on AI as much, on the other hand, may be easier to customize in this way by default. For instance, the ASSISTments system is made to support teacher-driven adaptability instead of more advanced types of adaptivity. This means that teachers can make or change their own assignments to better meet the needs of their students. This support for teacher-driven adaptability means that teachers don't have to use set tasks that they might not know how to use or that might not work well in their situations, like giving students word problems they can't relate to.

Lens 2 (Data): Use of Data that Reflect Historical Inequities

AIEd systems have a lot of potential to fix problems with unfair education, for example by making up for missing services that students would normally be able to get. But because these technologies are based on or shaped by past data, they might make any social problems that are shown in that data worse. In this third view, we look at how biases and unfairness in the ways that data was gathered or created can spread in AIEd systems. Figure 3 shows where this lens's focus is.

There are new research groups that are looking into fairness in machine learning because of the risks of "scaling up" unfairness through data-driven approaches. These groups, like the ACM Conference on Fairness, Accountability, and Transparency, have started to have an impact on research on educational data mining and learning analytics. From this second point of view, there are several ways that unfair situations could happen.

When machine learning or data-driven methods are used, biases in the data don't have to only show up in the first pathway. Here, we look at the effects of social distance that were talked about in the first lens through this data-centric lens, focusing on the roles of sample methods and biases in the system's design. But even if machine learning doesn't change the way an AIEd system acts, data may still be used to help form its design. Often, this data is made up of observations from a small number of situations and comments from a small number of stakeholders. Meaney and Fikes (2019) talk about "Early-adopter Iteration Bias" in the design of learning analytics systems and other educational technologies. This is the idea that the teachers and students who are most likely to be involved in the very beginning stages of the design process are usually from a more privileged group. When recruitment biases like these happen, new educational technologies may not be designed to meet the needs of underserved, marginalized, or otherwise risk-averse groups. Instead, they may be designed with the needs of these groups in mind more heavily in later design cycles.

Figure 3. Lens 2 (Data) highlights decisions regarding the data that an AIEd system relies upon (including the ways in which this data is used or generated). Designing datasets or data-generating mechanisms that support more equitable outcomes is a central goal.

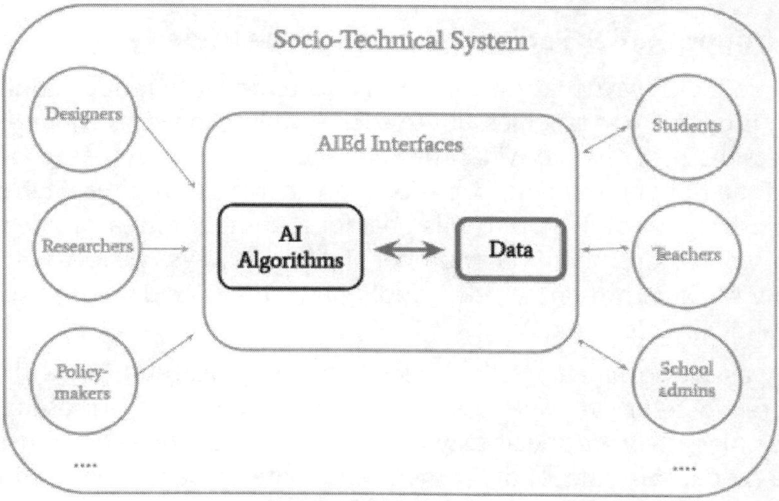

When the behavior of an AIEd system is built using data, there may be unfair outcomes because the educational goals of the people who built the system, the datasets used to train and test models, and the changing conditions in which the systems will be used in the future may not all match up. If some groups of students or learning situations are overrepresented in the datasets used to train and test models offline, the models that are created might store connections that don't work for other students or situations, and might even be harmful if used in these situations. For instance, using proctoring software during the COVID-19 pandemic has raised a number of concerns about fairness. For example, it has been hard to recognize the faces of students of color, likely because of biases in the datasets that the facial recognition technologies were trained on.

It's also possible for AIEd systems' assessment or teaching models to be shaped by the ratings or observed behaviors of human decision-makers, such as school administrators, teachers, parents, or students. This can lead to models that reinforce both good and bad behaviors displayed by these educational stakeholders, which we will talk more about in our fourth lens. For instance, it is known that K–12 teachers often show bias when judging the written work of students from underrepresented groups. This shows that teachers' actual assessment methods don't always match up with their stated educational goals. Also, past research has shown that assessment biases are easy to build into large-scale automated essay scoring systems when human teachers' scores are used as the "ground truth" for student success without being questioned. We will talk more about this in the next lens. The models and algorithms that were used to create an AIEd system may affect how much it reinforces or even makes past inequalities worse.

Lens 3 (Algorithmic): Factors Inherent to the Underlying Algorithms

There are a lot of ways that AIEd algorithms are meant to reduce equity gaps. One way is by trying to tailor lessons to each student. Concerns about one-size-fits-all lessons that tend to widen performance gaps can be eased by giving students the right amount and types of lessons at the right time. Still, using AI algorithms might not live up to this goal for a number of reasons, leading to unfair outcomes for students in a number of different ways. The focus of this lens is on how AI algorithms are used, including how they use data or are changed by it, as shown in Figure 4.

First, as we've already talked about, machine learning algorithms will tend to reinforce or even make worse biases that are already present in past datasets unless they are specifically made to fight these biases. For instance, if you fit a model to a dataset of teachers' automated essay grades that contain certain biases, the model will naturally make predictions that are skewed in the same ways. Keep in mind that these kinds of situations can happen even if no demographic variables are used in the machine learning model. This is because other variables can (and often will) relate to demographic variables in ways that aren't clear. Gardner, Brooks, and Baker (2019), for example, looked at a number of MOOC datasets and machine learning models used to predict dropout rates. They discovered that the models were less accurate for women than for men, even though none of the models explicitly used gender or other demographic variables. With our second lens, we can see that these differences may come from the types of data that were used to train the models. However, some models and learning methods may be more likely to make these differences worse than others.

Figure 4. Lens 4 (Algorithmic) highlights design decisions regarding an AIEd system's underlying AI algorithms (including the ways in which these algorithms use or are shaped by data). Designing algorithms that support more equitable outcomes is a central goal.

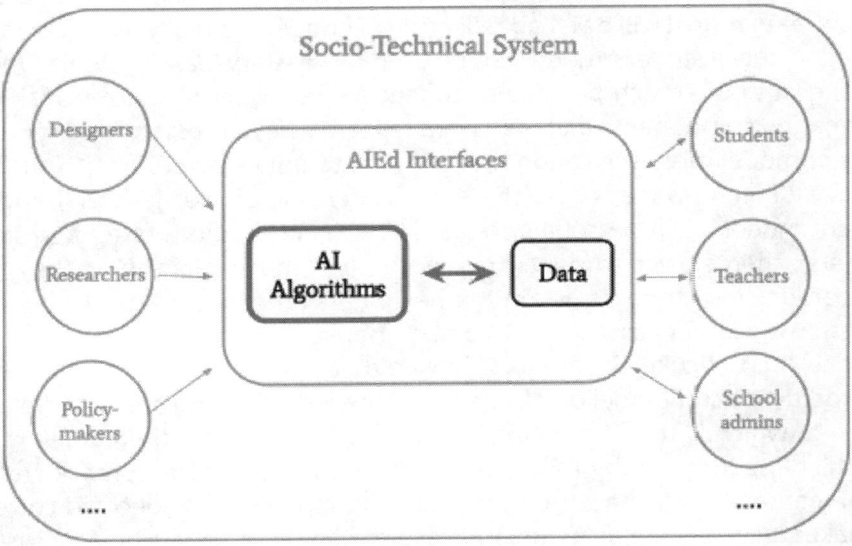

In theory, a dataset shouldn't have any unwanted past biases. However, machine learning algorithms could still be unfair if we have different amounts of data for different groups of people. In particular, most machine learning systems will be biased against groups that aren't as common in our data. This is because the algorithm will try to make the model as accurate as possible overall. If it can do that by making predictions that are more like those of a majority group (at the cost of those of minority groups), it will do that. For instance, a learning analytics algorithm that finds "at-risk" students trained on data from a college with a majority of white students can be very accurate overall. This is because it learns how to make more accurate predictions for white students while possibly making less accurate predictions for Black or Native American students for whom it may not have as much data. To say it again, this could happen because minority groups are naturally underrepresented in datasets where they are a minority. It's not always because of systematic historical biases, though. In real life, some groups may be undersampled in datasets because of historical biases. In some situations, this worry could be eased by purposely getting more information from minority groups, even if that information isn't typical of the whole population.

Due to model misspecification, machine learning methods can also lead to unfair decisions. This is very important when fitting statistical models of how students learn because learning is a complicated process that can't be seen, and any easy model will be a bad reflection of how things really work. One study looked at how a student model can be used for mastery learning, which means figuring out how much practice a student needs for each of a set of skills or information components that they want to learn. The authors showed two main types of model misspecification that can lead to unfair results. First, if students learn at different speeds (i.e., there are faster and slower learners) and the student model is not personalized (i.e., it fits data from both faster and slower learners), then slower students may not get as much practice as they need compared to fast students. Second, if the model's functional form is truly wrong, then slower learners could again be at a disadvantage (getting less-than-ideal practice). In particular, the authors showed that if students really do learn using the Additive Factor Model but a Bayesian Knowledge Tracing model for mastery learning (which is common in intelligent tutoring systems), then unfair results will still happen for both groups, even if different models are fit for slower and faster learners. This is because the underlying model is not specified correctly. To make sure everyone gets the same results, people who work on AIEd systems should not only try to make student models that better reflect how students learn, but they should also try to make algorithmic approaches that can handle model misspecification.

Last but not least, AIEd algorithms can be unfair even when they are not based on facts. For instance, using a heuristic for mastery learning—for example, thinking that students have learned a skill when they give N right answers in a row—could also lead to unfair results. By its very nature, this kind of strategy makes assumptions about how students learn that might not always be true in real life. In general, these kinds of risks can happen with algorithms that make decisions for students based on how well they do, even though they are very important for adaptive teaching. An example is a new game-theoretic way of encouraging students to correctly rate their own work that can naturally cause the grades of students who aren't doing as well to drop. So, students who don't do as well in school might get much lower grades than they would have otherwise if they weren't asked to grade their own work. This kind of scoring is also used to grade students in a number of university classes that are not related to research. Still, researchers haven't talked about what these incentive systems mean for fairness in educational results.

Lens 4 (Human-Algorithm): Interplay between Automated and Human Decision-making

Figure 5. Lens 4 (Human-Algorithm) highlights the complex interactions between AIEd systems and human decision-makers. Under this lens, designing to shape these (often bidirectional) interactions in ways that support more equitable outcomes is a central goal.

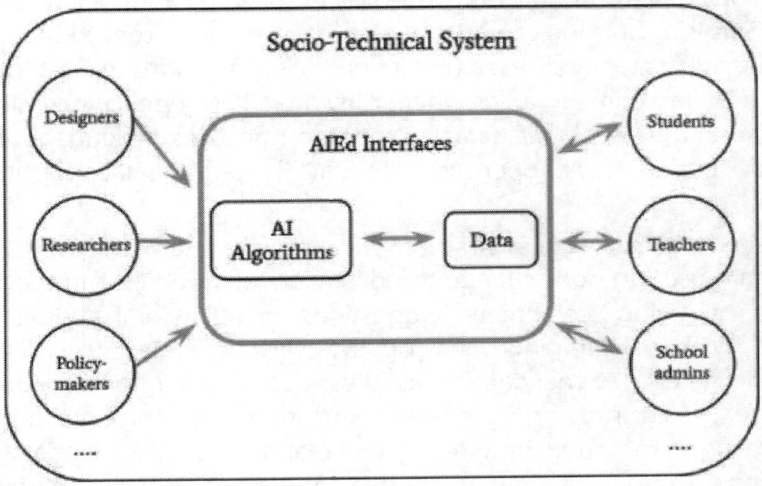

The use of AIEd systems in real-life schools doesn't leave kids alone when they're there. Instead, their effects come from the complicated interactions between the AI systems themselves, the people who create and build them, and the people who make decisions using them. To make the future of AI in education more fair, we need to carefully plan for how these parts will work together, rather than just focusing on AIEd platforms, datasets, or algorithms by themselves, as shown in Figure 5.

It's possible for an educational A or learning analytics system to have harmful algorithmic biases even if it doesn't show differences in how well it predicts the future for different groups of students. This is because the system may still contribute to unfair outcomes when it is used in the real world. For example, look at two different designs of a decision-support tool for teachers that both use the same core student modeling algorithms but show teachers the results of these algorithms in different ways. Different ways of presenting information may have very different effects on teachers' natural ways of making decisions, even if they use the same formulas. If the design of a tool makes teachers question what they think about each student's skills and growth potential, then that design might push teachers toward more fair working conditions. If, on the other hand, the main effect of a tool design is to make teachers feel supported in their beliefs, even if those beliefs are wrong, then that design could keep or even reinforce unfair patterns of teacher behavior.

When there are human-AI feedback loops in learning or making decisions, these kinds of relationships between human and machine biases may have effects that are stronger, for better or worse. In the case of predictive policing, Lum and Isaac (2016) found that PredPol, a popular predictive policing software, increased biases in the dataset and targeted Black people at twice the rate of white people, even though drug use was about the same between the two groups. This is a common example of an unfair outcome from the second lens. Simulating further, they showed that if PredPol's predictions make it more likely for police to find crime in areas where they are actively policing, then this will change the crime rates in the data that the algorithm uses, making the algorithm even more biased. This happens in a feedback loop that makes existing biases stronger.

It can be hard to guess how an educational system will work when AI systems are used to both change the behaviors of students and teachers (for example, by giving predictions, suggestions, or behavioral nudges) and be changed by these changing behaviors (by constantly learning and adapting based on new educational data). Since there has been a lot of work on making data-driven, self-improving systems for education for a long time, future work should focus on measuring, modeling, and planning for these kinds of looping interactions. These cycles might be able to work as positive, self-regulating loops if they are built that way. They could help people deal with the bad effects of algorithmic decision-making and help machines deal with the bad effects of human decision-making.

Achieving Equity Through AI in Education

We will now give you some short examples of some possible ways that AI in Education could lead to a more fair future. First, we talk about some promising ways to stop AIEd from making existing inequalities worse, taking into account some of the risks we talked about in the last part. Once we've looked at ways to lessen these bad outcomes, we'll go back to AIEd's promise as a way to fight inequality and show how it might be used to fix current problems in education.

Along with each path we show, we also give at least one criticism of that road, followed by possible solutions. We've had a lot of talks with AIEd researchers and practitioners, which is why we're writing each path as a dialectic. We want to draw attention to the problems we may face in the future while also recognizing how complicated they are. Our goal is to start new conversations and move conversations that are already going on forward. Keep in mind, though, that what follows is by no means a complete list of good ways to move forward or a full review of all the problems and criticisms that come with them.

Pathways to Avoid Amplifying Inequities

Path 1: Invest in developing tools and processes to support AIEd practitioners in developing and deploying more equitable technologies.

As a field, we could put more money into study and real-world tools for figuring out how to fix the unfair effects of AIEd technologies. For instance, we could create unique toolkits and organizational structures to help with designing, testing, and deploying AI-supported education in a way that takes fairness into account. Then, AIEd development teams could keep an eye out for any unwanted differences in how their technologies work in different educational settings and with different groups of students, and they could keep improving these technologies over time to fix these differences.

Critique 1: How will AIEd companies be held accountable?

Will businesses be able to say they are checking their technologies for unfair effects in order to boost their public relations, but not actually reporting or fixing all the problems they find?

Possible resolution: We can and should design mechanisms to promote increased accountability and transparency. For instance, support for company-internal auditing should exist side-by-side (and ideally in close coordination with) mechanisms for auditing and regulating AIEd systems from the outside.

Critique 2: In addressing one form of inequity, AIEd developers may inadvertently create others.

It's possible to hurt someone in another way without realizing it when trying to meet a certain idea of fairness, like following a certain quantitative meaning put forward in previous research.

Possible resolution: No matter what, we need to do our best. In the end, the ideas of fairness we choose for a given situation rely on what we and the people we work with find most important and relevant. When basic design trade-offs need to be made, we need to stand up and do so. In this case, it means taking responsibility, which is better than denying duty. Also, because we keep checking for fairness, we don't make small fixes that have long-term effects we didn't expect.

Path 2: Design AIEd systems that can clearly communicate their own capabilities and limitations, and hand off control to humans as needed.

In the future, AIEd systems could be made to tell the humans-in-the-loop about their doubts and possible biases (for example, when giving analytics). This would let the humans making decisions (like teachers and students) override their suggestions when necessary.

Critique: "Lifting the curtain" on AIEd systems will reduce trust.

By making things more clear and letting people know what AIEd systems can and can't do, we might make people less trusting of these systems. In the long run, these kinds of actions will make people less likely to use tools that would help students otherwise.

Possible resolution: It is possible to help teachers and students trust computers in the right ways if these systems are carefully planned and the ways that humans and computers make decisions are understood (for example, algorithmic reluctance or over-reliance). In an ideal world, AIEd systems would help teachers and students believe their predictions and suggestions only when they are reliable. If they aren't, they should help teachers and students question or ignore that information. More openness in AI systems may actually increase trust rather than decrease it, according to previous study. This is especially true when paired with meaningful control options for users.

Path 3: Incorporate equity-related outcomes, not just individual student learning outcomes, into the objective functions of AIEd systems.

In classes with AIEd systems, "rich get richer" effects happen a lot. This means that systems work in ways that help students who already know a lot about the subject more than they help students who don't know as much. On the other hand, AIEd systems might work well for one student, but they could make achievement gaps even bigger for the whole community. To fix this, we should work on making AIEd system algorithms that not only improve the learning outcomes for each individual student but also outcomes at higher levels, like the level of the class, school, area, or region. This problem is talked about in more detail by Kizilcec and Lee in this volume.

Critique: We should not suppress advanced students' progress simply to avoid widening achievement gaps across students.

The idea that AIEd systems can help advanced students reach their full potential faster than they would otherwise is a good way to look at the "rich get richer" argument. In the name of fairness, it might not be right or moral to stop these kids from making progress. We don't just want to close performance gaps because education is complicated.

Possible resolution: In the end, we might have to choose between different things. But we shouldn't make these kinds of trade-offs "by default." Instead, we should be aware of them and choose to make them. As a field, we should think carefully about our learning goals, both for individuals and for groups, as well as the choices we are ready to make to reach these goals. There's also a chance that we can get around some trade-offs by designing things carefully.

For instance, many AIEd systems that use adaptive problem selection will let smart students move on to more difficult material in a program as fast as they can learn it. A different design for these kinds of technologies, which might be better from an equity point of view, could keep different students fairly on track with the curriculum while giving students who learn faster challenging enrichment opportunities (for example, advanced students could learn more about a subject in depth without necessarily helping them get far ahead in the curriculum; they could help tutor their peers who are having trouble).

Pathways to Alleviate Existing Educational Inequities

Path 1: Broaden (meaningful) participation in AIEd system design to more equitably serve diverse populations.

In order for AIEd systems to be well-designed, they need to include views from a range of backgrounds that are typical of the students and teachers they are meant to help, such as those with different race, culture, and language. This could mean including students, teachers, and parents from a variety of backgrounds in the co-design process or hiring a more diverse team to lead the creation of the technology. However, this doesn't mean that teams should hire "token" members of certain groups just to get them off the list. It is important to always look for useful voices that aren't being heard and make sure that these voices can have a real effect on how AIEd systems are designed.

Critique 1: Students and teachers are not scientific experts.

By letting a lot of people join, we risk letting kids and teachers who don't know much about good teaching methods hurt the quality of these systems. For instance, what if a teacher wants to make a system that adapts to each student's "learning style," even though study shows that this might not work or could even be bad for the students?

Possible resolution: As learning scientists, designers, researchers, and writers, we don't lose our power when we let more people help make these systems. A more inclusive and team-based approach recognizes that there may be a lot we don't know that other stakeholders may know a lot about (for example, about their daily lives), and that we may also know a lot that other stakeholders may not know. Then, our task is to find the best way to balance the wants and needs of different stakeholders with what we already know about science or design. From this point of view, knowing the wants, limits, and problems of different interest groups doesn't limit us; it makes us stronger. Finding out what students and teachers think and have experienced can also help you guess if and how an AIEd tool could be used in different school settings. For instance, if teachers really believe in different ways of learning, they might use a certain tool in a way that tries to adapt lessons to different ways of learning. It is helpful for AIEd developers to know about both good and bad adoption trends and use that information when making these kinds of systems.

Critique 2: Can broadening participation yield discriminatory outcomes?

If you want to really meet the needs of different groups of kids, teachers, and learning environments, you might need to make different technologies for each group. Different groups may be treated differently, even if the tools are designed to meet their needs. This could make people in these groups feel bad about themselves in the long run.

Possible Resolution: Different treatment is already common in schools, and it's often needed to keep results from being different for different groups. As an example, mastery learning and all adaptive systems do different kinds of therapy. We usually want to give a student who is having trouble more chances to succeed than to a student who learns the same subject quickly. To make sure that these targeted interventions are seen as helpful and not discriminatory or stigmatizing, we need to design them with people from these groups.

Path 2: Fill existing gaps in educational services with AIEd technologies

AIEd systems can fill gaps, providing educational services where few or none previously existed; for example, by offering instruction in the midst of a multi-week teachers' strike, as in the Madaio et al. (2020) case study.

Critique: AIEd will function as such an attractive band-aid that we will neglect to heal the underlying wounds.

AIEd systems that fill in the gaps could be used as a "excuse" by policymakers not to spend money on better, longer-lasting solutions to the social problems that affect education. For example, these technologies could lead to less money for teachers and public schools or bigger classes. Also, schools that don't have enough resources might be more likely to choose this choice to save money, which could make inequality worse.

Possible resolution: This is a very important criticism that you should not ignore. Filling in holes in AIEd systems can do a lot of good, but in the end, researchers, practitioners, and policymakers all need to make sure that they don't hurt society more than they help. We need to keep talking about what we can do as a group to make sure that our work isn't just a "band-aid" or an excuse for not fixing bigger problems in our school systems.

Path 3: AIEd as a force to overcome harmful human biases.

As we've already talked about, AIEd systems have a lot of biases. However, a lot of the ways that they cause unfair outcomes come from human biases, like teachers' biases (for example, teachers' beliefs affect how they use educational technology in lenses 1 and 4; teachers' biases are stored in data used by AIEd technologies, like automated essay graders, in lens 2). AIEd systems can be used to push against human teachers when needed to help them see and get rid of their own biases.

Critique: If AI systems can encode harmful biases, how can they be used to help humans overcome harmful biases?

We might do the opposite of what we want by using AIEd tools to push teachers to make decisions that are more fair. For instance, AIEd systems might not understand when a teacher is using helpful heuristics because they are based on a lot of contextual knowledge that the teacher doesn't have access to, or they might even push their own harmful views onto teachers.

Possible resolution: As shown in Path 1 under "Pathways to Avoid Amplifying Existing Inequities," AIEd systems might be made with the knowledge that they aren't perfect and shouldn't give teachers surefire instructions on what to do. An AIEd system might have some damaging biases of its own, but they might be different from the biases of a human teacher. The AIEd system may help teachers learn and think by bringing to their attention differences between their own judgments and those of the system. Teachers can give input to AIEd systems, which can then be used to find and fix any biases the systems may have.

Conclusions

One way to improve education systems and lessen current inequalities is to use artificial intelligence in the classroom. But, like any other attempt to fix the tough problems in education, AIEd systems can easily have unexpected effects that make things worse instead of better. There are many ways to look at this and figure out how this can happen. Each one focuses on a different part of the complicated social and technological system that AIEd tools work in. In the end, we can only see how AIEd systems can really help reduce educational inequality if we look at all the different ways they can make things worse. As we look ahead, we need to have open, honest conversations about the many problems we will face. We hope that this chapter adds to the talks that are already going on and starts new ones about AI-supported education.

References

Amershi, S., Weld, D., Vorvoreanu, M., Fourney, A., Nushi, B., Collisson, P., Suh, J., Iqbal, S., Bennett, P N., Inkpen, K., & Teevan, J. (2019). Guidelines for human-AI interaction. In Proceedings of the 2019 CHI Conference on Human Factors in Computing Systems (CHI'19) (pp. 1-13). ACM.

An, P., Bakker, S., Ordanovski, S., Taconis, R., Paffen, C. L., & Eggen, B. (2019). Unobtrusively enhancing reflection-in-action of teachers through spatially distributed ambient information. In Proceedings of the 2019 CHI Conference on Human Factors in Computing Systems (pp. 1-14).

An, P.*, Holstein, K.*, d'Anjou, B., Eggen, B., & Bakker, S. (2020). The TA Framework: Designing real-time teaching augmentation for K-12 classrooms. In Proceedings of the ACM CHI Conference on Human Factors in Computing Systems (CHI'20) (pp. 1-17). ACM.

Arnstein, S. R. (1969). A ladder of citizen participation. Journal of the American Institute of Planners, 35(4), 216-224.

Baker, R. S., & Hawn, A. (2021). Algorithmic Bias in Education. https://doi.org/10.35542/osf.io/pbmvz

Baker, R., Ogan, A., Madaio, M., Walker, E. (2019). Culture in Computer-Based Learning Systems: Challenges and Opportunities. In Computer-Based Learning in Context, 1(1), 1-13. 2019.

Barocas, S., & Selbst, A. D. (2016). Big data's disparate impact. Calif. L. Rev., 104, 671.

Bickel, J. E. (2010). Scoring rules and decision analysis education. Decision Analysis, 7(4), 346-357.

Bietti, E. (2020). From ethics washing to ethics bashing: A view on tech ethics from within moral philosophy. In Proceedings of the 2020 Conference on Fairness, Accountability, and Transparency (FAT*20) (pp. 210-219).

Blikstein, P (2018). Time to Make Hard Choices for AI in Education. Keynote talk at the 2018 International Conference on Artificial Intelligence in Education (AIED 2018).

Bull, S., & Kay, J. (2010). Open learner models. In Advances in Intelligent Tutoring Systems (pp. 301-322). Springer, Berlin, Heidelberg.

Bull, S., & Kay, J. (2016). SMILI© : A framework for interfaces to learning data in open learner models, learning analytics and related fields. International Journal of Artificial Intelligence in Education, 26(1), 293-331.

Conati, C., Porayska-Pomsta, K., & Mavrikis, M. (2018). AI in Education needs interpretable machine learning: Lessons from Open Learner Modelling. arXiv preprint arXiv:1807.00154.

Corbett, A. T., & Anderson, J. R. (1995). Knowledge tracing: Modeling the acquisition of procedural knowledge. User modeling and User-adapted Interaction, 4(4), 253-278.

Chipman, S. F., Marshall, S. P., & Scott, P A. (1991). Content effects on word problem performance: A possible source of test bias?. American Educational Research Journal, 28(4), 897-915.

Cramer, H., Holstein, K., Wortman Vaughan, J., Daume III, H., Dudik, M., Wallach, H., Reddy, S., & Garcia-Gathright, J. (2019). Challenges of incorporating algorithmic fairness into industry practice. Tutorial at the ACM Conference on Fairness, Accountability, and Transparency (FAT* '19). ACM.

Datta, A., Fredrikson, M., Ko, G., Mardziel, P., & Sen, S. (2017). Proxy non-discrimination in data-driven systems. arXiv preprint arXiv: 1707.08120.

De-Arteaga*, M., Fogliato, R.*, Chouldechova, A. (2020). A case for humans-in-the-loop: Decisions in the presence of erroneous algorithmic scores. In Proceedings of the ACM CHI Conference on Human Factors in Computing Systems (CHI'20) (pp. 1-12). ACM.

Doroudi, S. (2020). Mastery learning heuristics and their hidden models. In International Conference on Artificial Intelligence in Education (pp. 86-91). Springer.

Doroudi, S., Aleven, V., & Brunskill, E. (2019). Where's the reward? A review of reinforcement learning for instructional sequencing. International Journal of Artificial Intelligence in Education, 29(4), 568-620.

Doroudi, S., & Brunskill, E. (2019). Fairer but not fair enough on the equitability of knowledge tracing. In Proceedings of the 9th International Conference on Learning Analytics & Knowledge (pp. 335-339).

Dwork, C., Hardt, M., Pitassi, T., Reingold, O., & Zemel, R. (2012). Fairness through awareness. In Proceedings of the 3rd Innovations in Theoretical Computer Science Conference (pp. 214-226).

Elzayn, H., Jabbari, S., Jung, C., Kearns, M., Neel, S., Roth, A., & Schutzman, Z. (2019). Fair algorithms for learning in allocation problems. In Proceedings of the Conference on Fairness, Accountability, and Transparency (FAT*19) (pp. 170-179).

Fancsali, S. E., Yudelson, M. V., Berman, S. R., & Ritter, S. (2018). Intelligent Instructional Hand Offs. International Educational Data Mining Society.

Ferguson, R. (2019). Ethical challenges for learning analytics. Journal of Learning Analytics, 6(3), 25-30.

Finkelstein, S., Yarzebinski, E., Vaughn, C., Ogan, A., & Cassell, J. (2013). The effects of culturally congruent educational technologies on student achievement. In International Conference on Artificial Intelligence in Education (pp. 493-502). Springer, Berlin, Heidelberg.

Garcia-Bulle, Sofia. (2021). The dark side of online exam proctoring. Observatory of Educational Innovation. https://observatory.tec.mx/edu-news/dark-side-proctored-exams

Gardner, J., Brooks, C., & Baker, R. (2019). Evaluating the fairness of predictive student models through slicing analysis. In Proceedings of the 9th International Conference on Learning Analytics & Knowledge (pp. 225-234).

Guo, A., Kamar, E., Wortman Vaughan, J., Wallach, H., & Morris, M. R. (2019). Toward Fairness in AI for People with Disabilities: A Research Roadmap. arXiv preprint arXiv:1907.02227.

Hansen, J. D., & Reich, J. (2015). Democratizing education? Examining access and usage patterns in massive open online courses. Science, 350(6265), 1245-1248.

Hardt, M. (2014). How big data is unfair. Medium. https://medium.com/@mrtz/how-big-data-is-unfair-9aa544d739de.

Heffernan, N. T., & Heffernan, C. L. (2014). The ASSISTments ecosystem: Building a platform that brings scientists and teachers together for minimally invasive research on human learning and teaching. International Journal of Artificial Intelligence in Education, 24(4), 470-497.

Holmes, W., Bialik, M., & Fadel, C. (2019). Artificial intelligence in education: Promises and implications for teaching and learning. Boston, MA: Center for Curriculum Redesign.

Holstein, K., & Doroudi, S. (2019). Fairness and equity in learning analytics systems (FairLAK). In Companion Proceedings of the Ninth International Learning Analytics & Knowledge Conference (LAK 2019).

Holstein, K., McLaren, B. M., & Aleven, V. (2018a). Informing the design of teacher awareness tools through Causal Alignment Analysis. In Proceedings of the 13th International Conference of the Learning Sciences (ICLS 2018).

Holstein, K., McLaren, B. M., & Aleven, V. (2018b). Student learning benefits of a mixed-reality teacher awareness tool in AI-enhanced classrooms. In International Conference on Artificial Intelligence in Education (pp. 154-168). Springer, Cham.

Holstein, K., McLaren, B. M., & Aleven, V. (2019). Co-designing a real-time classroom orchestration tool to support teacher-AI complementarity. Journal of Learning Analytics, 6(2), 27-52.

Holstein, K., Wortman Vaughan, J., Daume III, H., Dudik, M., & Wallach, H. (2019). Improving fairness in machine learning systems: What do industry practitioners need?. In Proceedings of the 2019 CHI Conference on Human Factors in Computing Systems (pp. 1-16). ACM.

Hu, D. (2011). How Khan academy is using machine learning to assess student mastery. Retreived from http://david-hu.com/2011/11/02/how-khan-academy-is-using-machine-learning-to-assess-student-mastery.html.

Kelly, K., Wang, Y., Thompson, T., & Heffernan, N. (2015). Defining Mastery: Knowledge Tracing Versus N-Consecutive Correct Responses. In Proceedings of the 8th International Conference on Educational Data Mining. ACM.

Kilbertus, N., Carulla, M. R., Parascandolo, G., Hardt, M., Janzing, D., & Scholkopf, B. (2017). Avoiding discrimination through causal reasoning. In Advances in Neural Information Processing Systems (pp. 656-666).

Kizilcec, R. F. & Lee, H. (forthcoming). Algorithmic Fairness in Education. In W. Holmes & K. Porayska-Pomsta (Eds.), Ethics in Artificial Intelligence in Education, Taylor & Francis.

Kizilcec, R. F., Saltarelli, A. J., Reich, J., & Cohen, G. L. (2017). Closing global achievement gaps in MOOCs. Science , 355(6322), 251-252.

Kleinberg, J., Mullainathan, S., & Raghavan, M. (2016). Inherent trade-offs in the fair determination of risk scores. arXivpreprint arXiv:1609.05807.

Labutov, I., & Studer, C. (2016). Calibrated Self-Assessment. International Educational Data Mining Society.

Lee, M. K., & Baykal, S. (2017). Algorithmic mediation in group decisions: Fairness perceptions of algorithmically mediated vs. discussion-based social division. In Proceedings of the 2017 ACM Conference on Computer Supported Cooperative Work and Social Computing (CSCW'17). (pp. 1035-1048). ACM.

Lum, K., & Isaac, W. (2016). To predict and serve? Significance, 13(5), 14-19.

Madaio, M., Yarzebinski, E., Zinszer, B., Kamath, V., Akpe, H., Seri, A.B., Tanoh, F., Hannon-Cropp, J., Cassell, J., Jasinska, K., Ogan, A. (2020). Motivations and Barriers for Family Engagement with a Home Literacy Technology in Rural Communities. In Proceedings of the 2020 CHI Conference on Human Factors in Computing Systems. ACM.

Madaio, M. A., Stark, L., Vaughan, J. W., & Wallach, H. (2020). Co-Designing Checklists to Understand Organizational Challenges and Opportunities around Fairness in AI. In Proceedings of the 2020 CHI Conference on Human Factors in Computing Systems (pp. 1-14). ACM.

Madnani, N., Loukina, A., Von Davier, A., Burstein, J., & Cahill, A. (2017). Building better open-source tools to support fairness in automated scoring. In Proceedings of the First ACL Workshop on Ethics in Natural Language Processing (pp. 41-52).

Martinez-Maldonado, R., Dimitriadis, Y. & Kay, J., Yacef, K., & Edbauer, M. (2013). MTClassroom and MTDashboard: Supporting analysis of teacher attention in an orchestrated multi-tabletop classroom. In Proc. CSCL2013. 1. 119-128.

Mayfield, E., Madaio, M., Prabhumoye, S., Gerritsen, D., McLaughlin, B., Dixon-Roman, E., Black, E. (2019). Equity Beyond Bias in Language Technologies for Education. In 14th Workshop on Innovative Use of NLP for Building Educational Applications, at ACL 2019.

Meaney, M.J. and Fikes, T. (2019). Early-adopter Iteration Bias and Research-praxis Bias in Virtual Learning Environments. In Companion Proceedings of the 2019 International Conference on Learning Analytics and Knowledge (LAK'19).

Nye, B. D. (2014). Barriers to ITS adoption: A systematic mapping study. In Proceedings of the 12th International Conference on Intelligent Tutoring Systems (pp. 583-590). Springer, Cham.

Ocumpaugh, J., Baker, R., Gowda, S., Heffernan, N., & Heffernan, C. (2014). Population validity for Educational Data Mining models: A case study in affect detection. British Journal of Educational Technology, 45(3), 487-501.

Ogan, A., Walker, E., Baker, R., Rodrigo, M. M. T., Soriano, J. C., & Castro, M. J. (2015). Towards understanding how to assess help-seeking behavior across cultures. International Journal of Artificial Intelligence in Education , 25(2), 229-248.

Ogan, A., Yarzebinski, E., Fernandez, P., & Casas, I. (2015). Cognitive Tutor use in Chile: Understanding classroom and lab culture. In International Conference on Artificial Intelligence in Education (pp. 318-327). Springer, Cham.

Olsen, J. K., Aleven, V., & Rummel, N. (2015). Predicting Student Performance in a Collaborative Learning Environment. In Proceedings of the 8th International Conference on Educational Data Mining (pp. 211-217). International Educational Data Mining Society.

O'Shea, T. (1979). A self-improving quadratic tutor. International Journal of Man-Machine Studies, 11(1), 97-124.

Pashler, H., McDaniel, M., Rohrer, D., & Bjork, R. (2008). Learning styles: Concepts and evidence. Psychological science in the public interest, 9(3), 105-119.

Raji, I. D., & Buolamwini, J. (2019). Actionable auditing: Investigating the impact of publicly naming biased performance results of commercial AI products. In Proceedings of the 2019 AAAI/ACM Conference on AI, Ethics, and Society (pp. 429-435).

Rafalow, M. H. (2020). Digital Divisions. University of Chicago Press.

Rau, M. A. (2015). Why Do the Rich Get Richer? A Structural Equation Model to Test How Spatial Skills Affect Learning with Representations. In EDM (pp. 350-357).

Reich, J., & Ito, M. (2017). From good intentions to real outcomes: Equity by design in learning technologies. Digital Media and Learning Research Hub.

Rideout, V. J. & Katz, V.S. (2016). Opportunity for all? Technology and learning in lower-income families. A report of the Families and Media Project. New York: The Joan Ganz Cooney Center at Sesame Workshop.

Rogowsky, B. A., Calhoun, B., & Tallal, P (2020). Providing Instruction Based on Students' Learning Style Preference Does Not Improve Learning. Frontiers in Psychology, 11, 164.

Rose, D. (2000). Universal design for learning. Journal of Special Education Technology, 15(3), 45-49.

Rummel, N., Walker, E., & Aleven, V (2016). Different futures of adaptive collaborative learning support. International Journal of Artificial Intelligence in Education, 26(2), 784-795.

Ryan, C. L., & Lewis, J. M. (2017). Computer and internet use in the United States: 2015. US Department of Commerce, Economics and Statistics Administration, US Census Bureau.

Saxena, M., Pillai, R. K., & Mostow, J. (2018). Relating Children's Automatically Detected Facial Expressions to Their Behavior in RoboTutor. In Thirty-Second AAAI Conference on Artificial Intelligence.

Shum, S. J. B. (2018). Transitioning Education's Knowledge Infrastructure. Keynote talk at the 2018 International Conference of the Learning Sciences (ICLS 2018),

Shum, S. J. B., & Luckin, R. (2019). Learning analytics and AI: Politics, pedagogy and practices. British Journal of Educational Technology , 50(6), 2785-2793.

Sims, C. (2014). From differentiated use to differentiating practices: Negotiating legitimate participation and the production of privileged identities. Information, Communication & Society, 17(6), 670-682.

Teninbaum, G. H. (2021, forthcoming). Report on ExamSoft's ExamID feature (and a method to bypass it). Journal of Robotics, Artificial Intelligence, and Law,

Uchidiuno, J., Yarzebinski, E., Madaio, M., Maheshwari, N., Koedinger, K., & Ogan, A. (2018). Designing Appropriate Learning Technologies for School vs Home Settings in Tanzanian Rural Villages. In Proceedings of the 1st ACMSIGCAS Conference on Computing and Sustainable Societies (pp. 1-11).

van Leeuwen, A. (2015). Learning analytics to support teachers during synchronous CSCL: Balancing between overview and overload. Journal of learning Analytics, 2(2), 138-162.

van Leeuwen & Rummel (2020). Comparing Teachers' Use of Mirroring and Advising Dashboards. In Proceedings of the 2020 Conference on Learning Analytics and Knowledge (LAK'20) (pp. 26-34). SoLAR.

VanLehn, K. (2011). The relative effectiveness of human tutoring, intelligent tutoring systems, and other tutoring systems. Educational Psychologist, 46(4), 197-221.

VanLehn, K. (2016). Regulative loops, step loops and task loops. International Journal of Artificial Intelligence in Education , 26(1), 107-112.

Veale, M., Van Kleek, M., & Binns, R. (2018). Fairness and accountability design needs for algorithmic support in high-stakes public sector decision-making. In Proceedings of the 2018 CHI Conference on Human Factors in Computing Systems (pp. 1-14).

Watters, A. (2014). The monsters of education technology. CreateSpace.

Wen, Z. A., Amog, A. L. S., Azenkot, S., & Garnett, K. (2019). Teacher Perspectives on Math E-Learning Tools for Students with Specific Learning Disabilities. In The 21st International ACMSIGACCESS Conference on Computers and Accessibility (pp. 516-518).

Young, M., Magassa, L., & Friedman, B. (2019). Toward inclusive tech policy design: a method for underrepresented voices to strengthen tech policy documents. Ethics and Information Technology, 21(2), 89-103.

Zhu, H., Yu, B., Halfaker, A., & Terveen, L. (2018). Value-sensitive algorithm design: Method, case study, and lessons. Proceedings of the ACM on Human-Computer Interaction, 2(CSCW), 1-23.

Chapter 8
AI in Education: Rapid Transformations in Learning

Students and teachers are facing a world of constant, ever-accelerating change. Those now exiting secondary school for the world of work or further study in the developed countries have never known a world without the ubiquity of the internet and the mobile phone. Although the first commercially-available mobile phone only appeared in 1985, by 1999 one phone was being sold in the United Kingdom every four seconds, and by 2004 — when these students were in grade 2 or 3 — there were more mobile phones than people in the UK[1]. A "Digital Divide" was quickly named for the difference in access to the internet and smart devices between the developed and developing worlds. As technology became more common in schools with the financial resources to do so, worries were raised that disadvantaged students of all nationalities would be left behind.

On the other hand, a lot of people thought that having access to technology and cheap mobile phones could help close the educational gap caused by problems in the formal education system. They thought that this could help people who had dropped out of school or never had the chance to go to one get a good education that could help solve big problems like the global problem of illiteracy.

In the event, the introduction of devices into the classroom did not bring about a commensurate improvement in exam grades — though it did help to enable new pedagogical modalities such as the flipped classroom — and illiteracy rates remained virtually unchanged[2]. The role of the teacher has been proven paramount, along with the need for adequate professional development

1 The Guardian. (2009). In just 25 years, the mobile phone has transformed the way we communicate. Retrieved from https://www.theguardian.com/business/2010/jan/01/25-years-phones- transform-communication

2 World Population Review. (2020). Literacy Rate by Country 2020. Retrieved from https:// worldpopulationreview.com/country-rankings/literacy-rate-by-country

supports which incorporate the building of digital skills[1]. Teachers are still needed even though technology can help students learn. In fact, teachers are seen as the most important part of using technology to improve teaching and learning.

Along with the rise of these new tools, there was a focus on what were called "21st century skills." In order to better prepare students for the world they would face after leaving school, the ability to work in teams, collaborate, and communicate effectively, as well as the development of analytical and digital skills, became the most important thing in the design of the curriculum and the way it was taught. People thought that getting digital skills and practice with basic technologies was closely connected to learning how to learn and how important it is to keep learning throughout your life.

Advancements in Technology

Data, Analytics and Personalized Learning

It became a main goal of educational reform to make personalized learning possible, which means being able to change the way, what, and how fast a student learns based on their own needs. Technology holds a lot of promise because it can help create personalized learning paths. However, this could not be done with just gear or software. To find out if students were learning 21st century skills, you would need to look at a lot of different statistics from different sources.

Student Information Systems (SIS) and Learning Management Systems (LMS) brought in new digital data sets, but most of the data that teachers needed to see about their students' progress and success was still on paper or in their heads. Before Artificial Intelligence (AI) or Predictive Analytics could be used to help make personalized learning paths, there had to be progress in how data was collected, kept, and made available.

The 'data journey' towards this state was comprised of the following key stages:

1. **Data collection**: the capturing of key student data relevant to some or all of the following core measures of student success: academic performance; attendance; participation; behaviour; consistency; resilience; persistence or 'grit'; confidence or self-belief; enjoyment or engagement; emotional development; social development; ethical development; physical development.

1 OECD. (2018). Teaching for the Future: Effective Classroom Practices To Transform Education. OECD Publlishing, Paris. Retrieved from https://doi.org/10.1787/9789264293243-en

2. **Data presentation**: the display of data in a form which allows for review and interrogation, including visualizations.
3. **Historical analysis**: the analysis of past performance and student progress to date to derive insights and to identify areas requiring course-correction or review.
4. **Predictive analysis**: the analysis of both current (real-time or near-realtime) data and historical data to enable projections with regard to such core concerns as student retention/dropout rates and to identify students in need of timely interventions, whether these relate to academic performance or issues of mental health or welfare, and to assist in future planning on a systemic, institutional, and individual student basis.

The majority of schools, colleges and education systems are currently at stage I of the data journey (data collection) but even at this stage Artificial Intelligence can deliver real benefits. Before we outline those benefits, we need to define what is meant by AI in an educational context.

Artificial Intelligence

Data is the first step in artificial intelligence. Using tools like predictive analytics and machine learning, AI can take in data from many sources, question that data, and find insights. This is what makes it such an exciting step forward in education technology, and it will change everything for everyone, from individual students to education ministries.

Perhaps the best way to think about AI in a school setting is to think about it as Augmented Intelligence. Utilizing AI gives everyone involved more data and new insights that can help them make better decisions. Here are some facts that important people in the situation need to think about:

Students: individual students need help to identify areas in their learning pathways where they need additional support or guidance, or where they require an increased focus in their studies

Educators: a typical primary-school teacher can have between 20-30 students in a class[1]. To measure progress against all of the core success metrics outlined in Stage 1 of the data journey above for each student in a class of 30 students would require them to track progress against 390 different data points. For a secondary school teacher, who might teach 6 or more groups of students in different grades or age groups, the challenge is exponentially greater. (It is a measure of the extraordinary dedication and skill that teachers as a profession

1 OECD.Stat. (2020). Average class size. Retrieved from https://stats.oecd.org/Index.aspx?DataSetCode=EDU_CLASS

display that they undertake to do this to the best of their abilities in service of their students and the students' families.) A professor or dean of faculty at a university may have an even larger cohort of students; and for all educators the student cohort will typically change on an annual or more frequent basis.

School Leaders: to manage an academic institution or to lead change, a school leader in K-12, Further Education or Higher Education needs to consider a vast range of factors and data points. In addition to student-centric data, he or she must consider staffing issues; financial and infrastructural management issues; matters relating to policy, governance and oversight; privacy, health and safety concerns, etc.

Curriculum Designers: those tasked with designing curriculum at an institutional, regional or national level need to consider information from a variety of sources, including the academic, the vocational and the societal, in order to ensure that evolving curricula can meet the current and future needs of students, and will adequately prepare them for the world they will face on leaving school. A curriculum based solely upon historic data, referencing a limited number of sources, cannot hope to meet future needs.

Having access to all of the relevant and available data is not sufficient. None of these challenges can be met with data alone. It is the ability of Artificial Intelligence to make connections across these different data points — to provide predictions of future outcomes in order to enable course-corrections in near-real-time and to derive insights which will allow all stakeholders to make more informed decisions — which constitutes its power and its promise.

Cloud Computing

It is not possible to query very large data sources without having access to the right amount of computer power. The main reason for the fast pace of creativity and technological progress we have seen over the last few decades is improvements in computer power. In 1970, Gordon E. Moore, one of the founders of Intel Corporation, said he thought computers would get twice as fast every two years. What became known as Moore's Law turned out to be true. Floating Operations Per Second (FLOPS) are a way to measure how fast a computer system (or CPU) works. FLOPS, which measure how much computing power a computer has, have grown by about a trillion times between 1956 and 2015. This increase in computing power has been accompanied by a commensurate reduction in cost, which also provided a vital contribution to the pace of change[1].

---

1 Max Roser and Hannah Ritchie. (2013). Technological Progress. Published online at OurWorldInData.org. Retrieved from https://ourworldindata.org/technological-progress

There has been a big change in the history of AI: from "on-premises" computing, where users connect to a computer or network of computers that are physically located nearby, to "cloud computing," where users connect to computing resources over the internet and have access to a virtually endless source of computing power that can grow as needed. Tools and programs like data storage, computers, databases, networking, and software are some of these resources. Computers and other electronics can get data and software as long as they can connect to the internet.

Three different types of services make up cloud computing: Software-as-a-Service (SaaS), Infrastructure-as-a-Service (IaaS), and Platform-as-a-Service (PaaS).

Software-as-a-service (SaaS) enables users to license a particular piece of software (for example, a productivity suite such as Microsoft 365[1]) on a pay-as-you-go or on-demand basis.

Infrastructure-as-a-service (IaaS) provides users with access to everything from operating systems to servers and storage as part of an on-demand service, meaning that organisations no longer need to purchase software or physical servers.

Platform-as-a-service (PaaS) provides users with a development platform for creating software, allowing them to develop, deploy and manage computer applications without having to build or maintain the infrastructure required to support this.

The key benefits of Cloud Computing — and the reasons why so many businesses and public enterprises have made the move to the Cloud — are the following:

1. **Reduced Costs**: computer server hardware and traditional desktop software can be very expensive and are often under-utilized, meaning that servers can sit idle for much of the time and that organisations end up paying a high price to license software that not all of their staff members use or require. A low-cost cloud service based on a pay-as-you-go model, whereby the organization only pays a license fee based on actual usage, can provide significant savings.
2. **Unlimited Storage**: Cloud Storage is virtually unlimited and is charged on a usage basis. The organisation no longer needs to worry about meeting changing storage needs via the purchase of expensive hardware which it will need to maintain, and storage provision can be scaled up — or scaled down — as needed.

1 https://www.microsoft.com/en-ie/microsoft-365

3. **Backup and Recovery**: all data stored in the Cloud is typically backed-up by the cloud service provider, with multiple fail-safes and automatic data replication across different locations, greatly reducing the danger of data loss and allowing for rapid data recovery in the event of a 'crash'.
4. **Ubiquitous Access**: key information can be accessed from virtually any place with an internet connection, at any time, and using any device. This in turn can improve communication and collaboration between team members and boost productivity.
5. **Security**: although many fears persist about placing sensitive or confidential information in the Cloud, cloud service providers often have enhanced levels of security and data protection along with services such as data encryption and remote wipe of lost or stolen devices which provide commensurate or improved levels of security compared to on-premises solutions.
6. **Flexibility**: organizations can scale services to meet their needs and increase or decrease capacity in line with demand to support fluctuating workloads.

Machine Learning

Machine Learning is a branch of artificial intelligence that lets computers do things without being directly told to, and to learn from their mistakes and get better without any help or input from a person. It's used to find answers to questions that can't be answered by doing research by hand. It's based on the idea that computers can learn to find patterns and make decisions. They can get better over time by learning from past calculations and making decisions and results that can be relied on.

It uses algorithms, which are pieces of code that contain a clear set of step-by-step directions that a machine can follow to reach a certain goal. Algorithms use training data, which is a subset of data that stands for the whole set, to set their settings. The program gets better at figuring out what's right as it uses more training data and looks at bigger and bigger sets of data.

There are various ways that computers look at data. Most of the time, they are put together by the type of machine learning they do: controlled learning, unsupervised learning, and reinforcement learning.

Supervised Learning: In supervised learning, algorithms make predictions based on a set of labelled examples that you provide. This approach is useful when you know what the outcome should look like. For example, you provide a dataset that includes city populations by year for the past 100 years, and you want to know what the population of a specific city will be four years from now. The outcome uses labels that already exist in the data set: population, city, and year.

Unsupervised Learning: In unsupervised learning, the key data points are not labelled — the algorithm labels them itself by organizing the data, or by describing its structure. This technique is typically used when you do not know what the outcome should look like. For example, you provide customer data, and you want to create segments of customers who like similar products. The data that you are providing is not labelled, and the labels in the outcome are generated based on the similarities that were discovered between data points.

Reinforcement Learning: In reinforcement learning, computers figure out what to do next by studying what happened and what happened in the past. The algorithm gets feedback after each move that helps it figure out whether the choice it made was right, neutral, or wrong. It works well for computer programs that need to make a lot of small choices without any help from a person. For instance, let's say you are making a driverless car and you want to make sure it follows the rules and keeps people safe. Since the car has been trained to stay in its lane, go the speed limit, and stop for people, it learns to do these things over time.

Machine Learning is already used in a lot of different fields. If you've bought things online before or searched for certain goods or services on a website, it can help that website figure out what items you might be interested in buying. Machine learning is often used by banks and other financial institutions to find, predict, and stop fraudulent activities. In healthcare, machine learning can help find trends or outliers, which can lead to more accurate diagnoses and faster access to important treatments.

The Vision and Promise of Artificial Intelligence

Students

Artificial intelligence can help students of all ages, skill levels, and socioeconomic groups in many important ways. These benefits can all lead to better learning outcomes and more enjoyable learning experiences.

It's possible that a lot of the data that is needed is already being gathered. For example, grade reports, attendance and punctuality records, school reports, scores compared to peers or classmates, Individualized Education Programs (IEPs), and other sources of these types of data.

Qualitative data often comes in the form of notes from observations in the classroom, staff meeting minutes, feedback from a teacher, teaching assistant, or department head, samples of a student's work with comments from their teacher, discipline or student welfare reports, and so on. These can be made stronger with the help of polls, interviews, and notes.

Some common types of quantitative data are individual and comparative test scores, groups of poll results, and any kind of numerical results or measures that are relevant to the student's progress. When used in this way, "quantitative data" basically means any information that can be written as a list of numbers.

More of this information will be available in digital form as schools and colleges move further along the "data journey." This makes it easier to analyze the data. One important thing to remember is that data in a data set doesn't have to be digital. Cutting edge technologies like Cognitive Services make it possible to get information from writing notes and recorded sound or video. Cognitive Services make it possible to see, hear, speak, find, understand, and make decisions faster. They also make it possible to collect and question data.

Personalization

AI, Data & Analytics, and Machine Learning make it possible for everyone involved in a student's education to access information and learn important things about the student's growth as well as other things that might be causing a change in their behavior, engagement, or performance.

AI can not only take in and analyze huge amounts of data, but it can also find links between different data sources. This can help find places where real-time help or solutions are needed. From this, AI can be used to create a personalized learning path for each student, one that takes into account their strengths, flaws, talents, and challenges.

There are huge effects from this. When learning is truly personalized, it gives each student the best chance to reach their full potential. A student's attitude toward school, level of involvement, sense of being cared for and valued, and overall happiness and well-being are likely to all get better along with their academic success.

Social and Emotional Growth

Social and emotional well-being has become an increasing area of focus in education. There has been a recognition that automation and AI are radically changing the world of work, and that interpersonal skills, empathy and creativity will become essential attributes for the jobs of tomorrow. Social and emotional skills, such as problem solving and collaboration, are increasingly necessary for the labour market. The link between a student's outlook and mood, their ability to interact and collaborate with others and their capacity to learn has also been recognised, and had led to a demand for educational reform which places these skills at the centre[1].

Students' exposure to the internet and social media has also contributed to an increased focus upon the development of these skills. The prevalence of 'fake news', disturbing images and stories, issues of privacy and data protection, and the pressures upon children and young people to project and protect an idealized image of themselves against a backdrop of cyber-bullying and health and welfare disorders, including body dysmorphia, eating disorders, depression and anxiety, have underlined the importance of students acquiring the knowledge and skills to navigate the world in which many of them now live.

Research[2] has shown that artificial intelligence and multimodal social computing can help to improve cognitive, social and emotional skills. Advanced analytics and machine learning have been used for a long time to help businesses, and more and more, these tools are being used in schools as well. Advanced analytics and machine learning have a lot of promise to help students learn social and emotional skills. This is because they let teachers tailor their lessons to each student and look at both qualitative and quantitative data to see how well they are learning these skills and help them improve.

21st Century Skills

There is agreement on the skills that kids need to be successful in both school and the workplace. What are now called "21st century skills" are a set of skills and knowledge that students will need to be able to reach their full potential after they graduate.

Different groups have different lists of 21st century skills, but most experts agree on a few key skills: critical thinking, perseverance, creativity, self-direction, global awareness, critical thinking, collaboration, digital literacy, and persistence.

These are all places where technology can help students improve their skills. For example, AI can help teachers plan and tailor the way students learn to meet their specific needs. The best example of how AI can help students learn is its ability to look at their progress across a wide range of different metrics, to collect data from a lot of different learning paths that aren't always related

1 The Economist Intelligence Unit. (2019). Emotion and Cognition in the Age of AI: white paper. Commissioned by Microsoft. Retrieved from https://clouddamcdnprodep.azureedge.net/gdc/ gdcWRrXfv/original

2 Cassell, J., Bai, Z., Paranjape, B., Sinha, T., Slebodnick, D., Luo Yi Tan. (2016). Sensing Curiosity in Play and Responding. The ArticuLab, Carnegie Mellon University. Retrieved from http://articulab. hcii.cs.cmu.edu/projects/scipr/

to each other, and to come up with insights that give a full picture of each student's progress.

Assisting a group of students in developing a wide range of 21st century skills involves gathering and analyzing huge amounts of data, which is sometimes called "Big Data." AI is needed to find useful insights that can help them on their way. "Without big data, you are blind, deaf, and in the middle of a freeway," said Geoffrey Moore, an organizational thinker.

Accessibility

Technology has helped kids with disabilities for a long time. The first people to benefit from education technology in schools and colleges were usually those who could use a laptop or similar device to help "level the playing field" as students. This meant that they had better access to learning objects and opportunities, weren't limited by set times or locations, and could use new tools and services that were made just for them.

Individuals who have trouble seeing can benefit from text-to-speech and screen narration, while students who have trouble hearing can benefit from voice commands, descriptive audio, and speech-to-text. Simple features like keyboard shortcuts and support for a variety of input devices and sensors have made it possible for people with severe physical disabilities to use computers, as the late Stephen Hawking's achievements show.

AI is opening doors for students with disabilities, which will profoundly alter their educational opportunities and levels of engagement. Among recent advancements driven by the use of AI have been Apps which can observe, analyse and describe the world around a visually impaired person through their mobile phone, with the ability to recognize the student's friends and acquaintances, and even to describe their emotions based on such factors as facial expression and posture[1].

Well-being

In recognition of well-being's impact on learning — and the education system's role in shaping the emotional and mental health of young people — the OECD has measured student well-being as part of its Program for International Student Assessment (PISA)[2] ranking since 2015.

PISA defines well-being as "the psychological, cognitive, social and physical functioning and capabilities that students need to live a happy and fulfilling life," which includes the following elements:

---

1 https://www.microsoft.com/en-us/ai/seeing-ai

2 http://www.oecd.org/pisa/

Psychological Well-being: comprising students' sense of purpose, selfawareness, affective states and emotional strength.

Social Well-being: students' quality of social lives, including relationships with family, peers and teachers, as well as a sense of social belonging within a school community.

Cognitive Well-being: referring to students' proficiency in using academic knowledge and soft skills to become lifelong learners, effective workers and engaged citizens.

Physical Well-being: the ability to follow a healthy lifestyle based on selfreported measures of physical activity and nutrition.

Everyone who has a stake in an educational school or system can use AI to find, predict, and stop crises in the well-being or welfare of students. It is possible to get data from all over the school, like attendance and punctuality records, performance ratings, and notes and reports from faculty, administrative, and counseling staff. This data can be used to make dashboards and alerts that help the school plan and allocate resources to help students who need help, are at risk of dropping out, or are having a mental health, academic, or personal life crisis. In this situation, AI's real-time ability to find students who need immediate help and its ability to use machine learning and other indicators to predict when other students may be in danger of having a mental health crisis in the future can actually save lives.

Educators

Using AI, Data & Analytics, and Machine Learning well can help teachers create fun, immersive learning experiences for all of their students and create personalized learning paths for each one by using the extra knowledge and insights that come from using these tools.

It is important to say again that AI will not replace teachers. "Any teacher that can be replaced by a computer deserves to be" is a controversial saying by Dr. Thornburg. However, it does show that there is currently no technology that can replicate, let alone replace, the many skills and qualities of a great teacher. It's not that these cool new technologies have made teachers less important; instead, they've made their job more important. AI holds promise for teachers because it can help them make their lessons more effective and create the best conditions for their students to learn and grow.

Effectiveness and Timesaving

AI can save teachers a lot of time because it analyzes all the available data sources and gives them insights that they can use to make personalized learning pathways. Without AI, teachers would have to spend a lot of time studying and collecting data, which is nearly impossible to do when the data is always changing and there are so many success factors and data sources to think about.

Giving teachers a clear picture of each student's progress lets them quickly find problems and gaps in their knowledge and fix them. This leads to better results for all students and happy, more involved classmates.

AI can also save time for teachers at the "other end" of the process by making detailed reports on each student that can be shared with the school, the parents or guardians, and the students themselves. These reports, which are more accurate and up-to-date than traditional reports or reviews, can be given to all stakeholders whenever they are needed and don't have to be historical reports that show past success at set points during the school year.

Freeing up time from laborious administrative tasks can also have an impact upon educator recruitment and retention. Teachers spend an estimated 3-5 hours[1] each day grading papers and tests, preparing lesson plans and completing administrative work outside of the classroom. Not only is this a leading cause of teacher attrition, it also serves as a powerful disincentive when trying to attract top talent to our schools and classrooms.

Engagement and Enjoyment

Students, who are engaged and interested, learn more and retain that learning for longer. Successive studies[2] in the late 20th and 21st century in both England and the US suggest that an absence of enjoyment is one of the foundational reasons for young people failing to achieve their potential. Though perseverance and an ability to deal with frustration and failure are also key to a successful learning journey, these studies have amply demonstrated that children in particular learn better when they are excited and engaged.

Student enjoyment is not only a beneficial condition for learning: it is a desired outcome, and in some national curricula is assigned the same importance as being healthy and safe[3]. When educators can devote more of their time to class preparation and learning delivery, and less on assessments

1 Murray, C. (2013). How Many Hours Do Educators Actually Work? Retrieved from https:// edtechmagazine.com/k12/article/2013/08/how-many-hours-do-educators-actual-ly-work

2 Goetz, T., Nathan C., Hall, B., Anne, C., Frenzel, A., Pekrun, R. (2006). A hierarchical conceptualization of enjoyment in students. Learning and Instruction, 16, 323-338.; Shernoff, D.J., Csikszentmihalyi, M., Schneider, B., Shernoff, E.S. (2003). Student engagement in high school classrooms from the perspective of flow theory. School Psychology Quarterly, 18(2), 158-176.

3 Department for Education and Skills. (2003a). Every child matters. London: DfES.

and the writing of reports, the benefits are felt by students in their classrooms and lecture halls. When students feel that their individual needs are 'seen' and considered by the educator, they feel supported and valued and are more likely to engage with their course of study.

Collaboration

Data and analytics can give schools useful information that can help everyone work together better. This information can also be used to create a personalized learning plan (PLP) or another type of whole-school support program. Based on a shared set of learnings and indicators, subject teachers, department heads, counseling and welfare services, and school leadership can work together to plan and carry out personal support programs. It helps team-teaching when teachers can match their skills and weaknesses with the needs of their students.

AI can help department and faculty heads figure out what their teachers' strengths and weaknesses are and how to set up joint methods that make the most of everyone's skills. Access to both quantitative and qualitative data all the time makes it possible to find and share the best practices that help students learn. It also makes mentoring and peer coaching relationships stronger.

Professional Development and Self-Reflection

Schools and colleges need to support the development of the increasingly complicated skills that students will need for work and further education in the 21st century. This can only be done through effective, ongoing professional learning. To teach students skills like critical thinking, complicated problem-solving, deep mastery of difficult material, effective communication and teamwork, and self-direction, teachers need to use more advanced methods. For teachers to help students learn 21st century skills, they need to be able to get professional development that helps them learn and improve the ways they teach these skills.

Many organizations and school systems don't meet these needs well, according to studies. Time, money, and resource limitations, along with the fact that a lot of professional development happens outside of school, make it hard for teachers to spend many hours or days each year working on their skills. Teachers also need chances to work together to learn, to try out the kinds of learning they will use in their own classes, and to share ideas and the best ways to do things. We can't help students learn important skills for the 21st century and build 21st century skills by giving teachers old-fashioned ways to teach during their professional development.

When teachers use technologies like AI well, they can get the same access to learning at any time and from anywhere. They can also learn the same skills that their students will need using the same methods and teaching styles that they will be expected to use in their schools and colleges. AI can also help with professional growth on the job and informally or on your own. Educators can better reflect on themselves and improve their skills when they have access to objective data instead of or in addition to emotional evaluations, which some educators may not be open to or willing to participate in.

Parents

Involvement and Engagement

Parents[1] are key stakeholders in the education of children and young people yet to reach the age of majority, and are typically deeply involved and interested in the education of their children above this age during the course of further and higher education. Their active participation can be a key factor in determining the successful completion of the student's learning journey. Students whose parents take an active part in their education are more likely to attend school regularly, adapt well to school, take advanced classes, and to excel academically. Such students also tend to have better social skills and are more likely to graduate from high school and to attend post-secondary school.[2] In fact, some studies suggest that parental engagement can prove the single most important determinant of student success[3].

There are also benefits for schools and colleges when parents are involved. Prioritizing relationships between parents and teachers not only helps the school but also makes the learning setting better, which in turn affects how well all students learn. Teachers who focus on getting parents involved in their children's education see that the whole class does better in terms of motivation, behavior, and results when more parents are involved. Also, when parents are involved in school governing and strategic planning, leaders are more likely to make decisions that are useful and have a big impact.

Parental participation can be seen as the first step toward parental engagement. A lot of schools and colleges have programs, fundraisers, and school events that parents can join in on. In turn, the school tells the parents

1 For the sake of concision, the terms 'parents' and 'parental' are intended as representative of all parents, guardians and care-givers.

2 Henderson, Anne T., Mapp, Karen L. (2002). A New Wave of Evidence. The Impact of School, Family, and Community. Connections on Student Achievement. Annual Synthesis 2002. National Center for Family and Community Connections with Schools, SEDL. Retrieved from https://sedl.org/ connections/resources/evidence.pdf

3 National PTA. (2000). Building Successful Partnerships: A Guide for Developing Parent and Family Involvement Programs. National Education Service, Indiana, USA.

about the student's progress in school and in social situations. In these situations, the information given to parents is generally from the past and is shared at certain times, like at the end of the school year or after a state or school exam. Parental involvement means that parents are involved in their child's education and work with the school or college to make sure the student meets his or her educational goals. Both sides must be ready to listen and share, bringing different points of view to the table so that they can work together to create and implement a learning path that fits the student's needs, abilities, and goals.

AI encourages parental involvement by giving them the chance to take part in their child's growth rather than just reviewing it. This is made possible by making sure that everyone has access to data and insights that can help them work together. All parties gain when parents can keep an eye on their child's progress, step in when needed, and talk to the child's teachers in a well-informed way. This includes the school, the teacher, the parent, and the child.

Reinforcing Values

Parents who are involved in their child's schooling show that they believe in the value of education. In turn, the child will be more likely to understand how valuable and important school is. Engaging parents can have effects that last for generations. Kids tend to copy how adults act, so if their parents are interested in their education, those kids will remember that lesson and be more likely to act in the same way when they become parents themselves. AI makes parents more involved by giving them a better view of their child's growth. This sends the message that they value education highly. To do this, though, schools and colleges need to be willing to let people access important data and the computer systems that store it. This will help build a culture of trust and shared responsibility.

School Leaders

Oversight and Insight

School leaders, deans, presidents and senior administrators are responsible for decisions which can affect every student and faculty member. Data and insights which can assist them in the decision-making process can have obvious benefits, a fact which is recognised by the majority of school leaders who regard digital technologies as an important supplemental resource which can be employed to personalize the learning experience based on each student's strengths, weaknesses, and preferences[1].

1 Education Week Research Center. (2018). School Leaders and Technology. Results from a National Survey. Retrieved from https://www.edweek.org/media/school-leaders-and-technol-

The challenge for school leaders[1] is an exponential one. Different levels of school have different responsibilities. A primary or elementary school teacher may be in charge of 25 to 35 students; a secondary or high school teacher may have up to 180 students in multiple classes; a university professor may have more than 100 students in a class but only tutor a smaller group; and a school leader is usually in charge of hundreds or even thousands of students.

There have been huge changes in how students are tested because of the focus on 21st century skills. In the past, it might have been enough to just keep an eye on a student's academic progress. But now everyone agrees that getting a student ready for life after school means helping them develop a wide range of skills and abilities, all of which need to be evaluated as important parts of their learning path. Teachers and school leaders need to look at more than just attendance and behavior. They also need to look at things like participation, persistence, optimism and self-belief, critical thinking, and many other important factors that will affect a student's future success. Simply put, without AI, it would be hard for a school leader to look at all of these different factors for every student in the school or get the information they need to help with timely interventions.

Efficiencies and Resource Management

Aside from duties related to teaching and learning, school leaders have many other duties. Aside from managing the institution's people and money, its real and digital spaces, and making sure it follows all legal and financial rules, there are often a lot of other administrative and logistical tasks that need to be done as well. A lot of the time, school leaders say that their first job is to "keep the lights on," which means making sure that the school can keep running and provide the facilities and services that are needed to teach.

The fact that the tasks involved are immediate makes the load that this puts on many school leaders even heavier. Sudden, unexpected costs for building upkeep and repairs, covering for teachers, facilities staff, or administrative staff who aren't there, and ups and downs in the number of students can all make it hard to run the school efficiently and affordably. Data and Predictive Analytics can help school leaders switch from managing in a reactive way to managing in a proactive way and see problems coming before they happen. AI solutions can help lower energy costs by making sure that heat and light are provided based on real demand. Machine learning can be used to make accurate predictions

ogy- education-week-research.pdf

1 For the sake of concision, the term 'school leader' is intended as representative of all school leaders at primary, secondary and tertiary level.

based on past patterns. Staff schedules can be better managed, and backup plans can be made before a problem happens at the last minute. It is possible to improve resource planning, automate reporting, and give all key staff members dashboard views with real-time data that are tailored to their jobs. Higher education schools are especially excited about the potential of AI and the Internet of Things (IoT) to make things run more smoothly and cut down on the number of unplanned events and the paperwork that often comes with them.

Teacher Retention

Getting and keeping talented students is one of the hardest things for any school boss. There are only so many great teachers in the world, and their effects can be hard to measure. Not only on the success of each student, but also on the organization's mindset and health as a whole.

However, globally a teaching crisis is driving what has now been recognised by the World Bank as a Learning Crisis[1]. School enrolments in developing countries, at both primary and secondary level, have shot up in recent years — but attracting and keeping qualified, motivated and effective teachers in those classrooms remains an enormous challenge, and graduation rates in a large proportion of those schools are often tragically low. This challenge is not restricted to the developing world. Even when educators are relatively well paid and have access to appropriate resources, the retention rate can be disturbingly low. The United States currently faces an annual estimated shortage of more than 100,000 teachers, and an additional 12% of teachers have indicated that the COVID-19 pandemic may lead them to leave the profession, even though they were not planning to do so before the crisis. Teachers with health challenges across the globe have been forced to consider early retirement, at a time when teacher absences are also expected to grow, and when an estimated 50% of new teachers were already choosing to leave the profession within the first 5 years[2]. The UNESCO Institute of Statistics (UIS) has estimated that countries need to recruit an additional 68.8 million teachers to provide every child with primary and secondary education over the next decade, and retention of existing teachers poses a significant additional challenge.

Computers and AI can't make new teachers or take the place of great teachers we already have. But school leaders can better handle and lower teacher turnover rates by getting to the bottom of some of the reasons teachers leave.

---

1 International Bank for Reconstruction and Development / The World Bank. (2018). The World Development Report 2018 (WDR 2018). LEARNING to Realize Education's Promise. Retrieved from https://www.worldbank.org/en/publication/wdr2018

2 Education Week Research Center. (2020). The Substitute Teacher Gap: Recruitment and Retention Challenges in the Age of COVID-19. Kelly Education.

Several surveys have shown that better pay is not the main issue for teachers and will not solve the problem of low retention rates by itself. What teachers want, it appears, is more autonomy, more time to spend teaching and preparing classes, less bureaucracy, and less time spent conducting tests and writing reports[1]. Also, what drives great teachers is their desire to make a change in the life of a student. An artificial intelligence (AI) system can help teachers do what they love most more effectively and with more satisfaction by giving them the tools to make personalized learning paths for each of their students, figure out and meet the unique needs of each student, and easily create real-time reports with the click of a button.

Student Retention and Welfare

There are many reasons why students at all stages of schooling don't finish. Performance problems in school are just one of these, and in many cases they are not the reason why a student drops out. Schools and colleges can better use their limited resources when they can find and/or predict which students are likely to drop out and act on them in time to keep them from doing so. AI can take in data from many different, unrelated sources, like student information systems (SISs), learning management systems (LMSs), and records of attendance or behavior reports, and turn it into insights that can be shown as real-time alerts. This is a huge step forward.

There are several reasons why keeping students in school or college is important. If a student drops out, the school may lose money in the form of lost tuition fees or government grants for each student. Also, a drop in graduation rates can make it harder for the college to get new students, and a drop in student numbers can also mean that teachers leave the school. For the students, this can mean fewer job possibilities, lower earning potential, and in some cases, a lot of student debt that they can't pay off because they don't have the skills to do so.

Students often drop out of college or university because they can't afford it, their health or family is in danger, or they are having a hard time adjusting to a new place with new people and more work. This is especially true for first-year students who are living away from home for the first time. More and more, schools and colleges are focusing on a threat that is deeper and more sneaky: the mental health of their students.

A recent survey of New Zealand students reported that 56% of all respondents had considered dropping out of tertiary study, the main reasons mentioned were feeling of being overwhelmed, living with mental illness,

1 Riggs, L. (2013). Why Do Teachers Quit? And why do they stay? The Atlantic. Retrieved from https:// www.theatlantic.com/education/archive/2013/10/why-do-teachers-quit/280699/

and fears of failure[1]. Student well-being and student welfare are increasingly important areas of focus for schools and colleges, with historic levels of anxiety, stress and depression being reported by students. Whether this represents an increase in mental health issues, or a welcome reduction in the stigma attaching to mental health (or both) what is inarguable is the benefit which accrues when a mental health crisis is averted.

Student suicides are on the rise in countries around the world. In the UK, a major survey in 2018 saw a significant increase in the rates of young people aged between 10 and 24 killing themselves, with the overall rate for that age group reaching a 19-year high and the rate for young females reaching an all-time high[2]. That same year saw a 33% increase in the number of Japanese elementary, junior high, and high school students who died by suicide[3]. The most recent survey by the National Crime Records Bureau in India found that of the total number of suicides in the country, 6.7% were by current students, the most common factors identified were stress and depression[4]. The use of Artificial Intelligence to interrogate vast amounts of data and to identify a specific individual in need of help is increasingly viewed by counselling services as a valuable, if not an essential tool in their efforts to prevent these tragic losses.

One practical way in which AI is being used is through the use of machine learning to add context to internet searches. Not only can AI help to avert cybersecurity breaches and protect sensitive student data, it can also generate an alert, if, for example, it noticed a student searching about self-harm.

Communications and Community

Parents benefit from AI because it makes them more involved and engaged, but school leaders also benefit when AI makes it easier for the school, parents, and the local community to work together. Communication that works well is the basis for closer connections, and AI can help keep and improve these. It is

1 New Zealand Union of Students' Associations. (2018). Kei Te Pai? Report on Student Mental Health in Aotearoa. Retrieved from https://gallery.mailchimp.com/b109fde7924adea2d-9afaa28d/files/ ad0db517-d37f-4075-9984-6236b5838f0d/Kei_Te_Pai_Mental_Health_Report_Main_.pdf

2 Office for National Statistics. (2018). Suicides in the UK: 2018 registrations. Retrieved from https:// www.ons.gov.uk/releases/suicidesintheuk2018registrations

3 The Nippon Communications Foundation. (2019). Child Suicides at Highest Rate Ever in Japan. Retrieved from https://www.nippon.com/en/japan-data/h00572/child-suicides-at-highest-rate- ever-in-japan.html

4 Saha, D. (2017). Every hour, one student commits suicide in India. Hindustan Times. Retrieved from https://www.hindustantimes.com/health-and-fitness/every-hour-one-student-commits-suicide- in-india/story-7UFFhSs6h1HNgrNO60FZ2O.html

not only possible to personalize the kids' learning paths, but it is also possible to personalize how each parent is communicated with. It is important to know which methods or tools work best for each parent and what they are most interested in or worried about. This will help make sure that the parents get useful information and aren't left wanting more or too much. When there is open communication between the school, the parents, and the community, the school leader's voice is boosted. This is because the leader can get immediate feedback and a variety of points of view, which can help them make decisions about policies and long-term plans for the institution.

Local, Regional and National Administration

Ministries of Education, local governments, municipalities, and other groups that are in charge of managing and keeping an eye on groups of schools or colleges depend on correct and up-to-date information. In the past, these groups have put a lot of emphasis on gathering data to help them make decisions. However, most of the time, this data is old and no longer relevant by the time it is gathered. It is not smart or necessary to plan for the future using only knowledge from the past.

AI, Data & Analytics, and Machine Learning technologies can take in all the available data and turn it into insights that can help with planning, even if different administrative groups are at different stages of their data journey. Because AI can come up with these insights in real time and keep updating that advice as new data comes in, it helps planners predict and measure important parts of the planning process. With enhanced intelligence, having your finger in the air can turn into having your finger on the pulse.

Resource Planning

AI can help with services like predictive maintenance of plant and industrial, IT, and electronic assets. This lets planners make sure they have the right resources as the environment changes. It can also keep track of important demographic information, capital needs, staffing and professional development needs, and more. The COVID-19 pandemic showed how important it is to have up-to-date information on hand so that quick plans for what to do in case of an emergency can be made. These plans can also be made ahead of time using accurate models to cover a range of possible situations. No one knows what the long-term effects of the pandemic will be on things like travel and traffic, working from home and childcare issues, a possible shift in population away from city centers as people don't have to travel to an office, or a continued reliance on online learning facilities and services.

Regional and national governments have mostly done a great job of handling the current problem. However, not all students have been served equally, and it took a while for best practices to be found and used again. With AI, it will be possible to look at all the different situations that could happen and have the knowledge and possible answers ready for when the next crisis happens.

Curriculum Design

It is always hard to make sure that college and school courses are up-to-date and prepare students well for the world they will face after they graduate. Knowledge is always growing and changing in many fields, such as, but not limited to, the sciences and technologies. This makes it hard to make sure that course material is current and up to date. As methods and emphasis shift and different skills become more or less important, the curriculum must also change and adapt. Lack of important skills and abilities can slow down economies and societies, which can stop or slow down growth for their countries. When there aren't enough skilled teachers or college spots in important subjects, demand can go over supply for a long time. There is more to education than just helping the economy of a country. Education is both an end and a means. It is the foundation on which all economies are built.

That's something AI can't do by itself. Changing a national curriculum on a big scale takes years of work and involves a huge number of stakeholders and people who are interested. Big data sets can be queried, analyzed, and insights can be found. These insights can then be shown through dashboards and visualizations that are customized to the needs and roles of those designing curriculum. This can make the information more up-to-date and accurate, and prepare those doing this important work better.

Challenges

Equity, Equality and Access

The term "digital divide" has been around since the late 1990s, but it was never meant to be a simple way to compare how easy it is for students and teachers to use computers and the internet. People came up with the phrase to show that there was a growing gap between those who "have information" and those who "have not." Information, not hardware, software, or broadband access, was the most important thing to look at back then and is still the most important thing to look at now when looking at unfair distribution of education tools.

The intervening years have seen significant advances, with hardware devices becoming cheaper, more powerful and more mobile, and increased battery life and alternate forms of connectivity enabling an additional number of learners to get online. However, the most recent global report on internet penetration[1] reported that 43% of the world's population still do not have access to the internet, and an estimated 40% of people have never once been online. The disparity between the most and least connected regions is stark. In North America and Northern Europe 95% of all citizens have access to information via the internet. In Middle Africa only 12% have the same opportunity.

This difference was made clear by the COVID-19 outbreak, which has been called a "homework gap." As of August 2020, most of the countries that were impacted had access to the internet, but it wasn't everywhere. A significant percentage of underserved students also report having access to only a single device — most often a smartphone — and insufficient internet access at home[2]. When you think about how hard it is to write a paper, look at data, or even read a lot, this different access puts these kids at a huge disadvantage.

AI starts with data. While teachers and institutions manually recording data can help close this gap, as more and more data is captured electronically, students who can't get to the information they need to help them with their studies or who can't create and share electronic data may not be able to get the help they need in creating personalized learning pathways that meet their needs.

The Ethical Dimension

For all students to benefit from AI in the classroom, rules and moral guidelines will need to be put in place. At the moment, private companies are the ones leading the way in using AI in education. This has raised worries about how student data is used, protected, and kept private. Organizations that make money can do a lot to promote the educational benefits of new technologies. However, their priorities will be different from those who are responsible for educating everyone, and the cost of these services may keep out groups of students who need them the most.

An ethical basis for AI is needed not only when the services and solutions that use AI are being deployed, but also when they are being developed. How

1 Pensworth, L. (2019). 2019 Internet Statistics, Trends & Data. DailyWireless. Retrieved from https:// dailywireless.org/internet/usage-statistics/

2 ACT Center for Equity in Learning. (2018). The Digital Divide and Educational Equity. Retrieved from https://equityinlearning.act.org/wp-content/themes/voltron/img/tech-briefs/the-digital-divide.pdf

can we make sure that biases based on gender, race, socioeconomic status, or skill don't show up in the programming? What can be done to stop the spread of social and cultural stereotypes? What can we do to make sure that all students, no matter where they live, have the same chance to benefit?

As these technologies become more powerful and influential, they will have an impact on education and, by extension, students' opportunities and values. To make sure that AI-enabled technologies respect and strengthen basic human rights, and that using AI in education helps to reach the Sustainable Development Goals, especially SDG 4, which says that everyone should have access to high-quality education and be able to keep learning throughout their lives, there will need to be openness and oversight.

Technology Dependence

All of the people listed in this brief can gain a great deal from artificial intelligence or augmented intelligence. People will always need to be involved in the right way to use AI effectively. AI may give people the most valuable thing it can: time. Time for teachers, administrators, and others to spend planning lessons, coming up with new and creative ways to help students learn, and evaluating and using AI's insights to create individualized learning paths for each student.

So, technology is more likely to make the job of the teacher stronger than to take it away. For the most part, relying more on AI will be good for us. In both the developed and emerging worlds, more and more jobs will likely be taken over by machines. It's also possible that the ability to give chores and mental abilities to machines could make us more dependent on technology while weakening our own abilities to do these things. This could be seen as a "use it or lose it" situation. Do kids who spend a lot of time on computers lose the ability to write clearly? Do people who use a spreadsheet or calculator for numbers get worse at doing math in their heads? Has our need for GPS made it harder to travel, or better yet, "find our own way"? It will be more important than ever to know where we want to go as these tools get smarter and better at what they do.

Continuous Professional Development

In order for AI to be useful in education, teachers and managers will need to be able to evaluate and understand the results. Luckily, you don't need to know a lot about technology to do this. People often think they know more about technology than they actually do when it comes to current AI solutions. Most teachers and managers already know enough about technology to be able to evaluate and use what they've learned if they know how to use a smartphone and/or a laptop. AI systems that work well create visualizations and dashboards that are easy to understand and let users query the data and learn from it in real time. It's easy to make views and reports that are specific to different roles and tasks. Continuing professional development (CPD) in this case is mostly about showing teachers how to use the insights they get to improve their lessons and help their students make their own unique learning paths.

Software and cloud services will probably change over time, just like all technologies. They may also be replaced by services or solutions from other companies or providers. Because of this, it is important for teachers to know about any new features and changes to the user interface (UI).

Adapting to Learning Speed while Scaling Change

If we believe in AI's promise, then maybe the hardest thing for governments and people in charge of schools will be how to make sure that all students can gain from it. It's clear that the use of AI in education has grown and changed over time, both at the formal and systemic levels:

1. Data Collection
2. Data Analysis
3. Data Visualization
4. Derive Insights
5. Predict Outcomes
6. Direct Outcomes

There is no way to skip any of these important steps and get to a point where AI is not only giving useful information but also helping lawmakers make decisions that will really make a difference. It's possible that different institutions or systems are at different stages of this process. The first thing that needs to be done is to figure out where they are on the continuum. The process of gathering data is ongoing, so it is still possible to move forward even if most of the data is not yet digitized and/or ready for analysis. The AI system will work better and be more accurate as more data is added.

An acceptable technology solution will need to be put in place in order to look at the data, make visualizations, and gain insights. The data needs to be kept somewhere, like in the cloud, an on-premises data store, or a hybrid cloud system that does both. Data privacy and security measures must be put in place, and all laws, like the General Data Protection Regulation (GDPR), must be carefully followed. Next, we need to create and/or use an AI solution that can take in Big Data, use Predictive Analytics, make detailed Dashboards and Visualizations, and use Machine Learning to make the insights and predictions that the AI solution makes more accurate and up-to-date over time.

AI in education solutions and services can be put in place at any time, unlike most technology deployments, which happen at set times (usually when the school is closed for holiday or some other reason). AI will continue to grow and change as it is used. Iteratively, sequentially, or at the same time, AI applications can be done. Some schools start with just one department or staff and then add data from other sources to their solutions and services as they grow across campus. At the systemic level, AI is usually used across the whole system with a focus on a specific data source or sources. For example, it might take in data from attendance records and grade scores to help find kids who are likely to drop out of school. Either way will work with a good technology solution that can make reports and dashboards that meet the needs of everyone involved as the AI implementation goes forward.

Data-mining is a term that is often used to describe these kinds of technological answers, and it fits here. Data sources are like fields of information that haven't been fully explored yet, full of "nuggets" that are just ready to be found. You just need to find the right tools to get to the important ideas you need. These things can help right away once they've been exposed. So, any plan to use AI in education needs to be in line with how people learn. Another way AI is transformative is that it can figure out when course changes or interventions are needed during the learning process, rather than after the fact. Most assessment methods are historical, which means they look at past performance based on tests that were given after the fact. AI is more than just another way to test students all the time. When used correctly, it lets teachers and managers guess how students will do in the future and make plans for how to meet their needs before they happen, so that things can change as quickly as they are learned.

The Future Unfolds

Cognitive Services

Cognitive Services are a group of new technologies that help programmers make apps that can see, hear, speak, understand, and even start to think for themselves. They let developers add features to their apps like detecting emotions and mood, recognizing speech and images, and understanding natural language, even if they don't have any direct AI or data science skills or knowledge. Large companies like Microsoft make these services available to developers as sets of AI algorithms and application programming interfaces (APIs). This makes it easy to add them to current solutions to make them better.

In the business world, these kinds of tools are already everywhere. A lot of people now use computer vision and speech recognition programs to get into their phones. National Language Processing (NLP) lets people search the web by asking a question in their own words and sentences by using natural language. Text to speech and speech to text services can be used to make papers and websites read aloud.

What this means for education is huge. They can help close the gaps in access and chance, especially for students with disabilities, and make education more open to everyone. Learning difficulties like reading and math problems can be fixed so that students with these problems can be involved in higher-level activities while they are still learning these basic skills. They don't have to wait until they are fully improved. When added to other AI solutions and services, they can speed up the creation of important insights. For example, a teacher can just ask the AI a question instead of typing in a long query with a computer or mouse.

Virtual, Mixed and Augmented Reality

Virtual reality (VR) puts the person in a computer-made world that they can't leave. Virtual reality (VR) experiences are usually done through a headset, which can be connected to a computer or gaming console or used on its own. The most advanced VR experiences can let users move freely within a digital world, hear sounds, and use hand controllers to move around and simulate tactile sensations.

Augmented reality (AR) lets people see and interact with the real world while also watching digital content. They can do this by wearing special glasses or headsets that put the digital content on top of the real world.

Virtual objects and the real world can be mixed together in mixed reality (MR), which lets the user communicate with both. Not only can the user see digital material, but they can also interact with virtual objects that can be rooted in the real world.

VR, AR, and MR learning material can change the way we learn by making it more immersive and interesting. With virtual reality (VR), students can go anywhere in the world from their classroom and experience a recreation of that world at any point in time. AR lets students see holographic instructions or information superimposed on top of a real object, giving them more knowledge about the object they are looking at. MR can be used, for example, in medical training or engineering, allowing students to 'dissect' limbs or 'repair' machinery which they view as holograms within the real-world environment, enabling learners to focus on practice rather than theory[1]. Although these new

1 Microsoft HoloLens. (2017). Windows Mixed Reality: An Evolution for Education. Re-

technologies are still evolving, the speed of change is exponential and some education technologists are already predicting that, in the future, low-cost versions of such technologies will supplant the textbook and free learners from the confines of their classroom.

AI will make it possible not just to deploy these exciting new technologies — but to analyze their effectiveness and to optimize the benefits they can provide to students and educators alike.

IoT and Edge Computing

The Internet of Things (IoT) describes the network of physical objects (things) that are embedded with sensors, software and other technologies, which allow them to connect and exchange data with other devices and systems over the internet, without involving a human being. An IoT device can be as simple as a lightbulb which can be turned on and off remotely, or as complex as a driverless car. There are already more connected 'things' than there are people, and researchers have predicted that there will be more than 40 billion such devices by 2025[1].

Many schools are already using the Internet of Things to help them run their buildings more efficiently and for less money. For example, sensors can be used to change the temperature and lighting in buildings and classrooms based on how many people are using them, which saves energy and money on costs. Remote cameras and biometrics can also be used to make campuses safer.

Edge computing is a way of organizing information technology (IT) in which data is handled at the network's edge, close to the user or the source of the data. This means that the data doesn't have to be sent to a central location (the cloud) to be saved or processed. This saves time and bandwidth. The main benefit of edge computing is that it might lower delay, which means that things can happen more quickly.

New Ways of Doing

Metacognitive Scaffolding

For example, scaffolding means giving a student help only when they need it and decreasing (or "dialing down") the help as the student gets better. The use of AI in education not only lets teachers know when and where a student

trieved from https://www.youtube.com/watch?v=7Xv8A9vqeBw

1 International Data Corporation. (2019). The Growth in Connected IoTDevices Is Expected to Generate 79.4ZB of Data in 2025, According to a New IDC Forecast. Retrieved from https://www.idc.com/ getdoc.jsp?containerId=prUS45213219

needs help, but also keeps track of when to give or take away help based on the student's growth in learning. As both resources and teachers' time are limited, this can have big effects on an institution's ability to meet the needs of all of its students effectively and efficiently. This helps them improve the way they teach and help as many students as possible graduate at the end of their learning journey.

There are many good things about new learning settings, but they can also be hard for some students. Students need to be able to manage their own problem-solving and learning more than ever before in order to do well in group or collaborative settings, to take advantage of the new learning methods and modalities that may come with flipped classrooms or remote learning, and to communicate clearly in a variety of media. Students will need help making plans and getting ready to learn, keeping track of what they're understanding while they're learning, and reviewing what they've learned at the end of a learning experience.

It is possible for AI to help with metacognitive support by letting students use the insights they gain along their learning paths. More and more, kids will be the main people who use AI services and solutions, not just the data that teachers, administrators, and system owners look at. When a student knows more about how they learn and how they think, they have more control over their education and important self-knowledge that will help them keep learning throughout their life.

Personalized Assessment and Credentialing

Technology is helping to open up education by letting students learn anywhere and at any time. This means that students who can't go to a real school or college can still reach their full potential. Building on the progress made in using technology in education over the last few decades, AI could make personalized learning a reality by allowing it to process huge amounts of data and derive insights that can be used to create a learning path that fits each student's needs and abilities.

AI will also be a big part of the next big problem that education technologists have to solve: how to make personalized testing possible. We know that the way our schools and colleges test kids now doesn't always match up with the skills that employers will be looking for when they come out of school. Remembering, comparing, analyzing, and drawing conclusions are some of the higher-order thinking skills that will be needed in the 21st century that can be tested by multiple-choice, long-form, and short-form tests. But it's hard to test "soft skills" like moral character, teamwork, collaboration, and the ability to work well with others, which are just as important to future employers and a graduate's ability to survive and thrive in the 21st century workplace.

Performance-based assessments, student portfolios, and standards-based projects and tasks that require students to use their knowledge and skills are being added to standardized tests by many schools and institutions. With these formative and summative types of tests, teachers can give their students quick feedback instead of looking at how well they did on past tests, which is what most state tests do. In real life, giving students more than one chance to be evaluated will inevitably lead to a huge increase in the amount of data that needs to be kept track of and examined by both teachers and administrators. If this data is to be used to give accurate and helpful feedback about a student's progress, AI will be needed.

There is also an increasing demand for new forms of credential which can provide a fuller picture of student capability and accurately represent the breadth of what students know and can do — and who they have become — as a result of their learning. Many institutions and an increasing number of school systems are investigating the use of micro-credentials that measure complex and general learning capabilities, including such 21st century skills as critical thinking, creativity, communication skills and entrepreneurship[1]. These micro-credentials are often created with employers and/or backed by them to show that they are useful and to help build a stronger relationship with the local business community.

The process of making new documents is a big job. At the systemic level, it will usually take months or years of work, involve many people, require a long consultation process, and change how the program is designed. If these new credentials are to stay useful after they are introduced, it will also be important to keep an eye on how well they work and show the results and insights using real-time dashboards that are specific to the interests or areas of expertise of each stakeholder.

When we look at how teaching and learning are changing along with technology, it is clear that AI and the use of data, analytics, and machine learning will be a big part of what students learn and the possibilities they have in the next ten years. AI is already making a difference in education for kids, teachers, school leaders, parents, administrators, and system owners. It will be a major force for change.

---

1 Milligan, S., Luo, R., Hassim, E., Johnston, J. (2020). Future-proofing students: What they need to know and how educators can assess and credential them. Melbourne Graduate School of Education, The University of Melbourne. 17-29. Retrieved from https://education.unimelb.edu.au/__data/ assets/pdf_file/0005/3397469/MGSE_Future-Proofing-Students_Web_Updated-9-7-20.pdf

Chapter 9

Artificial Intelligence and Personalized Learning: Realizing the Full Potential- An Analysis

Technology has been used in schools for a long time. The entrance of digital tools into the school was a turning point. In the 1980s, desk-top computers were first used in schools to start this trend. Since then, digitization has spread to every part of schooling. Computers were linked together by global networks, the Internet gave students access to a huge range of teaching materials and methods, and managerial tasks like keeping track of students and other tasks were carried out automatically. Along with computers, more and more other gadgets were brought into schools that either replace or work with desktop computers.

Along with the improvement of digital tools and their ability to connect to more devices, the huge amount of data that these tools create and their computer power has also grown a lot. As a result, more and more intelligent systems are being used. These systems can find patterns in huge amounts of data and are getting better at mimicking human behavior, particularly reasoning. Because of this, these systems can either do things on their own or help users do them.

These new developments in AI could change the way we learn by making personalized apps possible. An artificial intelligence (AI) system could decide what students learn and how well they do in school. Bloom (1984) says that students who get one-on-one tutoring do two standard deviations better than students who go to school the old-fashioned way. Personalized one-on-one learning is not usually possible for everyone because there are not enough teachers and it costs a lot. There is also evidence that teachers are having to deal with more work. This means that learning apps that use AI could be good for both students and teachers, making them more productive.

From a sociotechnical point of view, this chapter looks at how AI has changed schooling. We look at new ideas that could hit the market in the next five to eight years. First, we look at the tools that make AI possible, especially machine learning. We look at how AI is being used in schooling right now. As a final touch to this section, we will give an outline of how AI systems can be used in education. The next step is to look at these AI systems' effects on society, the law, and ethics. Finally, we list the top five possibilities and threats that come with using AI in education and suggest ways to deal with them.

Methodology

To answer the study question, more than one method was used. The study of AI's uses and applications in education is mostly based on reviews of the literature and talks with people inside and outside of education. A workshop of experts was also set up to come up with the final list of possibilities and risks. One problem with this part is that it only talks about one situation: the Dutch school system. Still, a lot of the results can be used to improve education systems in a wider way. The uses of AI and social issues are especially important for education in general. The legal advice and, to a lesser extent, the policy advice are more situational and will be most useful for the Netherlands and other countries with similar schooling and legal systems.

Interviews

The people who were interviewed were Dutch scientists who work in AI, educational science, and educational innovation. In order to get a full picture of what AI can do in education, interviews were also done with school leaders, teachers, and developers of AI apps for education. Last but not least, ethicists were asked to think about the moral problems that come up when AI is used in schooling. People who were interviewed were chosen in part based on their name and the assumption that they were experts in the subject, and in part based on snowball sampling. Snowball sampling is a way in which people who took part in the chapter suggest that other people take part in follow-up interviews. One benefit of this method is that it lets people who are hard to reach, like teachers, still be a part of the chapter through links.

Literature review

Most of the analyses that look at the foreign situation, technical options, and legal issues are based on scientific literature. First, as much information as possible about how AI can be used in education was gathered. Then, the information was organized and framed, using some of what was learned from conversations. A methodical technique was used to look at the legal aspects, beginning with a legal interpretation of AI in education. This is then turned into acts and actors that are legally important so that laws and rules can be found that apply to them. This evaluation leads to a talk about the legal effects based on action and control.

History of AI

AI has been around longer than most people think. The idea of automating human behavior and thought goes back to ancient times. Greek stories talk about bronze robots called Talos that kept pirates away from Crete. Stories about the Golem of Prague from the Middle Ages also have AI ideas. Ideas about AI today can be traced back to the early days of computers, to people like Turing, Walters, and Minsky.

Scientist John McCarthy came up with the word "artificial intelligence" in 1956. Since then, the field of science has gone through a number of cycles, with high points when AI was getting a lot of attention and then low points when it was criticized and disappointed. So far, there have been three big waves in the field of AI. Pioneers at MIT and Stanford sparked the idea in the 1950s and 1960s, around the same time that the term was formed. During the 1970s, however, study budgets were drastically cut because AI wasn't really able to do things like translate texts from Russian to English, which was needed at the time because of the Cold War and was thought to be something AI could do. An AI made a bad translation from Russian to English of "The mind is willing but the flesh is weak," which means "the vodka is good but the meat is spoiled."

Japan made a strong commitment to AI in the 1980s so that it could help its economy move forward. Soon after, the United States and the United Kingdom did the same. Expert systems were in charge of AI at this time. Expert systems do certain jobs and actions that people do. All of these systems' "intelligence" is designed by hand. That's why the AI couldn't learn how to do new things without someone writing the new rules it needs. The systems work like a pre-programmed "decision tree" that checks if/else lines in a planned way to make a choice. In the end, expert systems did not work as well as planned because the rules they used were made by hand. It was often too hard for the AI engineer to write all the rules by hand into an expert system. Because of this, AI lost a lot of attention again in the 1990s.

AI has recently come back to life thanks to people like Andrew Ng, Geoffrey Hinton, and Yann LeCun. They set the stage for deep learning. A type of machine learning called "deep learning" It is a group of programs that can learn from data. With deep learning, problems that were thought to be impossible before were suddenly seen as possible. Let's look at AlphaGo, a computer program made by Google that beat the world winner at the Go game in 2016. A lot of people thought that humans were the only ones who could play Go at a high level until that point. There are 10172 possible moves in Go, which is a lot more than in chess. The number of moves is too high for standard methods (like a minimax tree search) to find the best plan.

Deep learning searches for a connection between what goes into a model and what comes out of it over and over again using a number of mathematical changes. The basic idea behind these changes comes from the way our brains work, which is called a "neural network." The things we sense activate brain cells called neurons. When these neurons sense a stimulus, they might or might not send messages to other neurons. Hundreds of billions of neurons work together to make complex behavior possible. When using machine learning, a general rule is that as more data is used to teach the model, it gets better at what it does. Because more and more tasks are being done digitally, a lot of data is being created that can be used for this. This, along with computer power that keeps getting stronger and academic breakthroughs, makes it possible for progress in the area of machine learning to grow very quickly.

Deep learning is a technology that can be used for many things, not just schooling. It can be used in many ways that are as good as or better than human performance. Deep learning is used in medicine to find skin cancer and sort CT pictures into different groups. Deep learning is used in self-driving cars to figure out the car's speed and direction based on data from the camera. In the fight against fake news, Facebook uses deep learning to figure out how real a text is.

Educational AI Applications

In the area of educational AI applications, there are different kinds of groups working. On the one hand, we can see that some companies give digital learning materials a "machine learning layer." In this case, machine learning methods are being used to replace classification based on rules that were made by hand. Additionally, several start-ups are testing how AI can be used in schooling. Big tech companies like Google and Facebook are leading the way in AI development, but they aren't very present in the Dutch schooling market. This is likely because AI needs specific contextual info from students (in this case Dutch students) that is hard to get.

There are different kinds of fundamental research that can be done in the area of AI. Experimenting with different ways to use AI in schooling is another way to learn useful skills. We can also see that schools and teachers have begun to use AI in their own lessons. IT teachers who know how to use AI do this to make their work easier. These skills can be used in the classroom, especially by business teachers who have worked with machine learning before.

In general, AI can be used in education to teach and test knowledge and skills, to keep teachers up to date on their students' growth and accomplishments, and to transfer knowledge and skills. Here is a list of all the ways AI can be used in education that were found and grouped during the study.

Adaptive learning systems

An adaptive learning system is a computerized tool for learning that changes as little as possible to fit the user. This makes the learning process more effective and/or helps students do better in school. In order to do this, a flexible learning system has the following parts:

1. **Expert model**. This is a model that possesses all the information that will eventually have to be transferred to the student. This model is also aware of the degree of difficulty of the information, and the hierarchical structure between the concepts.
2. **Student model**. This model keeps track of what information the learner has already learned and what skill level the learner has. In fact, it models the way a learner learns.
3. **Instruction model**. This model is specialized in teaching methods. The model knows what the best way to give feedback to a specific student, and when to apply certain didactic strategies such as productive failure (first let the student try it himself before the correct answer is given). The model combines information from the expert model and the student model in order to determine the most suitable instructions.

There are both simple statistical methods (like Bayesian statistics) and more complicated deep learning techniques that can be used to build the models listed above. A study from Stanford University researchers shows that a Deep Knowledge Tracing model is better at modeling what the student knows than a Bayesian model, but it is also (much) less clear. Similar things happen when you compare deep learning-based models to more traditional statistical methods: a deep learning model learns a connection between input and output, but it's not clear what factors make up that connection. It is easy to see and understand the path from an input parameter to an output in a smaller statistical model. But with millions of parameters in a deep learning model, the path is not as clear.

At some point, all three parts are put together in a user interface that the student can use. It's not easy to make a system for flexible learning. Several goals need to be improved at the same time in an adaptive learning system. There are times when these goals are at odds with each other and times when there is a way to balance them. A system that adapts to learning might try to teach the student as much complicated information as quickly as possible. But what does this mean for the student? Any questions that are too easy make it hard for the student to learn quickly enough, and any questions that are too hard make them lose interest, which can hurt their performance in the long run. A system for flexible learning can also "go crazy." Something like this could happen: a student might be good at statistics in general but have trouble with regression. In the long run, an adaptable learning system might only offer this student work on going backwards. But on the test, questions are asked about everything, and the student hasn't studied enough for the parts that aren't regression.

Automated essay scoring

AES, or automated essay scoring, is a way to grade written works like essays and papers without a person being involved. Natural language processing is what AES uses to judge a written text based on its content and style. In automatic essay scoring, texts that have already been graded by hand are used to train a model. Next, methods for machine learning are used to find out how closely new texts match or contain parts of the texts that were used to make the model.

Analytical dashboards

More and more digital learning tools are being used in schools, and these systems are making more and more data. This information can be used to let the teacher know how the kids are doing. These kinds of screens are often used to do this. One example of a dashboard that shows student growth and performance is a pie chart that shows what percentage of students have mastered a certain skill. Another example is a line chart that shows how well a student has done over time. Even though these summary statistics aren't always very "smart" on their own, predictive modeling is being used more and more. For instance, combining data from a system that tracks students' whereabouts with information about their personalities could help make a model that can predict how well students will do in and out of school.

Classroom monitoring

Not only is AI used to help people learn and take tests in China, but it is also used to keep an eye on kids by using cameras to see who is paying attention.The teacher can talk to a student or use another method to get their attention based on this knowledge. People in Europe are also interested in and researching this kind of technology. In Switzerland and France, for instance, tech is being tested that uses cameras to look at kids and give real-time feedback to the teacher. In Europe, methods for keeping an eye on a classroom are mostly used for research purposes. These technologies are already being used in schools in China. It's important to note that putting the systems in Chinese classes doesn't seem to improve students' attention. If anything, it could be because of the effects Jeremy Bentham talks about in Panopticon. A panopticon is a type of jail where the prisoners are kept in line by making them feel like they are always being watched. A Chinese student's response says it all: "I dare not be distracted now that there are cameras in the classroom." It feels like a strange pair of eyes are always watching me.

Augmented reality, virtual reality & simulations

In more and more places around the world, people are trying to combine AI with other digital innovations. In Germany, research is being done that combines AI with augmented reality using smart glasses sc that the student can see directions right in front of their eyes. German researchers are looking into a lot of different things, such as how to combine augmented reality with smart teaching systems. Simulations, virtual reality, and AI are all being studied in Canada as well to see how they can be used together to make learning better. In these simulation settings, students are given real-world directions by an AI, and then they can start working on a problem right away.

Teachable robots

AI is being tried to work with other digital innovations in more and more places around the world. In Germany, smart glasses are being used in research that blends AI with augmented reality. This way, students can see directions right in front of their eyes. German experts are interested in many things, such as how to hook up augmented reality with smart classrooms. Along with AI, simulations are also being looked into in Canada to see how they can be used together to improve education. In these simulations, an AI tells students what to do in the real world, and then they can start working on a problem right away.

Properties of AI Applications

There are a lot of different ways that AI can be used in schooling, as you can see from the examples above. In order to make decisions about AI applications in the difference, it is necessary to look into which features of AI applications are important and set them apart. Here is a list of the most important things that make them different.

Didactical versus pedagogical

A lot of the ways AI is used in education are to make teaching tasks easier to do automatically. Some of these are choosing what to teach (usually in adaptive learning systems), going over tests (like automatically scoring essays), and giving students helpful comments (usually in intelligent tutoring systems). Teachers and instructors are also expected to do more than just pass on information. We also want them to learn how to get along with others, follow rules and ideals, and do other social skills. These things can also be done with an AI. Based on the skills and weaknesses of each student, an AI can choose the most diverse group of students for a group project, for example.

Subject specific or cross-curricular

Artificial intelligence (AI) can be used to teach someone about a subject or help them learn a skill. These AI apps that are focused on a certain subject are already being used to help students learn new languages or do math. When an AI app is used across multiple areas, it doesn't just teach one skill; it also looks at how well the student is doing in all of them. This way, the AI can tailor not only one skill but also the whole program to each student. More than in elementary school, the teacher already knows which student is working on what across subjects. But in higher and academic education, this is not as easy. Higher and academic education make it harder for teachers to see what's going on in the world outside of school. To make up for this, teachers in higher education are being renamed mentors to do these jobs that cross over into other subjects. An AI can help with this mentoring job by keeping an eye on a student's progress in all of their classes and, if necessary, identifying them.

Need for differentiation between students

Under the Dutch school system, a student's level and the year decide what subjects they are taught and how hard they are. The student can only go to a certain year or level if they have met certain performance standards in a number of courses. For example, at VWO, a student should be able to learn both math and a foreign language at the same level of difficulty. Artificial intelligence (AI) used as a flexible learning system can make it less important to tell the difference between years and levels. A student may be able to learn one subject more quickly and well than another with the help of an AI app. With an AI application, you can confirm each subject separately instead of all of them at once.

Level of autonomy

The level of autonomy in AI apps for education varies a lot. There are three main types of independence for AI applications in education:

1. The AI provides insight into student performance to the teacher.
2. The AI interprets and provides information on student performance to the teacher.
3. The AI gives direct recommendations to the student (and perhaps parents) without the intervention of the teacher.

When an AI is only used for sending signals and gathering information, it doesn't have a lot of freedom. In this case, the person who is using the information (the teacher) can choose whether to use it or not. The person can also choose for himself how to handle the information in this case. In the case of this helpful AI, for instance, picture a screen with advanced pattern recognition that shows how well students are doing. When AI is part of a flexible learning system, it already has some freedom. Adaptive learning systems can decide on their own which students should study which course material when and how they should be taught it. In the future, we might find even more self-driving devices that can do things without any help from a person.

The way the AI talks to people is another thing to think about. When it comes to giving information about how well students are doing, choices are made. How is the information given? How is the student's success made clear (over time or between students)? This also assumes that a teacher knows how to correctly interpret these facts. Because of this, the teacher should know how to read probabilities, what a confidence interval is, what statistical significance means, what a type 1 and 2 mistake is, and so on. There are also different things to think about when it comes to how information is presented.

Educational styles

AI applications can be used to help with both standard (often classroom-based) learning and new ways of learning. Digital learning tools today can be used in and out of the classroom, of course. It is also possible for other uses to occur that fit in with the way schooling works now. AI can be used to find absence in administrative systems, for instance. AI can also be used to make schedules work better. Blended learning is one more step toward using new ways to teach. Traditional schooling is mixed with digital tools for learning in blended learning. AI is used in more than just digital learning tools. It is also used to keep an eye on the classroom with different types of devices. Virtual reality and game-like elements can be used to keep students interested and motivated. VR can be used in places other than school. You can also teach more useful skills with VR than with, say, an adaptable learning system. Lastly, AI might make learning from afar better. Huge amounts of data are being gathered because Massive Online Open Courses (MOOCs) are digital and the material is digital. This information can be fed into an AI. Different kinds of information are gathered about students by MOOCs:

1. **Data on the learning process**: while students are studying, all kinds of data are collected, such as: what exercise the student did, how long the

student spends on an exercise, and what explanation the student received. These data can be used as input for an adaptive learning system.

2. **Data on the student**: Personal characteristics such as gender, country of origin and age, but also which other MOOCs the student has followed on the platform.
3. **Linking with external sources**: For internet-based services, it is often easier to achieve link with other systems. Many MOOC platforms offer the option of logging in with a Facebook account. Once this has been done, the MOOC platform can enrich existing data with external social media data. In this way, a MOOC can incorporate data that is generated outside the platform.

Accuracy and Interpretability

In general, AI apps use advanced models for making predictions. Additionally, a prediction is almost never 100% correct, though that doesn't mean a person would do better. The correctness of a model and how easy it is to understand are often two sides of the same coin. It's harder to understand more complicated AI-algorithms, especially the new deep learning algorithms, but they work much better. More and more, machine learning is being used to automate jobs that used to be done by people. This makes interpretable models even more important. When a model is used in real life, questions like "what is a model good at? what is a model bad at? how does a model come up with a prediction?"

Because of this, ways have been found to give people more information about complicated machine learning models. One way to figure out how a change in input affects the output of a model is to use Shapley Additive Explanation (SHAP). This makes it possible to show, even for the most complicated models, which traits it uses to make a choice and how it does so. The SHAP method can also be used with almost any algorithm, which makes it a unified way to understand what a model says will happen.

A lot of progress has been made in the area of convolutional neural networks to help us understand these models better. It is possible to see how each layer of a neural network is activated with feature visualization. To sum up, this shows that basic geometric shapes like edges and corners are picked up in the network's lower levels. And as we look deeper into the network, we see these geometric patterns put together in more complicated ways. Each layer of the network builds on the patterns of the layers below it to make traits that are more complicated. You can use these details to figure out what inputs the network looks at when making a prediction.

Modularity and Portability

An important thing about many AI apps is that they combine data from different sources. This means that service providers are likely to offer full solutions that include both the AI program and the dataset. It is usually hard to connect and share data between the different training systems that are used (even when AI isn't involved).

At the national level in the Netherlands, efforts have been made to standardize different parts of (mostly) digital learning tools. For example, these kinds of standards make it easier to create a single 'student identity" that can be used across multiple platforms. AI doesn't have a lot of this kind of standardization; instead, it has a lot of little pieces.

Societal Impact

AI and educational institutions

AI can be thought of as a computer tool for learning. Similarly, certain conditions must be met in order for AI to work well. A good digital system must be in place at the very least. At the very least, the digital infrastructure includes a fast internet connection and devices for teachers and kids. Also, data must be provided so that AI models can be trained. This can include data from systems that manage things like schools, the resources themselves, and the data that is made when people use those resources.

The conditions needed for AI systems to work well are not just technical. The people who run schools and teach must also be able to see the value in AI apps and know how to use them properly. For this to work, people who work in education need to know how to use technology well. Next, AI apps that are tailored to a certain subject can be used to help teach. Last but not least, an institution can move toward integrating different AI systems once users have enough experience using AI in a responsible way.

AI and students

AI will have different effects on different areas of schooling. When it comes to elementary school, AI can make it less likely for students to get a classroom explanation of a subject and more likely for them to get an explanation that is tailored to their skill level and way of learning. Students will have to spend more time in front of a computer screen in class because of this. Even so, we believe that there will still be a lot of face-to-face contact between the teacher and the student.

In secondary school, AI will not have as much of an effect on students as it will in primary school. Mostly, AI will be used in ways of teaching that are already being used on their own. At the moment and in the near future, AI systems are best for learning facts and checking what you know. AI will have a bigger effect on STEM subjects than on "alpha" subjects because STEM subjects are more set in stone. An AI is better at checking to see if a math problem was solved properly than it is at checking the arguments in an essay.

Large changes may happen because of MOOCs in higher education. It is possible that the same information and skills could be learned through a MOOC when AI is added to them. This would be faster, cheaper, and from a more reputable school than standard higher education. These changes will make it easier for students to follow classes put on by foreign institutions because they won't have to be in the classroom in person.

AI and teachers

The teacher is very important in the Dutch school system. The teacher could set up the lesson in any way they want. An AI must be designed using design thought, so this is the way to go about it. When you use design thought to make a technology, you put the user's needs first. For AI to be useful in education, it needs to be able to be used in a variety of ways and work with teachers' different ways of learning.

Along with the people who use the apps (students and children), teachers will be the ones who feel the effects of AI the most. There will be new tasks added to the curriculum, some tasks that are already there will become more important, and some tasks that are already there will be handled by AI. We see that choosing course material and grading are two of the main jobs that can be taken over. Another thing that an AI can do is give comments to the student. Some tasks can be done automatically by AI, which means the teacher has more time to focus on tasks that are hard or impossible for AI to do automatically, like social tasks like coaching and guiding. When AI is used, it will also create new jobs. As a teacher, you need to be able to understand what an AI says and act on that information in order to use it properly.

AI and the educational system

AI has the ability to have a big effect on the Dutch school system. Students are put into groups based on their skills because that's how the current school system works. Being able to teach a subject at a certain level of difficulty is made easy by this. It will be less about general "education levels" and more about the topics when AI is used for personalized learning.

AI can get rid of the need for tests that are all the same. One thing that people don't like about standardized tests is that they only show how well a student did at one time. With AI, a learner's progress can be tracked as they go through the learning process. This gets rid of the need to test at certain times and gives a more accurate picture of a student's skills.

Legal Impact

Dutch law says that rights and duties can only belong to people. People who are real people and legal organizations, like a BV, a foundation (like some schools), or the State (like the Ministry of Education, Culture, and Science), are the two types of legal subjects. AI: Can we count it as one or the other?

One could say that an AI is like a person in some ways, since it can learn and make choices without help from people. However, AI is not a real person, and the Dutch legal system says that AI cannot be a legal body because it is not allowed to be one. Finally, we can say that AI technology is not a real or legal person, so it does not have its own rights and duties.

This means that there is always a person behind "the actions of an AI" who has the rights (like intellectual property rights) and/or duties (like being responsible for AI decisions that cause harm). This is possible as long as the law rules for aid cases, assistants, and legal representatives are followed.

After looking at Dutch laws, we can say that the legal status of an AI in education will always rest on what it is used for. In any case, the following can be said about this in a broad sense:

1. The application of AI in education touches on various generic regulations of various kinds. Some of these regulations are of supplementary law, which means that they can easily and often be deviated from by contract, such as the regulations of the Copyright Act and the Database Law.
2. The flexibility of these private laws is much less evident in the rules of public law, such as the rules on disclosure and re-use of administrative or public sector information. The applicability of these regulations may discourage developers from entering into partnerships with institutions if this would mean that their knowledge would become obsolete. Supplementary contracts on intellectual property rights can (partly) offer a helping hand here. However, it has to be ensure that cooperation with market parties does not ultimately lead to the creation of dominant positions that may conflict with rules on competition.
3. Decisions taken by institutions are, of course, entirely governed by the general rules of administrative law, including the general principles of

sound administration. Applying these principles to AI can be difficult because they inherently clash with the black box that AI creates. But it does not seem to be an unsolvable problem.

4. Rules on the protection of personal data (GDPR) are highly applicable to AI. The nature of the personal data in education and the character of AI very difficult to imagine that large-scale AI would be permitted without a statutory regulation. Of course, this will change completely if the data to be used are no longer personal data.
5. If something goes wrong due to the application of AI, there do not seem to be any noteworthy problems with the application of the laws on liability. This set of laws is very open and flexible so that those who are disadvantaged by AI applications should not be put at risk.
6. The education-specific sectoral rules in themselves leave a great deal of freedom and do not seem to contain any harsh restrictions. However, it will always be necessary to act with regards to the principles of education law. In addition, the interests of the child will always have to form a central and ethical point of reference, and the question will always arise as to whether this is the case with AI.

Ethical Impact

The question of whether or not certain AI uses are technically possible or legal is not relevant; what matters is whether or not those uses are needed and desired. People in the education field think that this moral decision should eventually rest with teachers and schools. We will now talk about some ethical issues that are especially important when AI is used in schooling. Norms and standards show what people in a society want. But not all of them were written into the law. Not only do norms and ideals affect how you use technology, they can also be built into it, whether you are aware of it or not. On the other hand, an engineer might plan for uses that are different from those of the user (because they are in line with the engineer's standards and values).

There are many people with a stake in education, mainly the teachers and schools, the students, and the parents. Each has their own set of rules and ideals. An AI program also has (implicit) rules and values that might not match the rules and values of the different people involved.

Several social issues connected to the use of AI in education have been talked about in this chapter. The people involved can form an opinion about AI uses based on this set by weighing the factors in light of their own standards and values. Keep in mind that many of the things that were talked about are not brand new and are also important in a broader sense, whether it's for AI or for schooling in general.

Transparancyy, explainability, and predictability

When an AI is used to help people make choices or makes decisions on its own, the person using it gives some of the ethical issues over to the AI. When the driver of a self-driving car gives up control, he is still responsible for what happens. Because of this, it is important for the user to know what could happen and be able to decide if those results are morally okay for him. When making an AI program, you need to know the following:

- On what data was the AI trained, and is it possible that certain biases may occur in it (which may lead to a bias in decisions or conclusions of the AI)?
- To what extent does the AI continue to learn, and how is it ensured that no bias arises?
- How is the underlying algorithm of the AI structured, and how does the AI deal with examples it has never seen before? Under what circumstances are outcomes of the algorithm correct or incorrect?

Unbribable

An AI should (as much as possible) make decisions that are based on facts and shouldn't be affected by outside factors. If AI can be controlled, it can be used for bad things. People often say that AES systems are bad because they praise students for how they use words instead of what they know. One way to trick an AES system is to use language that is linked to complex thinking without paying attention to the content. Think about how often you use "nevertheless" instead of "but."

Privacy and self-determination

People's privacy and right to make their own decisions can be violated when AI is used. For example, modeling a student (even if only partially) could be seen as a breach of these rights, especially if there are no limits on how the model can be used.

AI in different ethical theories

Different ethical models can be used to look at the above issues. Kant says that rules are set ahead of time and that an AI program can't break them under any circumstances (i.e. the end never justifies the means). From a practical point of view, morality depends on the result: if an AI that can't be explained clearly does better than other options, it probably wouldn't be moral not to use it. Lastly, virtue ethics says that arguments should be based on the application's own qualities. In this case, this means that the AI's design principles should be judged on their morality. Goals are also very important in virtue ethics, which is also called teleology. For this reason, AI can be used in an ethical way when it is used for good things. We will look at these ethical theories in more detail below as we talk about how they can be used with an adaptive learning system that makes decisions that can't be explained.

On the basis of Kant's ideas, using an AI with an adaptive learning system that can't be explained by its methods can't be called ethical use. No matter how good an AI program is, it will always have to follow the rules of ethics. Even if the learner learns a lot faster in the adaptive setting, it is unethical to use because it is not clear how the personalized learning material is made.

The pros and cons are weighed against each other from a practical point of view. For the adaptable learning system, it will be important to see if the better learning makes up for the fact that it can't be explained. When everyone agrees that using AI will make things better, When compared to what would happen without AI, it may be morally okay to use AI.

In virtue ethics, goals are very important. Because the adaptive learning method is hard to explain, one might wonder if it is being used for a good cause. Does the method help students do better in school or help the school trim down on the number of teachers it needs? In the first situation, there is a valid goal. In the second, it is possible to question whether using systems with unclear logic to cut costs is a valid goal.

Opportunities and Threats

AI is a tool that can be used in many ways to achieve many goals in the field of education. In the next section, we'll talk about the biggest pros and cons of using AI in education that were found in this chapter.

Opportunities

Reducing the workload of teachers

One of the best things about AI in education is that it can help teachers deal with problems linked to their work load. In the past few years, the teacher has often shown unhappiness with the large amount of work that comes with teaching.

The extra work teachers have to do is partly because they are getting fewer new teachers and partly because they are given more management tasks on top of their regular tasks. AI can help the teacher by taking care of routine tasks automatically, which will make their job easier.

What we think AI will soon be able to do automatically or make easier are mostly proofreading tasks (like pointing out what's good and bad about an essay so the teacher can focus on those areas) and writing course materials (with the help of automatically sorting content).

Personalized learning

From what we can see, using AI for individual learning is seen as a great chance. Teachers only have so much time and attention to give each student, so they can't teach each one directly. AI doesn't have this problem. This lets an AI better match what students want to learn with what they are being taught. This way, the teacher can focus more on "problem students," and each student can go through the lessons at his or her own level and pace. The process of automating jobs will move along slowly. At first, we think it will start with small jobs like choosing and practicing course material. Deep learning algorithms could help make adaptive learning systems better, which could help with these jobs.

Supporting the teacher with data-driven insights (learning analytics)

AI can help the teacher by putting together facts and making it easy to understand. With these learning statistics, the teacher can learn more about each student in a complete and sound way. AI can show cognitive biases, which can make schooling more fair when it comes to things like race or gender. In the case of school advice, an AI that doesn't know about race or gender can't take these things into account. It is known that students who came to the United States from outside the Western world usually get worse school advice than students who were born in the United States. An AI can help a teacher get rid of any unconscious biases they may have.

Improved assessment

AI can help the area of assessment move from doing assessments every so often to doing assessments all the time. One big problem with standardized tests is that they only show a picture of what a student knows and not a good reflection of what they know. With AI, a student's level of knowledge can be constantly checked without having to take tests on a regular basis.

Synergy with other digital learning applications

Lastly, AI can make digital learning tools more useful by replacing rules that were programmed by hand with rules that the AI has learned. AI can work well with new technologies like VR, AR, and serious games, making them work better together. These technologies make it possible to fully control a virtual area, which helps students learn more. There is a chance that knowledge gained in a virtual world won't be applied fully to "the real world," and that students won't pay as much attention to other, less formalized knowledge they gain at school, like social skills.

Threats

Educational objectives can be jeopardised by AI if the emphasis is on technology

As AI grows into more focused data and technology, there is a chance that its uses will no longer be in line with educational goals. For instance, an AI that is designed to share information might not have been able to include other things like motivation. There is also a chance that companies from other countries will get into the Dutch schooling market. There is no way to know for sure that these actors have the same training goals. We might lose control of schooling because of this.

Some people might wonder if education won't become cruel when it's fully automatic and students go through the steps of learning without any help from a teacher. This risk goes up when simulations are used for training too much. If you learn something in a game, you might not be able to use it in the real world.

Bias in humans in translated to data, and incorporated by AI

One big risk of using AI is that there might not be enough data to teach the models. Aside from the fact that data is available, there is also the chance that it has been tainted by human error. There may be biases against racial and gender groups in historical statistics. There is a chance that AI will pick up on these attitudes and make them stronger. This can cause a feedback loop that makes it harder for some minorities to get ahead.

The labour market for teachers

Teachers might need to learn new skills in order to use AI in a smart way. At the moment, teachers are not trained in data-driven education, but AI does expect users to have at least basic computer skills. If teachers can't keep up with this change, the next teacher might be a data expert with less schooling. Of course, there is a very small chance that "the teacher" will be replaced by a computer. An AI would need to have a certain level of Artificial General Intelligence to be able to do all of a teacher's work. We don't think this will happen any time soon.

Dependency on black-box models versus the responsibility of teachers

One danger is that AI systems that we don't fully understand could be used in schools. To get rid of this risk, teachers and AI both need to change. It is necessary to make machine learning models easier to understand and for teachers to learn more about AI in order to avoid this risk. A teacher can't be responsible for methods that don't make sense.

Applying AI without the necessary prerequisites

There are a few things that need to happen before AI can be used effectively in schools. For instance, AI can't be used without a technical framework and data. It is possible for AI to not live up to promises if it is put into use too quickly. Because of this, AI can be very disappointing, just like other new learning tools. This could finally make people not want to use AI in education, which could also slow down other digital innovations in this area. Also, there are many legal issues (often for good reason) that make it impossible to fully adopt AI right away.

A shift in power

Some people worry that putting AI into the world will give more power to one group. This could be a tech giant or a company that already publishes training materials. However, recent events seem to show that this risk can be handled. There was a recent decision that confirmed the school, not always the person who made the digital educational resources, owns the data that is generated by those resources. But policymakers are still worried about it.

Policy Recommendations

It's clear that using AI in schooling can be helpful in many ways. The education field doesn't seem to be against or even excited about using AI to automate some tasks, especially those that are administrative or teaching. Think about going over tests again and making a program fit your needs. But we can also see that in order for AI to be used in a way that has a big effect, some basic legal and moral questions need to be solved.

It is also being talked about what the teacher's job should be when AI is used. AI can help teachers in some ways, which means they can give better lessons. But teachers are asked to be responsible for the choices made by an AI that they can't explain, to work with data and judge the usefulness of AI results, and to be able to explain why AI is being used to those involved.

There are several things that lawmakers (specifically those in the Ministry of Education, Culture, and Science) can do or decide in order to encourage the use of AI in education as follows:

1. Stimulate the acceptance of AI in education by teachers, parents and students.

We're going to ask schools to come up with a plan for how they want to use AI in their own institutions. Our staff, parents, and kids who aren't directly in the school can use this vision to understand how much AI is used and what the goals are. Of course, schools need to be helped to come up with this kind of plan. This kind of AI vision should have at least these parts:

- Why does the school apply AI
- For which tasks does the school apply AI (for which tasks not)?
- How is the accountability of the AI guaranteed?
- How is it ensured that the AI is not prejudiced?
- How is it ensured that educational goals are not compromised by AI?
- How is the privacy of the student ensured?

2. Increase the digital skills of teachers

To use AI responsibly, you need to know how to use computers. This is needed in all areas of schooling (PO, VO, and HO). These digital skills include not only knowing how to use a computer, but also knowing how to read data in a way that makes sense of what an AI says. Think about having a strong background in statistics and knowing a few basic machine learning methods. In this case, three things can be done:

- More attention should be paid to digital skills on teacher-training courses. Make digital skills an obligation, such as didactic and pedagogic skills.
- The current teacher population must be given further training in order to be able to use AI responsibly.
- Stimulate teachers with a background in data or AI. This can trigger a chain reaction within a school that can promote the adoption of AI.

3. Creation of a data infrastructure

All things considered, AI programs need a lot of data to work well. Because of this, the availability of data is a key factor in the growth of AI uses in Dutch schools. It's possible that the Ministry of Education, Culture, and Science could help get more data and set up the right conditions for studying and creating AI applications for use in schools. There is also the worry that data might be biased. These sources of data can be gathered and made public by the Ministry of Education, Culture, and Science. They can be used to train AI models that are fair.

4. Facilitate experiments with AI in education

To the boundaries of experiments, policy must set limits. In terms of policy, one of the most important problems that could be fixed is the lack of data that can be used for research. When you experiment, you should also not be too strict about what the results of a pilot project should be. It's also necessary to have money to carry out these trials. There should be more room for AI experiments in research funds that are already out there.

5. Stimulate a multidisciplinary approach to the development of AI applications in education

It is very important to use a variety of fields to make sure that the goals of education are not lost, that user needs are met, and that the best technological standards are reached. New research funds that aren't just focused on one area can be made to encourage this kind of multidisciplinary thinking.

6. Develop a certification for responsible AI use

To make AI easier for people who need to understand it, like schools (which buy AI apps), parents, and kids, one idea is to create a certification system where AI apps must meet certain requirements. One example is that a person who isn't an expert in AI can choose an AI app in a smart way. At the very least, this kind of approval should cover these things:

- Stimulate standardization, data portability, interoperability, in order to ensure that the market for educational AI application functions properly. It should be noted that far-reaching 'top-down' standardisation could actually slow down innovation.
- Develop legal frameworks (in order to creating clarity) and solving legal bottlenecks in the use of AI in education.
- Benchmarks for transparency and explainability of an AI. To what extent must an AI be transparent, which data has been used, which algorithm is used to process it, and which requirements must a explanation of

an AI model meet? In practice, the Ministry of Education, Culture and Science can contribute to the establishment of benchmarks that an AI must meet as a minimum requirement. For example, benchmarks for reviewing essays.

References

Piech, C., Bassen, J., Huang, J., Ganguli, S., Sahami, M., Guibas, L. J., & Sohl-Dick- stein, J. (2015). Deep knowledge tracing. In Advances in neural information processing systems (pp. 505-513).

Cornelisz, I., & Van Klaveren, C. (2018). Student engagement with computerized practising: Ability, task value, and difficulty perceptions. Journal of Computer Assisted Learning, 34(6), 828-842.

Norris, C. (2005). From personal to digital: CCTV, the panopticon, and the technological mediation of suspicion and social control. In Surveillance as social sorting (pp. 263-295). Routledge.

Balfour, S. P. (2013). Assessing Writing in MOOCs: Automated Essay Scoring and Calibrated Peer Review™. Research & Practice in Assessment, 8, 40-48.

Chase, C. C., Chin, D. B., Oppezzo, M. A., & Schwartz, D. L. (2009). Teachable agents and the protege effect: Increasing the effort towards learning. Journal of Science Education and Technology, 18(4), 334-352.

Lundberg, S. M., & Lee, S. I. (2017). A unified approach to interpreting model predictions. In Advances in Neural Information Processing Systems (pp. 4765-4774).

Olah, C., Mordvintsev, A., & Schubert, L. (2017). Feature visualization. Distill, 2(11), e7

T. Bjerkedala, P.K. G. A. S. J. I. (2007). Intelligence test scores and birth order among young Norwegian men (conscripts) analyzed within and between families

Grace, K., Salvatier, J., Dafoe, A., Baobao, Z., en Evans, O. (2018). When Will AI Exceed Human Performance? Evidence from AI ExpertsJournal of Artificial Intelligence Researc

Liang Jun, B. (2018). Facial recognition used to analyze students' classroom behav- iorsChina: People's Daily Online

Connor, N. (2018). Chinese school uses facial recognition to monitor student attention in class Beijing Telegraph

Collaboration.ai (2018). Education: shape the minds of the future by adding intelligence to the way students work and collaborate together

Lelei, D., en McCalla, G. (2018). How to Use Simulation in the Design and Evaluation of Learning Environments with Self-directed Longer-Term Learners vol. 10947, Cham: Springer

Mansson, K., en Haake, M. (2018). Teaching Without Learning: Is It OK With Weak AI? vol. 10948, Cham: Springer

West, D. M. (2012). Big data for education: Data mining, data analytics, and web dashboards. Governance studies at Brookings, 4(1).

Herodotou, C., Rienties, B., Boroowa, A., Zdrahal, Z., Hlosta, M., & Naydenova, G. (2017, March). Implementing predictive learning analytics on a large scale: the teacher's perspective. In Proceedings of the seventh international learning analytics & knowledge conference (pp. 267-271). ACM.

Chapter 10
Enhancing Educational Outcomes: AI in Delivery and Assessment

In the past few years, artificial intelligence technologies have grown very quickly. An important reason for this is the progress made in generative AI (Table 1). This type of AI can now do many things, including creating realistic text, images, music, and video.

Some lawmakers and education experts think that AI technologies, if used correctly, could help students learn more and make teachers' jobs easier in educational settings like schools, colleges, and universities.

AI isn't used as much in education as it is in other fields, and it's still in its early stages and being tested. People don't know what the pros and cons are.

There are some problems with using AI in schools. There are worries about bias, safety, and the use of personal data (PN 708) in general. Also, many AI tools were not made with kids in mind, so they might show them inappropriate material.

People with a stake in the issue are worried that relying too much on AI tools could hurt teaching, writing, and thinking skills, and could completely change the way adolescents learn. For instance, some teachers have said that using creative AI too much could hurt the growth of some teaching skills. Another thing is that AI trainers might not be able to provide the kind of emotional support that human teachers can.

The Department for Education (DfE) explained its views on using AI in English schools in March 2023. These views included the pros and cons, issues related to data and intellectual property, and suggestions for how students could be helped to learn about and use AI.

In November 2023, the DfE released a report on the use of generative AI in education. This came after a call for proof. It found that early adopters of AI in education mostly had good feelings about it, but a lot of people also had serious concerns. The DfE held a two-day "hackathon" in October 2023 with teachers and data scientists to figure out the best way to use AI in schools.

Educating people is a decentralized policy. The Department for Education in England is in charge of education policy, which is what this talk is mostly about. Unless otherwise stated, all statistics, strategies, policies, and funds are for England.

Table 1: AI definitions

Artificial intelligence (AI)	The UK Government's 2023 policy paper on 'A pro innovation approach to AI regulation' defined AI, AI systems or AI technologies as "products and services that are 'adaptable' and 'autonomous'". The adaptability of AI refers to AI systems, after being trained, often developing the ability to perform new ways of finding patterns and connections in data that are not directly envisioned by their human programmers. The autonomy of AI refers to some AI systems that can make decisions without the intent or ongoing control of a human.
Generative artificial intelligence	Defined by the Alan Turing Institute as "an artificial intelligence system that generates text, images, audio, video or other media in response to user prompts." Generative AI systems are often trained on huge datasets by employing a machine-learning approach.
Large language model (LLM)	AI systems trained on a vast amount of text that can carry out a variety of language tasks, such as generating text (generative AI), answering questions, and translation. LLMs work by recognising patterns and predicting text but are limited in their understanding of context. Examples include OpenAI's ChatGPT and Google Bard.
Educational technology (EdTech)	Technologies specifically developed to facilitate teaching and learning which may or may not encompass AI.

Definitions are not universally agreed, move at a fast pace and are interlinked.

AI in Action: Improving Education Delivery

Reducing educators' workloads

The DfE's "Working Lives of Teachers and Leaders" study, which came out in April 2023, asked more than 10,000 English state school teachers and leaders questions. This is what the report said:

- 72% of teachers felt that their workload was unacceptably high
- high workloads were reported as the biggest reason for teachers considering leaving the state school sector

- 66% of teachers reported that they spent less than half of their working hours teaching due to time spent on activities including lesson planning, marking, and tracking pupil data, as well as administrative tasks

Staff have also reported increasing workloads in higher and further education institutions.

The DfE set up the Workload Reduction Taskforce in September 2023. Their goal is to cut the work of primary and secondary schoolteachers by 5 hours a week in 3 years. As part of this plan, we are looking into how AI-powered educational tools can help with planning lessons, giving grades, and making administration easier.

The government said in October 2023 that it would put up to £2 million into Oak National Academy, a platform for learning and teaching resources. This would give all English teachers free access to AI-powered lesson planning resources.

AI could cut down on work by helping with planning and making things in many different ways. One example is that AI tools can

- scan text and make it more concise, or put it into language more suitable for specific age-groups
- generate definitions for key-terms found in a section of text
- produce questions and quizzes with model answers, which can be tailored to address specific weak points in learners' understanding
- automate or support administrative tasks such as the production of emails, reports, or seating plans

AI tools that can grade students' work and give them comments are also being made. Some of the digital tools that are used to assign and grade work are also being used to find students who might need more help or a harder level of challenge in a certain area.

In November 2023, over 9,000 teachers were asked to fill out a poll on the app Teacher Tapp. Of those teachers, 42% had used AI to help students with their work at least once.

Limitations in reducing workloads

Because AI teaching tools are new, study into whether they can be used in real life in schools is still in its early stages. People think that making lessons and giving grades are important parts of teaching because they help students understand and make progress,48,49 so AI tools might only be able to help in some ways. Administrative jobs like writing reports might be easier to give to AI systems, but this could depend on the subject and the teacher's style.

Large Language Models can give results that aren't suitable, are biased, or aren't based on facts. Their outputs might need to be reviewed by a person first before they can be used in schools, which takes away from the time savings that using them can give.

83% of 284 academics working in UK universities surveyed in 2023 said they planned to use generative AI more in the coming years. However, some respondents were worried that work that was outsourced to AI tools could be replaced by other, possibly more time-consuming tasks.

Personalised education and support

Platforms for online learning where students talk to AI teachers directly can be customized for each user. Certain claims say that these kinds of sites can provide more help than is usually present in lectures or classes.

These systems can be like one-on-one tutoring in some ways by talking through chatbots that use clear, natural-sounding language made by LLMs. Based on information about each learner, platforms can tailor lessons to their individual skills and weaknesses. However, some experts question how personalized many AI-based EdTech tools really are.

It's possible that some AI teachers will be easier to find and less expensive than human tutors, but they might not be able to teach as well or offer psychological support or extra context to lessons.

This is because AI can help students with challenges or learning problems, like dyslexia, get better access to education. The power behind screen reader technologies, which turn text and pictures into speech or braille so that visually impaired students can use computers, comes from AI. Speech-to-text tools can write down what teachers say for students who have trouble hearing or who are learning English as a second language.

AI chatbots can also be programmed to answer general questions or questions about homework. This gives students and pupils more online help and might also stop school staff from feeling like they have to answer texts outside of school hours.

Several AI experts say that AI tools could change the way we learn and help close achievement gaps if they are used correctly.

But some education experts are worried that relying too much on AI for tasks like planning lessons or grading work could make teachers less skilled and hurt the relationships between teachers and students. This could mean that education results are more general and less specific. Customized LLMs that are fine-tuned using teaching material might help make sure that outputs are more in line with the relevant school curricula. However, fine-tuning alone can't stop LLMs from producing false or biased outputs sometimes.

Educator training

AI systems can use information from lessons to give teachers feedback on how they're doing. Some systems are being worked on that will use recordings of lessons to help teachers improve their skills by giving them feedback on how they connect with their students.

Generative AI can also be used to start conversations during professional development by simulating how teachers and students interact in the classroom.

Performance data could help teachers do their jobs better, but some teaching groups are worried that the same data could be used to punish teachers or keep an eye on their work.

AI use by educators in assessment

AI could be used to set up, grade, and mark tests and graded homework, as well as to give and oversee tests that are given from a distance. These tools are still in their early stages of development, and teachers don't trust AI for big tests like GCSEs or national exams because of concerns about fairness, responsibility, and validity.

Markers who are people can make mistakes and be biased, which can change the grades that students get. In contrast to AI markers, human markers can be affected by things like mental tiredness when making decisions. Additionally, there may be some variation based on the type of test. The Office of Qualifications and Examinations Regulation has said that human examiners don't always agree on certain types of questions, like those that need longer answers. For example, multiple choice questions have a higher rate of agreement between examiners.

When AI is used to grade, it might use the point of view and biases that were most popular in the training data. This could lead to bias and/or limit the kinds of answers that are ok. Human marks can also explain their choices very clearly, which is different from many AI systems that make decisions in a less clear way.

According to surveys done by Jisc in 2023, some college students don't mind if AI marks their short answers and quizzes, but they are less happy with AI marking other types of assignments.

Assessment experts say that because test results are so important, there are big problems with giving full control of marking exams to AI. However, there may be room for AI-powered tools to help with marking.

Learner use of AI

The UK government made a 10-year plan for AI in 2021 with the goal of "making the UK a global AI superpower." This included steps to help people learn about AI, such as working with the National Center for Computing Education (NCCE) to get kids interested in AI.

Some people and places in the education sector, like schools that offer the International Baccalaureate and the Russell Group of universities, are actively pushing students and pupils to use AI tools in their work in different ways. They say this will help students get a balanced view of AI and its limits, which will stop it from being abused, and it can give younger people some of the skills and information they'll need in the future workforce.

However, some education experts have expressed several concerns including:

- learners may develop an over-reliance on AI in education, impacting their development of writing and critical thinking skills
- a negative impact on literacy skills
- the syntax and grammar of text produced by AI-tools may flatten individual writing styles
- less personal creativity when used in subjects such as art and music

In addition, there are concerns that the online text LLMs are trained on may overrepresent the writing style, culture and biases of English-speaking nations such as the UK and the USA. LLM outputs may therefore lack the social and cultural nuances of any given community.

Learner use of AI in assessment

A lot of people are worried about how creative AI will change performance on school tests.

Recent studies have shown that the newest forms of generative AI software can make results that can sometimes pass certain tests at the high school or college level.

Because of this, generative AI could make it harder to grade many types of work, such as articles, dissertations, online tests, and course applications.

Generative AI can make highly graded coursework, which could give some students an unfair edge in the job market if they are tested in this way instead of through exams that are graded by real people.

It is very hard to figure out when creative AI is being used. Some experts think that because generative AI and AI-detection tools are always getting better, it is unlikely that detection tools will ever be able to correctly spot text that was generated by AI.

Several studies have shown that publicly available AI-detection software is often wrong and prone to "false positives," which are situations where learners are wrongly accused of using generative AI.

Rethinking assessment

There are growing calls on schools, colleges and universities to implement new ways of evaluating learner progress that are less likely to be undermined by AI. Proposed approaches include:

- **exams under invigilated conditions**: for example, returning to handwritten exams to prevent AI misuse. Several stakeholders including the Quality Assurance Agency see this as a regressive response that may reduce the accessibility of examinations.108 Exams delivered through secure online browsers have been proposed as a more accessible alternative.
- **oral examinations**: the assessment of student understanding and reasoning through oral examinations, as is already done in some circumstances, could be expanded to other subject areas. This approach comes with significant logistical challenges. These include time constraints, and the possibility of students assessed at the start of the process discussing exam content with those assessed later.
- **observed examinations**: commonly used in medical teaching, in these examinations, students conduct a series of tasks in a controlled environment. However, this approach may be limited to subjects which include practical elements.

Alternatively, the Joint Council for Qualifications and some education experts argue that the large-scale abuse of AI can be reduced through preventative measures including:

- openly discussing AI with learners and explaining how its exploitation could lead to diminished learning outcomes (as is already done in relation to essay- mills)

- providing greater levels of support during writing tasks
- setting more specialised assignments which are less readily completed by using generative AI

Other interested parties want new ways to check students' work and knowledge, with a bigger focus on learning and skill development through activities like internships, presentations, and group projects that help students get ready for the real world of work.

But making big changes to the way assessments are done now could cause a lot of problems for students and teachers.

Policy considerations

It's hard to say what will happen with AI technologies, like those used in schools, in the next few years.

Several experts on the use of AI in education say that AI will completely change the way we teach and learn. This makes me think about the future of schooling and the kind of relationship with technology that young people might be encouraged, as well as how this might be different in different settings.

Stakeholders have also raised a number of practical issues that need to be addressed. These include showing proof that AI-powered EdTech works, giving teachers training and direction, addressing "digital divides," and making the laws that govern how AI collects and uses data on teachers and students clearer.

Evidence of effectiveness

A lot of people are using AI-powered EdTech, but only a few studies have looked at how well it works, and those studies were limited to certain use cases. Also, this is very true for tools that use creative AI.

Most of the information out there comes from EdTech businesses, which makes it less unbiased. Strong, independently produced proof on the pros and cons of AI, like independent certifications, could help educators decide if and how to use AI in their classrooms. Schools have also said that they don't have much time to think about whether EdTech is right for them.

In England, there are a number of programs that help with study and learning about AI in schools. These include pilot studies like the ones funded by the Northern Council for Further Education and Oak National Academy's projects funded by the government that are looking for the best ways to use AI. Some places of learning are looking into how AI can be used in their respective situations.

China, Singapore, South Korea, and the United States are just a few of the countries that have put a lot of money into EdTech research and are starting to use AI teaching tools in schools and colleges.

Many high-tech AI tools for education are being made outside of the UK. Some parties have said that AI EdTech that was made outside of the UK might not work as well in UK schools.

Training and guidance

Oxford University Press released a study in 2023 that found that even though many teachers thought AI would be good for education, only 23% of UK teachers were ready for the move toward an AI-enabled classroom. The DfE asked for evidence on creative AI in education, and almost all of the people who answered said that teachers should be trained in AI.

Some non-government groups, like the Teacher Development Trust, have put together online guides on how to use AI in education. But education experts say that teachers may need to learn more about AI and be better at using it through professional development and training programs if AI tools are to be widely used by teachers. Interventions like these might also be useful in higher and further education.

Tackling 'digital divides'

Inequalities in regions and differences in socioeconomic situations, among other things, can make it harder for some people to get effective internet, computers, tablets, or smartphones. A "digital divide" is another name for this.

Because of digital differences, some schools may not have the right equipment to use AI tools effectively and efficiently.

Pearson, a business that works with schools, released a report in 2023 that said half of English secondary schools don't have access to reliable WiFi and that only 44% of secondary schools have laptops for used in class. Jisc studied how learners felt during the 2022–2023. They found that more than half of students in UK further and higher education said that WiFi problems got in the way of their learning.

The DfE has released research that shows that limited budgets are the main reason why schools don't use technology more. They have also promised £200 million to connect all English schools to high-speed internet by 2025.

However, some stakeholders have said that the biggest benefits of AI might only be available to schools and students with more money if they can't keep paying for the upkeep of IT infrastructure. The price of some paid or premium forms of AI tools may also be out of reach for some students, giving them an edge when they work from home or do their homework.

Safety and data security

The UK Government put out a white paper in 2023 about how to regulate AI in a way that is "pro-innovation." This is based on current legal frameworks instead of making new laws, and it aims to regulate through the regulators that are already in place. The white paper talks about data, safety, and security.

Some lawyers have talked about how important it is to regulate things in a way that is specific to each situation, even in education. Stakeholders have pointed out that data protection laws, especially the UK General Data Protection Regulations (UK GDPR), are important for making sure that AI tools handle data properly. The UK held a global meeting on AI safety in November 2023. This was followed by the creation of the UK's AI Safety Institute.

In the UK, the DfE and the educational offices of devolved executives have put tips on how to use AI on their websites. But teachers and AI experts have said that more, more detailed instructions are needed.

The NASUWT teachers' union has made a list of 12 rules for how AI and other digital tools should be used in schools in an ethical way. This emphasized how important it is for teachers to be involved in choices about the growth and use of AI and Edtech in schools so that the technology supports educational goals and is easy to use. NASUWT also stresses how important it is to carefully regulate and keep an eye on all AI and Edtech that is used in schools.

The Digital Futures Commission published a report in 2023 recommending three key legislative priorities to ensure that EdTech is used in a way that protects children's personal data and is not detrimental to learning:

1. Clarification of how existing regulatory frameworks including UK GDPR, The United Nations Convention on the Rights of the Child, and The Age-Appropriate Design Code apply to EdTech tools. Where necessary, these frameworks may require extension so that they comprehensively cover the use of EdTech in education. Additionally, the development of legislation which ensures high standards, transparency, and compliance from EdTech companies.
2. Certification frameworks so that high-quality, peer reviewed EdTech products that have proven educational value and safety standards are easily identifiable by schools.
3. Development of secure data infrastructure which serves the best interests of children and educational institutions, whilst also allowing for controlled data- sharing which supports the development of new EdTech tools.

A lot of different groups, like UNESCO, Jisc, and the Russell Group, have also put out advice on how to use AI in education.

A big issue is intellectual property. The DfE says, "Education institutions must not allow or cause pupils' original work to be used to train generative AI models unless they have the appropriate consent or exemption to copyright."

Some people may still disagree about what kinds of data can be gathered and how they can be used by AI. Concerns about privacy and safety arise when AI tools are given access to pupil data. There are groups like Defend Digital Me that are wondering if it is legal for companies to use data about children to teach AI and make new tools.

But putting strict limits on how data can be used could stop AI tools used in education from being trained and improved.

Chapter 11
The Evolution of Artificial Intelligence: A Theoretical Review of its Impact on Teaching and Learning in the Digital Age

Introduction

An important paradigm change in the way we teach and learn has happened with the introduction of artificial intelligence into schools. In the past few years, the fast development of AI technologies has led to their widespread use in many fields. One area that has seen big changes is education. Machine learning, natural language processing, and adaptive algorithms are all coming together to make new apps that can help people with a wide range of learning styles and tastes. An increasing level of sophistication in AI makes it clearer that it has the ability to change the way we teach and improve student outcomes. It's important to know how AI has been used in education in the past so that you can understand where it is now and what will happen in the future. This review looks at the history of AI in education to lay the groundwork for further research into its theory bases and real-world applications.

Using AI in education opens up a lot of possibilities, but it also brings up important questions and problems. Traditional ways of teaching and new AI-powered tools are interacting in a very interesting way in the world of education. Some important issues that need to be carefully looked at are how to fairly distribute AI resources, how to use student data in an ethical way, and how this will affect teachers' jobs. As AI technologies become more common in schools, it is important to think about how they might affect teaching methods, student participation, and the overall learning process. This chapter talks about the important worries people have about using AI in school, with the goal of giving future study, policymaking, and teaching methods a theoretical base to build on.

The main goal of this theory review is to bring together what is already known about how AI has grown and how it has changed teaching and learning in the digital age. Through looking at the theoretical foundations that support using AI in education, this chapter aims to give you an idea of the possible pros, cons, and moral issues connected with this technology shift. It also wants to add to the current conversation about AI's role in education by giving a more complete picture of how these technologies can be used to improve outcomes in the classroom. We hope that the theoretical discussion in this chapter will help teachers, researchers, and lawmakers figure out how to use AI in schools, which can be tricky.

This review uses a theoretical framework that includes ideas from constructivist, sociocultural, and cognitive learning theories to look at how AI affects teaching and learning in a broad way. Based on the ideas of constructivism, this chapter looks at how AI can help with active learning and personalized, student-centered methods. The study of AI's role in promoting social interaction and collaborative learning environments is based on sociocultural views. Cognitive learning theories also help us understand how AI can adapt to different learning styles, handle large amounts of information, and improve general cognitive processes. By combining these different theoretical views, this chapter aims to give a complete picture of how AI affects education, which will serve as a strong base for the rest of the review.

Historical Development of AI in Education

Overview of AI in Education:

Putting artificial intelligence (AI) into schools has been a slow but significant process that has changed the way we teach and learn. The main goal of using AI in schools is to make learning faster and better while also meeting the needs of each student. AI is used in many different ways in education, such as smart tutoring systems, adaptive learning tools, and virtual reality simulations. These technologies use machine learning algorithms to look at how well students are doing, give them personalized feedback, and make learning settings that are always changing. The introduction to AI in education sets the stage for looking at how these technologies have changed over time, focusing on the area where new technology and better teaching methods meet.

Evolution of AI Technologies

The progress made in the field of artificial intelligence can be seen in how AI tools are used in schools. At first, rule-based systems and simple decision trees were the main types of AI used in education. But when machine learning, especially deep learning, came along, AI in education moved into a new era with more advanced tools. Natural language processing (NLP) and computer vision technologies have made AI-powered educational tools even more useful by letting students connect with them in more complex ways and create their own unique learning experiences. AI technologies in education have changed over time from rule-based systems to more complex, adaptive algorithms that can look at huge amounts of data and make learning material and experiences fit the needs of each student.

Key Milestones in AI-Driven Educational Tools:

There have been a number of important steps forward in the development of AI-based teaching tools, showing how they have grown from simple apps to complex learning systems. One important turning point was the creation of intelligent teaching systems (ITS) in the 1970s. For example, the PLATO system did groundbreaking work in this area. These methods paved the way for personalized learning with computer help. Adaptive learning systems have become more popular in the 21st century. Knewton and DreamBox were among the first companies to offer data-driven adaptive learning experiences. Adding virtual reality (VR) and augmented reality (AR) to education has also created new ways for students to learn that are more engaging and interactive. To understand the history of AI in education and the wide range of uses that have changed the field, it is important to know about these important turning points.

Theoretical Foundations

Constructivist Learning Theory

AI as a Facilitator of Active Learning

Using AI in education is a great way to support constructivist learning theory, which stresses how important it is for students to be actively involved and build their own knowledge. AI technologies can help people learn actively by creating simulations and engaging situations where people have to solve problems. For example, AI-powered Intelligent Tutoring Systems (ITS) can give students quick feedback, adaptive tests, and learning experiences that build on each other, which makes them more involved in the learning process. This fits with the ideas of constructivism, which says that students learn best when they explore and work together. New study shows that AI can help encourage active learning, especially when it comes to making classrooms that are always changing and encouraging students to find meaning through hands-on experiences.

Personalised Learning Environments

Personalized learning is also very important according to constructivist principles, which take into account the different types of learners and how they think. When used in education, AI is great at making personalized learning spaces by changing lessons and material based on each student's needs. Machine learning algorithms look at data about students to find out their strengths, weaknesses, and preferred ways of learning. They then make educational tools that are more relevant to those needs. Individualizing learning experiences makes the focus more on the student, giving them the freedom to study topics at their own pace. Personalized learning environments have been shown to improve student motivation, involvement, and knowledge acquisition. This supports the constructivist idea that students actively shape how they understand the material.

Socio-cultural Learning Theory

Social Interaction and AI in Educational Settings

Vygotsky's sociocultural learning theory stresses how important social interactions are for brain growth. AI in education could improve social relations by creating smart agents that make it easier for students to work together to learn. Chatbots and virtual tutors can have useful conversations with students, help them figure out how to solve problems, and encourage them to work together to build knowledge. Recent studies show that social interactions facilitated by AI are good for students' cognitive and metacognitive growth. This shows that AI has the ability to improve the social and cultural aspects of learning.

Collaborative Learning with AI

Adding AI tools to collaborative learning, which is an important part of sociocultural theory, makes it even better. Students can work on projects together, share ideas, and get feedback in real time with the help of virtual collaboration tools that use AI. AI-powered teamwork tools not only make it easier to talk to each other, but they also make it easier to share different points of view, which creates a more culturally and socially diverse learning environment. New study shows that AI can help people learn together, and it has the potential to break down barriers like geography and culture, making global classrooms that welcome everyone.

Cognitive Learning Theory

Cognitive Load and AI Integration

Cognitive learning theory tries to explain how our minds work when we learn, and it includes the idea of cognitive load. AI in education is very important for managing brain load because it changes how lessons are taught to fit the needs of each student. Intelligent tutoring systems can change the level of difficulty of jobs based on how smart the student is, finding the best balance between skill and challenge. Recent studies have shown that AI can help reduce cognitive load that isn't needed and increase cognitive load that is needed, which leads to better learning results.

Adaptive Learning Systems

Using adaptive learning methods is in line with cognitive learning theory, which takes into account the fact that learners' thought processes are not always the same. AI-powered adaptive systems look at how each learner learns and change the way material is delivered and the speed of learning to match each learner's cognitive abilities. This personalized method not only makes learning more effective, but it also meets the different cognitive needs of each student. New study in the field shows that adaptive learning systems can help students learn more, remember what they've learned, and do better in school overall.

AI Applications in Teaching and Learning

Intelligent Tutoring Systems

Intelligent Tutoring Systems (ITS) are one of the most important ways that AI is being used to improve education (Anderson et al., 1995). These systems use machine learning techniques to give each student personalized, flexible lessons. ITS can give specific feedback, find places where students can improve, and adapt the lessons to meet the specific needs of each student by checking their performance and learning in real time. Recent improvements in ITS have added advanced data analytics, which give us a better picture of how students are learning and how they are progressing. Research shows that ITS can help students do better in school by getting them more involved, helping them solve problems better, and helping them understand the material better. Intelligent Tutoring Systems show how AI could change the relationship between a teacher and a student by providing personalized, data-driven help.

Adaptive Learning Platforms

AI is used by adaptive learning tools to make learning experiences that are both dynamic and tailored to each student. These platforms use algorithms to look at data about each learner and change the pace and material to make the learning journey better. By figuring out what each student is good at and bad at, flexible learning systems can make sure that each student gets the right amount of challenge and help. Recently conducted studies have shown that adaptive learning platforms can improve student achievement, engagement, and retention. These systems also allow for self-paced learning, which works for people with a variety of learning styles and preferences. The use of adaptive learning in schools is in line with differentiated and student-centered teaching concepts. This shows how AI can be used to meet the specific needs of each student in a scalable and effective way.

Virtual Reality and Augmented Reality in Education

Technologies like Virtual Reality (VR) and Augmented Reality (AR) are changing the way we learn by making lessons more immersive and involved. Virtual reality puts people in a computer-made world, and augmented reality adds digital material to the real world. VR and AR can be used in schools to help students learn by doing, by letting them explore difficult ideas in a three-dimensional place. For example, VR simulations can take students to foreign countries, scientific labs, or historical events, which can help them understand and be more involved than traditional methods. New studies show that VR and AR can help students stay motivated, remember what they've learned, and learn how to think critically. Using these tools in teaching and learning is in line with constructivist and experiential learning theories, which stress the value of hands-on experiences and being involved in the learning process.

Natural Language Processing and Language Learning

Natural Language Processing (NLP) is one of the most important parts of AI applications for language learning because it gives computers advanced ways to read and understand human language. NLP is used by AI-powered language learning tools to give students personalized feedback on their grammar, pronunciation, and language skills. NLP-powered chatbots and virtual language teachers put language learners in real-life conversational situations that help them learn in a more natural way. Research shows that NLP can help people learn languages by improving their language skills and making them more motivated to learn. Socioconstructivist ideas support using NLP to help people learn languages because they stress how important social relationships and real language use are in the learning process. AI's ability to change based on each person's language learning needs makes language learning more personalized and effective.

Gamification and AI

Combining gamification and AI in education is a powerful way to get kids interested in learning and help them do better in school. Adding game features to non-game situations, like learning, such as competition, challenges, and rewards, is called gamification. AI technologies improve gamification by giving students adaptive challenges, personalized feedback, and material that changes based on their progress. AI-powered gamified learning settings can help students feel like they've accomplished something, stay motivated, and work together. New studies show that gaming and AI can help students stay interested, remember what they've learned, and learn how to solve problems. This app fits with theories about what motivates and engages people, stressing how important intrinsic motivation and a good learning setting are for students to do well.

Implications for Pedagogy

Redefining the Role of Educators

When artificial intelligence (AI) is used in education, the traditional job of teachers needs to be rethought. With the rise of AI-powered technologies like Intelligent Tutoring Systems (ITS) and adaptive learning platforms, teachers are no longer just people who pass on knowledge. Instead, they help students have personalized, data-driven learning experiences. Teachers need to get used to a classroom that is more flexible, where AI helps with teaching, testing, and giving each student personalized help. Research shows that for AI to be successfully used in education, teachers need to learn how to manage technology and help students find their way around AI-enhanced learning settings. This change shows how important it is for schools to have professional development programs that teach teachers how to use AI tools correctly. This way, teachers and AI systems can work together to improve student results.

Enhancing Student Engagement

AI has an effect on pedagogy by making learning more interesting for students by making it more personalized and engaging. Students are interested in adaptive learning platforms and gamified AI applications because they adapt content to each student's needs and add challenge and competition aspects. Modern educational theories stress the importance of active and involved learning, which is in line with the way AI-driven educational tools work because they are dynamic and responsive. Studies have shown that students like learning experiences that include AI. They say that AI makes them more motivated, curious, and like they own their learning path. As AI keeps getting better, teachers can use these new technologies to make the classroom more interesting and focused on the students. This will help students remember things better and understand them better.

Addressing Equity and Inclusivity

One important thing to think about when putting AI to use in education is how it might affect fairness and inclusion. Although AI has the potential to make learning more personalized, it could also make educational gaps worse if it is not used carefully. To improve fairness and inclusion, we need to carefully look at who can use AI technologies, taking into account things like their socioeconomic level, where they live, and their different learning needs. Researchers stress how important it is to build AI applications with inclusivity in mind, so that students from all backgrounds can benefit from personalized learning experiences. AI can also be used to help students with specific learning problems and to provide tailored interventions for students with a range of needs, making the educational landscape more open to everyone. It is important for policymakers and teachers to work together to create rules and frameworks that put fair use of AI tools in education first.

Ethical Considerations in AI-Driven Education

When AI is used in education, there are many social issues that need to be carefully thought through. As AI systems gather and study huge amounts of student data, concerns about privacy, safety, and permission come up. Ethical rules for the responsible use of AI in schools need to be made by educators, lawmakers, and technologists working together. For students' privacy and trust to be protected, there must be clear information about how data is used, informed consent, and strong security measures. Also, fixing bias in AI systems is important to make sure that all students are treated fairly. When creating and using AI-based tests, it is important to keep ethics in mind to make sure they are in line with educational goals and protect students' rights. Educators can create a safe and responsible learning setting that puts students' rights and well-being first by incorporating ethical concerns into AI-driven education.

Challenges and Considerations

Technical Challenges

Using artificial intelligence in schools comes with a lot of technology issues that need to be carefully thought through. One big problem is making sure that different AI systems can work together and be added to current educational systems. Technical standardization is important to make sure that different AI apps can talk to each other and share data without any problems. This will stop siloed systems that make it hard for people to work together. Problems with the system's dependability, its ability to grow, and the need for constant upkeep and updates are also technical problems. Because school environments are always changing, AI systems need to be able to adapt to new tools and changing ways of teaching. To solve these technical problems, educators, technologists, and lawmakers need to work together to build strong frameworks that allow AI to be used in a way that is sustainable and scalable.

Privacy and Security Concerns

Concerns about privacy and security become the most important things to think about when using AI in schools. When AI systems gather and look at private student information, there is a higher chance that privacy will be broken or that someone will get in without permission. To protect data privacy, strong encryption methods, safe storage, and strict access controls must be put in place. Furthermore, being open and honest about how data is used and getting permission from kids and their parents are important ethical issues. New laws, like the General Data Protection Regulation (GDPR), make it clear how important it is to protect people's privacy rights in the digital age. It is important for researchers and policymakers to work together to make clear rules and standards that protect data privacy and security while still using AI to help education.

Bias and Fairness in AI Algorithms

Concerns about bias and unfairness in AI algorithms are very important, and they also apply to teaching uses. Since AI systems are taught on old data, if those datasets contain biases, the algorithms can keep and even make differences worse. This problem is especially important in educational settings where fair treatment is very important. To fix bias in AI algorithms, we need to keep looking at the training data, making sure it is diverse and representative, and using methods that make things more fair. According to research, educators and AI writers need to work together to find and fix biases in algorithms so that all students get fair results. By using fairness and openness as guidelines when creating and testing AI algorithms, people can lower the chance that these algorithms will reinforce social biases in schools.

Balancing Automation with Human Touch

AI's automation features make educational processes more efficient than ever before, but it's hard to find the right mix between automation and human touch. As educators, it's not just their job to teach; they also need to be mentors, offer mental support, and help students grow socially and emotionally. No matter how powerful AI systems are, they might not be able to replicate the complex social connections that are necessary for teaching and learning to work well. To find a good mix between AI-driven automation and human touch, you need to think carefully about the strengths and weaknesses of each. To make the most of AI-enhanced classrooms, teachers need to know how to use technology to their advantage while still keeping the essential human aspects of education.

Future Directions and Recommendations

Anticipated Trends in AI and Education

When we think about the future, we can see that a number of expected trends in AI and schooling will change the way we learn. As natural language processing, machine learning, and adaptive algorithms continue to get better, AI-driven teaching tools should be able to do more. Immersive technologies like virtual reality and augmented reality are expected to make learning even more fun and involved, which will help students understand and remember things better. With the rise of predictive analytics and learning analytics, teachers will also be able to use the power of big data to learn more about their students' progress, interests, and possible problems. On the horizon are also collaborative and socially intelligent AI applications that will help students learn from each other and make it easier for them to interact socially in digital learning settings. As AI in education continues to change, it's important to stay on top of these trends and support research and development that meets the needs of both teachers and students as they change.

Ethical Guidelines for AI in Education

Strong moral guidelines are becoming more and more important as the use of AI in schooling grows. To make sure that AI technologies are used in schools in a fair and responsible way, clear ethical standards must be created and followed.

These rules should cover things like data protection, security, reducing bias, and being clear about how algorithms make decisions. To set up ethical frameworks, educators, policymakers, technologists, and ethicists must work together to make standards that are thorough and can be used anywhere in the world. These rules should stress how important it is to get informed consent, own your data, and keep testing AI systems to find and fix any errors they may have. To keep a balance between the possible benefits of AI in education and the ethical concerns that protect students' rights and well-being, it is important to keep having talks across disciplines and involve all stakeholders.

Professional Development for Educators

Teachers must be ready to learn how to use and handle these advanced technologies in order for AI to be successfully used in education. So, it's very important to put money into comprehensive professional development classes for teachers. These programs should give teachers the skills they need to successfully use AI tools in their lessons, understand the insights that AI systems give them, and encourage teachers and AI systems to work together. The training should also cover the moral issues connected to using AI in schools, giving teachers the knowledge to make smart choices about data safety, security, and reducing bias. It is important for educational schools, technology developers, and professional development providers to work together to make programs that are specific to the needs of teachers. Professional development is important for teachers so they can use AI to its fullest to improve their lessons and students' results. This will make the switch to AI-enhanced classrooms go smoothly.

Conclusion

Summary of Findings

In conclusion, studying the growth of AI and how it affects teaching and learning has shown that the area where technology meets educational theory and practice is very complex. Intelligent teaching systems, adaptive learning platforms, and virtual reality apps are just a few of the big steps forward in the history of AI in education. These advances have paved the way for big changes in the way we teach. We can see how AI can help with active learning, social relationships, and personalized learning through the lenses of constructivist, sociocultural, and cognitive learning theories. A variety of AI-based uses in education, from smart tutoring systems to game-based learning, have shown that they can get students more involved, create more personalized learning settings, and offer new ways to learn languages and play educational games.

Theoretical Implications

The ideas that this review is based on show how important it is to have a deep knowledge of AI in education. Some learning theories, like constructivism, show how AI could help with active learning and make learning more personalized. Sociocultural views stress how AI can improve social interactions and places where people work together to learn. Cognitive learning theories help us understand how AI can handle a lot of information and adjust to different ways of learning. Combining these different academic views helps us fully grasp how AI fits in with well-known educational ideas while also pushing the limits of conventional teaching methods. Theoretically, putting AI to good use in education needs a careful combination of technology and teaching methods, taking into account how they change and interact with each other.

Call for Further Research

At the end of the chapter, it's clear that using AI in education is an area that is changing quickly and has big effects. However, problems like technical limitations, privacy concerns, algorithmic biases, and the fine line between automation and human touch make it clear that more study and careful thought are needed. In the future, researchers should focus on solving the technical problems that make it hard to use AI in a variety of school settings. There are also ethical concerns about privacy, security, and bias in AI systems that need to be looked into more and strong rules need to be made to protect students' best interests. Furthermore, the call for more research includes ongoing exploration of successful strategies for professional development, which will make sure that teachers are well-equipped to use AI in their teaching. Future study will focus on how AI is changing, how it should be used ethically, and how professionals can keep improving their skills. This is because technology and education are always changing.

References

Anderson, J. R., Corbett, A. T., Koedinger, K. R., & Pelletier, R. (1995). Cognitive Tutors: Lessons Learned. The Journal of the Learning Sciences, 4(2), 167-207.

Blikstein, P., & Worsley, M. (2016). Multimodal Learning Analytics and Education Data Mining: Using Computational Technologies to Measure Complex Learning Tasks. Journal of Learning Analytics, 3(2), 220-238.

Boyle, B. (2017). Virtual Reality and Augmented Reality in Education. Retrieved from https://www.westpoint.edu/sites/default/files/inline-images/centers_research/center_for_teching_excellence/PDFs/mtp_project_papers/Boyle s_17.pdf.

Chan, T. F. I. (2015). Predicting the probability for adopting an audience response system in higher education. Doctoral Dissertation

Dede, C. (2010). Comparing Frameworks for 21st Century Skills. In J. Bellanca & R. Brandt (Eds.), 21st Century Skills: Rethinking How Students Learn (pp. 51-76). Solution Tree Press.

Deterding, S., Dixon, D., Khaled, R., & Nacke, L. (2011, September). From Game Design Elements to Gamefulness: Creating Interactive Leisure with Gameful Design. In Proceedings of the 15th International Academic MindTrek Conference: Envisioning Future Media Environments (pp. 9-15). ACM.

Diakopoulos, N. (2016). Accountability in Algorithmic Decision Making. Communications of the ACM, 59(2), 56-62.

D'Mello, S. K., & Graesser, A. C. (2014). Feeling, thinking, and computing with affect-aware learning. In R. A. Calvo, S. K. D'Mello, J. Gratch, & A. Kappas (Eds.), The Oxford handbook of affective computing (pp. 419-434). Oxford University Press. https://doi.org/10.1093/oxfordhb/9780199942237.013.032.

Floridi, L., & Taddeo, M. (2016). What is Data Ethics? Philosophical Transactions of the Royal Society A: Mathematical, Physical and Engineering Sciences, 374(2083), 20160360.

Hattie, J., & Donoghue, G. M. (2016). Learning Strategies: A Synthesis and Conceptual Model. npj Science of Learning, 1(1), 1-13.

Jackson, E.A. (2019). Use of Whatsapp for flexible learning: Its effectiveness in supporting teaching and learning in Sierra Leone's Higher Education Institutions. Sage Preprint, 1-18. https://doi.org/10.31124/advance.8947415.v1.

Jackson, E.A. (2017). Impact of MOODLE Platform on the Pedagogy of Student and Staff: CrossCurricular Comparison. Education and Information Technologies, 22(1), 177-193. https://doi.org/10.1007/s10639-015-9438-9.

Jackson, E.A. (2015). M-Learning Devices and their Impact on Postgraduate Researchers Scope for Improved Interaction in the Research Community. International Journal of Advanced Corporate Learning, 8(4), 27-31. http://dx.doi.org/10.3991/ijac.v8i4.5024.

Jackson, E.A. (2015a). Role of information science in sustainable development: Sierra Leone as a case study. Management of Sustainable Development, 7(2), 23-29.

Johnson, L., Adams Becker, S., Cummins, M., Estrada, V., Freeman, A., & Ludgate, H. (2013). NMC Horizon Report: 2013 Higher Education Edition. The New Media Consortium.

Koedinger, K. R., & Corbett, A. T. (2006). Cognitive Tutors: Technology Bringing Learning Science to the Classroom. In K. Sawyer (Ed.), The Cambridge Handbook of the Learning Sciences (pp. 61-77). Cambridge University Press.

Lajoie, S. P., & Derry, S. J. (1993). Computers as Cognitive Tools. Lawrence Erlbaum Associates.

Luckin, R., Holmes, W., Griffiths, M., & Forcier, L. B. (2016). Intelligence Unleashed: An Argument for AI in Education. Pearson.

Mayer, R. E. (2008). Learning and Instruction. Pearson.

Russel, S., & Norvig, P (2010). Artificial Intelligence: A Modern Approach. Prentice Hall.

Selwyn, N. (2017). Education and Technology: Key Issues and Debates. Bloomsbury Publishing.

Siemens, G., & Long, P (2011). Penetrating the Fog: Analytics in Learning and Education. EDUCAUSE Review, 46(5), 30-32.

Siemens, G. (2005). Connectivism: A Learning Theory for the Digital Age. International Journal of Instructional Technology and Distance Learning, 2(1), 3-10.

VanLehn, K. (2011). The Relative Effectiveness of Human Tutoring, Intelligent Tutoring Systems, and Other Tutoring Systems. Educational Psychologist, 46(4), 197-221.

Vygotsky, L. S. (1978). Mind in Society: The Development of Higher Psychological Processes. Harvard University Press.

Index